CHANGING CHANNELS

CHANGING CHANNELS

The Civil Rights Case
that Transformed Television

Kay Mills

University Press of Mississippi

Jackson

www.upress.state.ms.us

The University Press of Mississippi is a member of the
Association of American University Presses.

12 11 10 09 08 07 06 05 04   4 3 2 1
∞
Library of Congress Cataloging-in-Publication Data
Mills, Kay.
Changing channels: the civil rights case that transformed
television / Kay Mills.
p. cm.
Includes bibliographical references and index.
ISBN 1-57806-519-4 (cloth : alk. paper)
1. United States. Federal Communications
Commission—Trials, litigation, etc. 2. WLBT (Television
station : Jackson, Miss.)—Trials, litigation, etc. 3. Television
broadcasting—Law and legislation—United States—History.
4. Fairness doctrine (Broadcasting)—United States—History.
5. Blacks in television broadcasting—Civil rights—United
States—History 6. Blacks on television—Civil rights—United
States—History. I. Title.
KF228.U53M55 2004
343.7309'946–dc22   2003020228

British Library Cataloging-in-Publication Data available

CONTENTS

CHANGING CHANNELS

INTRODUCTION

Young Willie Pinkston and his friends often gathered on Saturday afternoons around the black-and-white television set at a neighbor's house to watch *Teen Tempo* on Channel 3, NBC affiliate WLBT. It was the mid-1950s, and Elvis was the rage. All the kids on *Teen Tempo* were white, and, frankly, they couldn't dance. Or at least not dance the way the older girls in Willie's group thought was cool. The girls knew all the dances, and they read the fan magazines. Willie was only six or seven at the time, and he and his young friends giggled at the dancers. "We'd laugh. 'Look at him. The one with the T-shirt and blue jeans.'"

Black teenagers never appeared on WLBT. *Teen Tempo* played Elvis's music, maybe some Chuck Berry, but never anything more soulful. Watching *Teen Tempo*, Pinkston said years later, "was my first recollection of 'We're not there,'" of black faces being invisible on much of American television.[1] What he and his friends were experiencing was but one aspect of an especially effective blackout of African Americans on southern TV stations. A program featuring Oprah Winfrey, born in Kosciusko, Mississippi, would not have been carried on any television station in her native state. She simply could not have launched her highly successful career in the 1950s or 1960s, at least not in the South. Singer Nat "King" Cole's show did not appear on many southern stations. Network interviews with newsmakers like civil rights attorney Thurgood Marshall were not broadcast on many southern stations. Local newscasts and television commentaries presented civil rights activists as "outside agitators," bent on fomenting trouble in a local black community supposedly content with second-rate schools and second-class citizenship. The station manager at Channel 3 editorialized on the air against integration in front of a backdrop that proclaimed "Never."[2] In short, television in the South—indeed, in most of the United States—was not giving a full and accurate portrayal of the world in which its viewers lived.

Until the battle for Channel 3—WLBT—no one had any idea how to challenge these discriminatory practices effectively. Until the Channel 3 case, blacks in Mississippi saw only distorted pictures of their lives on television. Many southern television stations were not fairly covering the civil rights movement for social justice and economic opportunity. That blatant misrepresentation had political ramifications within both the white and black communities. Whites could not fully understand what they could not see. Blacks could not feel the courage of their numbers when they could not see those numbers, when they could not see their leaders argue the merits of their cause on television. Many southern newspapers, especially those in Jackson, reported the civil rights struggle with even more bias. But they were not licensed by the federal government to serve the public interest; WLBT was.

Even in the battle for Channel 3, it was not the federal government agency charged with protecting that public interest that finally took up the issue. Instead, it was a small band of blacks and whites who defied local customs of segregation to work together to challenge the WLBT license. That challenge, filed in 1964 by the Office of Communication of the United Church of Christ and two black Mississippians, started changing the face of television. The challengers charged that WLBT did not serve the public interest because it failed to cover issues of interest to a substantial portion of its audience, that is, the black community, and that the station distorted those issues that it did cover. A federal appeals court panel, headed by Warren Burger before he became chief justice of the United States, ruled twice in favor of the challengers. Even after the challengers won their case, there was no assurance that the station's practices would change substantially over the long haul. That depended on who won the permanent license to operate Channel 3. It took another group of citizens, again black and white working together, to end the battle. The license was awarded to a group with majority black ownership.

This is the story of that sixteen-year legal struggle. It was a fight in which all the money and all the power were arrayed on the station's side at first. The money and power shifted when a Texas banker took up the cause by helping an integrated group seek the permanent license. A liberal Democrat, he was drawn to the case because he believed that the old ownership at WLBT had treated its black audience unfairly. *Changing Channels* takes us through almost fifty years of change in television history—from 1955, when WLBT, without fear of sanction, could pull the plug on a network interview with Thurgood Marshall to today, when Oprah Winfrey reigns supreme as the Queen of Television.

Changing Channels tells the story of people like Willie Pinkston, whose life was changed by the challenge to WLBT's license, and it shows how news coverage by a reconstituted WLBT helped alter the racial and political dialogue in Mississippi and throughout America. *Changing Channels* illustrates how citizens were able to make government work for them because they had the perseverance—and later the money—to remain in the labyrinthine legal fight.

The issues dramatized in this landmark case have not gone away, as Americans saw in the controversy in 2002 over Mississippi senator Trent Lott's seeming endorsement of Strom Thurmond's 1948 segregationist candidacy for president. Aftershocks from the WLBT case itself are felt even today. In 1998 a federal appeals court struck down a Federal Communications Commission (FCC) affirmative action plan that had been put in place during the same years the struggle over WLBT's license was occurring. The court said that the policy brought undue pressure on broadcasters to hire minorities.[3] The FCC made several stabs at revising its policy and in November 2002 approved new rules requiring only that broadcasters widely circulate information about their job openings—without specifically targeting minorities or women.[4] Because much of the broadcast industry is being deregulated, citizens, especially minorities, no longer feel that they have the force of law behind their efforts to secure employment and have a voice in broadcast issues. Citizens are at a loss, for example, about how to protest the dearth of minority characters on network television programs. *Changing Channels* explores the background of the affirmative action rules and the sense of public participation that the WLBT case generated.

Changing Channels has a distinguished cast of characters, names famous and not—Warren Burger, Medgar Evers, Martin Luther King Jr., Andrew Young, Everett Parker, Earle K. Moore, Aaron Henry, R. L. T. Smith, Gordon and Mary Ann Henderson, Paul Porter, Ann Aldrich, E. William Henry, Kenneth Cox, Nicholas Johnson, William Dilday, Walter G. Hall, Martin Firestone, Hodding Carter III, Patricia Derian, and more. In its telling, it is a story as layered as *Driving Miss Daisy* and as dependent on personal perspective as *Rashomon*. It is, most fundamentally, a story that must not be forgotten, lost in the dust of government archives.

Connie Curry, author of *Silver Rights*, suggested that I write this book. *Silver Rights* is the moving story of the Carter family of Drew, Mississippi, who enrolled their children in the all-white public schools at considerable risk and yet triumphed. Connie and I met in the late 1980s when I was starting my work on *This Little Light of Mine*, a biography of Fannie Lou Hamer, the Mississippi civil rights crusader. In 1997 Connie was preparing a book about Aaron Henry, a complex and too-unheralded figure of the state and national civil rights movement and one of the two Mississippians who joined in challenging the WLBT license. People kept telling Connie the story of that case merited its own book.

With Fannie Lou Hamer, Aaron Henry had led the integrated Mississippi Freedom Democratic Party that challenged the all-white Democratic delegation to the party's 1964 convention. That political challenge brought black Americans and then other minorities and women more fully into the Democratic Party. Connie knew that I was not only familiar with Mississippi's civil rights history but also had covered the FCC in the 1970s as a reporter in Washington, D.C. This book would tap into both areas of my background.

I had covered the public interest communications law movement that emerged in the wake of Warren Burger's first WLBT decision. I had reported about Everett Parker, the brains behind the challenge, and some of the other players from those days. I had gone to Mississippi in 1973 and interviewed William Dilday at WLBT. He had just been named the first black TV station manager in the South by the group operating WLBT on an interim basis while the ultimate licensee was determined.

I had come of age politically in the 1960s, and Mississippi always seemed to loom large in any discussions of the profound changes that era brought. As a young broadcast news scriptwriter for United Press International (UPI) in Chicago in the mid-1960s, I wrote about the events in Mississippi as they unfolded: the violence that lingered after Freedom Summer in 1964, when young people from around the state and around the country had sought to register blacks to vote, and the dramatic attempts by Mississippi blacks to assert other civil rights. Since then, I had written two books in which Mississippi figured prominently, the Hamer biography and a book about Head Start, the federal program for low-income children which became entangled in Mississippi politics in the 1960s and 1970s. Here was another story of those turbulent times, played out more in law offices, courtrooms, hearing rooms, and broadcast studios than in the streets or in Congress, but of critical importance in helping a community find its voice and in making government do its job.

Not that many years after Willie Pinkston had laughed innocently at the dancers on Channel 3, he became the first black anchor regularly doing WLBT's 6 P.M. weekday newscast, broadcasting to the heart of the Old Confederacy. The door of opportunity opened at WLBT as a direct result of the case being presented against the station at the FCC and in the federal courts. As an eleven-year-old, Pinkston had read the racist commentary on the front page of the *Jackson Daily News*, which he delivered on his paper route. Not that many years later, he became the newscaster to whom a "good ole boy" colleague (who drove a pickup truck with a gun rack) once reported: "My little boy loves watching you on TV." Since those days in Jackson, Willie Pinkston dropped his first name and became Randall Pinkston, anchoring evening newscasts in other cities, covering the White House for the CBS network, and reporting breaking news around the world.

Talking to Randall Pinkston helped me put a human face on the battle for Channel 3. He had grown up with WLBT, and his experience taught him how much this case meant, to his own life and to the American public. It was a story known by few with whom he worked at CBS. Not that it was a secret, but in television, as in life, too little time is spent examining how we got to be who we are and where we are. Journalism is a world of deadlines—you can't stand around telling your life history. But that is what I asked him to do one morning as we sat in the cafeteria at CBS headquarters in New York. As I would soon discover, others who had been the first black newscasters and technicians at WLBT had similar stories.

Randall Pinkston was born in Mississippi in 1950, still dangerous times for anyone who was black. Five years later, two white men murdered fourteen-year-old Emmett Till, visiting from Chicago, because they contended he had flirted with a white woman. Or because these two men knew they could get away with it. They beat Till severely, tied a weight around his neck, and dumped his body in the Tallahatchie River. Even then, this murder drew national attention. Even back in 1955, some people in America were as shocked as they would be more than forty years later when white supremacists dragged a black man to his death behind their truck in Jasper, Texas. The difference then was that the Mississippi men got away with it.

Pinkston began his education in segregated schools, despite the Supreme Court's decision in 1954 that such education was inherently unequal and therefore unconstitutional. Mississippi acted with no deliberate speed, and it was not until families like the Carters of Drew took action, enrolling their children in all-white schools and filing lawsuits, that the state opened those schoolrooms to black children. Many white children then headed for private, segregated academies. WLBT had not covered the issue of segregated schools with any balance, not when Thurgood Marshall's appearance on an NBC network show encountered "cable trouble" and was not broadcast, when NAACP field secretary Medgar Evers unsuccessfully sought airtime to discuss desegregation in Little Rock schools. Station WLBT and others across the South distorted coverage of racial matters or omitted them entirely in their local newscasts. Stay tuned after the national news for the true story, their viewers would be told; then they saw one-sided reports about an epic struggle that was reshaping the country.

Pinkston started listening to the news early on. His great-grandmother turned on the radio every morning at six o'clock, he recalled, partly because she was a news fanatic, partly because she needed to get everyone else out of bed. Pinkston grew up listening to *Monitor* on the weekends and shows like *Johnny Dollar, Ma Perkins*, and *The Shadow*. Late at night he would turn the dial to see what distant stations he could find. He wrote the station call letters in a notebook. He was fascinated with radio, but he never had any thought of becoming a journalist—"no dream, no thought, no notion." Once his family bought a television set, he saw signs announcing that WLBT was experiencing "technical difficulties." He wasn't aware at the time that programs might be blacked out. "We didn't know what we weren't seeing." He could not remember "a particular moment of realizing that no people of color were on TV. I can only tell you that I do remember my family and I being very excited whenever someone black *did* appear on TV. Nonappearance was the norm."

After graduation from Lanier High School in Jackson, Pinkston enrolled in Wesleyan College in Connecticut. He went to the campus radio station and asked, "What courses do you have to take to work here?" He found out that all he needed to do to work at the station— an extracurricular activity—was to take one brief test. Pinkston signed up on the spot. He sent home some photographs of himself at work, pictures his proud dad showed his minister, the Reverend Wendell Taylor. "My boy Billy's on the radio," he said, using the name his immediate family called him.

Pinkston had transferred to Millsaps College in Jackson during the second semester of his freshman year when his dad became ill. Taylor had learned that Channel 3 was looking for staff members and told Pinkston. "I didn't know anything about news," Pinkston recalled, but Taylor insisted. "Tell them I sent you." The station had started reaching out to the black community as a result of the challenge filed against its license. As the case moved back and forth between the FCC and the courts in the 1960s, WLBT began making changes. It fired its former manager and was recruiting black staff members by the time Taylor prodded Pinkston to apply in 1969.

Although Pinkston felt ill-equipped to begin his broadcast duties, he knew something about news because of his relatives' devotion to listening to the events of the day. He had grown up listening to the *Monitor* woman pronounce Phnom Penh, Djakarta, and other world hot spots. He started working for WJDX-FM, a station owned by Lamar Life Broadcasting, which also ran WLBT. The radio and TV stations were all housed in the same building. One day Dave Mieher, WLBT's news director, said, "Willie, we want you to take a crack" at doing the Saturday night television newscast.

"Well, I wanted to be a lawyer," not a broadcaster, Pinkston recalled. "I had visited Harvard Law School. I had made the connection about how the law had changed things at home." But he started his first job as a TV journalist—writing, producing, and anchoring the Saturday night news. He was not yet twenty years old.

"There was only one negative event that happened in that building in the entire time that I was aware of," Pinkston said. He was still working full time at the FM station and was playing a long cut of music on the air. He went into the control room to explore, as he frequently did. There, hanging over some of the electronic equipment, was a little noose, made of twine, with a sign that said emphatically: "Do Not Touch." In Mississippi in that era, when lynching of black people for supposedly "getting uppity" or "not staying in their place" was still an open wound, a noose was not a playful object. Pinkston, who said he did not feel threatened, left his own note in reply: "You shouldn't leave things like this lying around. You never can tell who'll see them."

Generally, however, WLBT staff members—still mostly white in those days—gave Pinkston helpful tips. "When you read [the news], you should smile," one person said. Another explained the technical material he needed to know. "The white guys were all very supportive, and it was rough initially because I hadn't done TV before." Pinkston learned his trade and became the station's first full-time black anchor on the weekday evening news. Viewers seemed to take that in stride, he felt, because the ratings in the October sweeps didn't go down, nor did they the following February.

In 1974 Pinkston thought he had not gotten the raise he deserved, so he left for the CBS-TV affiliate in Jacksonville, Florida. Later he worked as weekend anchor and public affairs producer for the CBS affiliate in Hartford, Connecticut, then spent ten years with WCBS-TV in New York City, where he won two Emmy Awards for outstanding spot news and covered political affairs. He joined CBS network news one month before the start of the Gulf War in 1990. He covered the White House for two years, traveling with President George H. W. Bush to Europe and the Far East. When Bush collapsed while dining with the Japanese prime minister, Pinkston broke the story on CBS radio.

Before Pinkston left WLBT, another staff member at the station made the suggestion that would change his public persona. "He said, 'You're doing a nice job but did you ever think about changing your name? Willie doesn't sound like the authority that you are.' I had never liked Willie anyway. So I left Mississippi and I left Willie. I went back to the name my family had called me. You know how they always say your whole name when they want to make a point. *Randall Pinkston!*" he said, recalling for everyone that call home for dinner or out to the kitchen for a scolding.

Not long after our first interview, I talked to Pinkston by phone. He was in London as backup for CBS correspondents who had gone to Yugoslavia to cover NATO attacks on Belgrade at the beginning of the military action over Kosovo. It was the end of his workday, around 5 P.M., and he said he was looking out of the CBS bureau window at Hyde Park.

"Did you ever think you'd be doing what you're doing?" I asked this man who had first watched television regularly as a child on a farm outside Holly Bluff, Mississippi.

"I did not even dream about it."

Langston Hughes, he said, wrote about what happens to a dream deferred. "It shrivels like a raisin in the sun." But "in that case at least there was a dream," Pinkston added. Growing up where he did, when he did, "you don't even think about what you can do. I have often wondered what I could have done if I had had a dream."

I. SEEKING A VOICE

WLBT-TV was a symbol. To many white people in Jackson, Mississippi, in the 1950s and early 1960s, it was a sign of their progress. They had entered the world of television with a network-affiliated station that broadcast bandleader Mitch Miller's show and other entertainment as well as news to much of the state. A major institution in town, Lamar Life Insurance Company, once run by writer Eudora Welty's father, owned the station. To many black people in Jackson, WLBT was a sign of how little progress they had made. This new medium in town had no black staff members on the air or behind the cameras, rarely interviewed black people who made news, and didn't show black teenagers on its dance programs. WLBT, like other Jackson institutions, was controlled by whites for whites. In those earliest days of television, blacks were invisible, except as troublemakers or criminals.

That time-honored Mississippi approach clashed with federal policy. Licensed by the government, WLBT was guaranteed certain freedoms. It also had responsibilities. WLBT's response to those freedoms and responsibilities virtually assured that it would become a target of the forces that were altering the way Americans thought about race and democracy at midcentury.

WLBT went on the air in Jackson on December 28, 1953. Fred Beard, a thirty-two-year-old World War II veteran, was part owner and station manager. The following December, another veteran, Medgar Evers, who was twenty-nine, became the Mississippi field secretary for the National Association for the Advancement of Colored People (NAACP) in Jackson. The television station and its white manager would be at cross-purposes with the black activist most of the next decade, engaged in one skirmish of a statewide civil rights confrontation.

In 1953 the nation was at peace. The Korean War had just ended. But domestic tranquility would not last long in Mississippi. The U.S. Supreme Court was considering a case arguing that separate public schools for white and black children—the system that operated in Mississippi and across the South—were inherently unequal. Locally, Medgar Evers was seeking to win admission to the University of Mississippi law school, which did not admit black students. In 1954 Evers lost his bid to go to law school, but the Supreme Court acted, striking down school segregation. Overturning the law did not mean enforcing it, however. Evers and his allies fought legal battles for black Mississippians that would rock the state.

Network television focused its cameras on those battles and helped shape the national response. Local TV in the South was another story. WLBT was not an isolated case; in many ways, thanks to its news director, Richard Sanders, its news coverage may have been better than many other stations in the South. Most southern television stations failed to provide balanced coverage of the civil rights movement. Had that not been the case—had local television not reflected the standpat white point of view but instead stepped back to cover all sides of the news—the South might have changed faster than it did. Indeed, in the eyes of the 1968 *Report of the National Advisory Commission on Civil Disorders*, all of television shared at least part of the responsibility for racial tension and misunderstanding because the medium had not adequately presented news about the African American community.[1] The little-known story of this Mississippi TV station thus illustrates a key element in the struggle for civil rights.

Race was, of course, central to the defining event of the nineteenth century in America, the Civil War. Race continued to be an overriding issue in Mississippi throughout much of the twentieth century as well because of the restrictions enacted on its black population when the Reconstruction era ended. Legislative restraints and capricious local registrars—coupled with nightriders' violence—kept blacks from voting. With no political influence, blacks also had other freedoms curbed. The state perpetuated black economic and political inequality by maintaining a separate and decidedly unequal school system. Black children attended classes in run-down buildings, black teachers sometimes had little more education than their students, and textbooks were worn-out hand-me-downs from white schools.

Black Mississippians knew that they could not progress without better education, so by the 1950s the core public policy issue concerning race was school desegregation. In the eyes of many white Mississippians, nothing less than the southern way of life was at stake in maintaining separate schools. Many whites considered black people inferior. Once, most blacks in Mississippi had been slaves, the property of plantation owners. Now many were sharecroppers or domestic workers. Whites' refusal to educate black children adequately had been one way to ensure this supposed inferiority. Segregation kept blacks untrained, working in other men's fields or cleaning other women's bathrooms. Segregation literally kept black and white young people, friends perhaps in childhood, apart as they started to form more permanent attachments. Segregation gave poor whites someone over whom they could feel superior, blunting any likelihood of cooperation to improve their lives. Thus the U.S. Supreme Court decision of

May 17, 1954, in *Brown v. Board of Education* rolled like thunder over the state. "Never!" cried many (but not all) white Mississippians. A few whites looked for leadership that would allow southern states to obey the court order, but for many years they got little or none from politicians, preachers, or businessmen.[2]

WLBT had been broadcasting for less than six months when the court dropped its bombshell. Before the TV station went on the air, its station manager, Fred Beard, had been running the radio stations that Lamar Life Insurance owned. Lamar wanted to get into television and so lobbied to get Channel 3 assigned to Jackson. Beard and four partners applied for the license, which, as the insurance company's subsidiary Lamar Life Broadcasting Company, they received in August 1953.[3]

Lamar Life Insurance had been chartered in 1906. Its ten-story office building, constructed in 1924–1925, was hailed as "Jackson's first skyscraper."[4] Lamar had established its network radio station in 1929. In 1953 the family that owned much of the stock sold a 40 percent interest to Clint Murchison, a conservative Texas oilman who was moving into life insurance, book publishing, and other ventures. In 1955 Murchison's sons, Clint Jr. and John, purchased a majority of the stock.[5] Years later, Fred Beard insisted that the Murchisons had little to do with day-to-day operations of the television station. But it was the Murchisons who later would hire the influential Washington law firm of Arnold & Porter to represent WLBT.

Beard, born February 1, 1921, was a native of Columbus, Mississippi, in the northeast section of the state. He attended public schools there and graduated from the University of Mississippi in 1942, "just in time to go into the army." He became a major during the war and afterward earned a master's degree in business administration at Harvard. Beard then moved to Jackson to work at the R. E. Kennington department store, first as a buyer, then as merchandise manager.

"To be perfectly honest with you, I had no desire to get into radio and television," Beard said in an interview.[6] He had gone to P. K. Lutken, the president of Lamar Life, for some career advice, and Lutken suggested that Beard work for him, running Lamar's radio station. " 'Television's coming,' " Lutken told Beard. " 'We'll most probably want to get into that,' and so he hired me."

Not long after WLBT went on the air, its news director, Jim Perry, hired Richard Sanders, soon to turn twenty-eight, as a radio and television news reporter. About five months later Perry died. Sanders was promoted and served as news director until he moved to ABC News in Washington, D.C., in October 1965. Born in Chicago, Sanders had served in the U.S. Navy during World War II, although he never saw combat. He was originally drawn to advertising when he majored in journalism at the University of Missouri, but he took a broadcast-writing course, made straight A's, and was hooked. Sanders worked for radio stations in New Orleans and Spartanburg, South Carolina, before getting the job in Jackson, where his wife had grown up.

While still in South Carolina, Sanders had reported on attempts by Governor James Byrnes to establish a school equalization program. Byrnes and other white politicians thought that if they could bring the buildings, books, and teachers' salaries for black schools up to the same quality as those in white schools, they might avoid having to desegregate the state's public schools. Sanders covered the county board of education as it was discussing these plans. "I don't recall ever seeing a black at any of the meetings, and certainly none were invited to take part in the discussions. Blacks really weren't expected to embrace the program."

When he went South, Sanders said, "I didn't know anything about blacks." Chicago's schools had been segregated. He never saw a black person during almost two years of service in the navy. The University of Missouri was segregated (and a highway sign not far away proclaimed that he was in "The Heart of Little Dixie.") "I had always been told that blacks were very happy with their life." His thinking would change during the years he spent in Mississippi. He clearly came to disagree with many of the opinions of his boss, Fred Beard, but had a businesslike relationship with him. "Beard was difficult but never nasty. We never had any shouting arguments. Our discussions were held in a decent manner."[7]

Beard's tenure at WLBT drew few neutral reactions. Maurice Thompson, WLBT's program director in that era, wrote a history of the station that made its way into the files at the Mississippi Department of Archives and History. In it, he said that Beard was "detested and loved. He was kind and unforgiving. None of these evaluations had to do with his employer-employee relations. He was generous and understanding to a fault in his relationship with employees. Fred Beard was one of the strongest willed men I have ever known. His religious, civic, political and philosophical principles were imbedded in iron, unmovable. He was instinctively polite and gentlemanly, but the nerve-ends of his convictions rode near the surface at all times and I have seen many an unwary person fall into the trap of his smile only to be torn to shreds by his, at times persuasive, and at others, devastatingly abrasive preachments.

"I greatly admired Fred Beard," Thompson wrote, "although differing with him radically on many occasions and over many policies. I will always remember Fred with deep devotion and I hope he will always remember me as an understanding friend."[8]

Those who watched the television station did not always share Thompson's devotion. And not just black viewers. Hodding Carter III, then a Greenville, Mississippi, journalist, told the Federal Communications Commission (FCC) in June 1964 that Jackson's television stations were, almost without exception, "geared to a far right-wing, rigid segregationist approach." He added that there was no pretense of balance or opposition to racist or ultraconservative groups, with the exception of WLBT's news director, Dick Sanders. Despite being under great pressure from his station's general manager, Beard, Sanders attempted to present a fairly rounded news program, Carter said.

Carter called Beard "little more than . . . an unofficial mouthpiece for the total resistance line of the Citizens' Council."[9] In the wake of the Supreme Court desegregation decision, Citizens' Councils had been formed across the state to resist black and white children attending school together. Their members were upper- and middle-class business leaders who sought to maintain segregation through legal means, which at the beginning was relatively easy because they controlled politics and the laws. They didn't need to put on the white sheets of the Ku Klux Klan, the white supremacist organization that often terrorized black citizens. But historian John Dittmer has written that council activities in effect gave others permission to act with lawlessness. "Through its unrelenting attack on human rights in Mississippi," Dittmer said, "the Citizens' Council fostered and legitimized violent actions by individuals not overly concerned with questions of legality and image."[10]

By supporting these defiant attitudes against school desegregation, WLBT-TV almost immediately became a target of black criticism. In 1955 Thurgood Marshall, the attorney who had argued against school segregation before the Supreme Court, appeared on the NBC network program *Home* to discuss the case. WLBT viewers did not see that interview. The station reportedly flashed a sign that said "Sorry, Cable Trouble"—although station manager Beard later denied that any such sign had been used. Beard did acknowledge that he had cut off the interview.[11] The NAACP's Washington office got word of the incident and protested to the FCC.[12]

In response to an inquiry from the FCC, Beard wrote on December 8, 1955, that neither the NAACP nor the Citizens'

Council had been permitted to appear on WLBT. "We have covered from a news standpoint the activities of both groups. . . . The policy not to provide time to either group was established by both television stations in this market to prevent the stations from becoming involved in this issue. It now appears that it will be impossible for the radio and television stations to continue a 'hands off policy.' "

"Regarding the specific complaints about my activities," Beard continued, "I was only one of the many Southern television stations that complained to the National Broadcasting Company about certain television programs promoting social equality and intermarriage of whites and Negroes. . . . As it has been our policy not to permit local or network propaganda on either side to be broadcast or telecast, Thurgood Marshall's interview on the NBC-TV program, 'Home,' was not telecast. If it had been telecast then we would have been obligated to make equal time available to the other side. Statements I made at the Citizens' Council meeting [about using 'Sorry, Cable Trouble' signs] were not quoted correctly in the newspapers.

"It is true that I am a member of the White Citizens' Council Association. It is a group that has been formed to keep racial elements in the state from taking hold and causing acts of violence. The Council's membership is made up of the most outstanding business men in the state. It is to the advantage of every one that such an organization exists."[13]

Another issue arose at this time, as it would again and again at WLBT—the use of courtesy titles such as Mr. and Mrs. when referring to black people. Whites didn't use them, newspapers didn't use them, and WLBT didn't use them. But Sanders was scheduled to interview Clarence Mitchell, the NAACP's representative in Washington, D.C., who had traveled to Jackson to address a rally. Sanders used people's last names in reporting the news without courtesy titles for blacks or whites, following the University of Missouri School of Journalism stylebook. But, he asked himself, how would he greet Mitchell, and how would he refer to him once he introduced him on the air? He even had to rule out using "Mr. Mitchell" when they met. "I was concerned that the control room might have the microphone open for a mike check, and I was a Yankee from Chicago in the Deep South."

It was awkward, Sanders recalled. He introduced himself, thanked Mitchell for coming, and chatted briefly until the interview began. Sanders never used the word "mister," and Mitchell "never indicated by so much as a glance that he was offended. He was there to get his message across, and he knew the situation only too well."

Sanders continued to grapple with the issue, especially when he referred to black women. "I had no problem with calling a married woman 'Mrs.' or a single woman 'Miss,' no matter what her color," Sanders said. "But white viewers and listeners in Mississippi and the South weren't ready for such a drastic change . . . not yet. Actually the use of 'Mrs.' to refer to a black wasn't a big problem because not many black women were in the news. We didn't usually do stories about black-on-black violence unless it was out of the ordinary, and black women just didn't make much news in the media." Sanders did confront the issue in 1958 when NAACP attorney Constance Baker Motley came to Mississippi to argue a voter registration case. Sanders referred to her by her full name on first reference and then called her "attorney Motley." The Jackson newspapers, however, called her "the Motley woman."[14]

At WLBT as well as throughout the nation, one of the first flash points in the fight over school desegregation occurred in September 1957 in Little Rock, Arkansas. Nine black students had tried to begin classes at previously all-white Central High School, but Arkansas National Guardsmen, acting under orders of Governor Orval Faubus, blocked their way. The next time they tried to enter, a white mob cursed and threatened them. On September 25, U.S. Army paratroopers and the National Guard, which President Dwight D. Eisenhower had federalized to remove it from Faubus's control, escorted the students into the school. That day, the *Jackson Daily News* front page headlined: "Bayonet Rule Opens Little Rock School to Nine Negro Students; Soldiers Club, Stab Foes of Integration." Under front-page photographs of Eisenhower at a news conference, the newspaper carried these words:[15]

TO THE PRESIDENT:
(An Editorial)
NUTS!

The next night WLBT broadcast a discussion of the Little Rock crisis, which included the views of U.S. Senator James O. Eastland of Mississippi, an outspoken opponent of integration. Little Rock had galvanized the Citizens' Council and the Ku Klux Klan, Sanders recalled. There was talk of people arming themselves, and the station believed that it ought to assemble the state's leaders together in a program. "I thought it was important," Sanders said. "The blacks weren't going to do anything. That community was quiet. But we were right across the bridge from Rankin County, where there were diehard, overt segregationists and Ku Klux Klansmen."[16]

Medgar Evers protested, first to the station, then to the FCC. He said that the station had aired only the viewpoints of whites adamantly against school integration.

Evers understood the frustrations encountered in Little Rock. He could find few people willing to enroll their children in white schools, or, if he found sufficiently daring parents, he could do nothing to protect them from reprisals. He had gone to segregated schools himself while growing up in Decatur, Mississippi, in the east-central part of the state, not far from Meridian.

Evers's parents were hard-working people who taught their children pride mixed with the caution they would need to survive in the world as they knew it. That was a world in which a friend of Evers's father, Willie Tingle, could be dragged through the streets of Decatur and lynched for supposedly insulting a white woman. It was a world run by people like Senator Theodore Bilbo, a fuming, racist stump speaker. Evers's older brother, Charles, remembered that when he and Medgar were youngsters, they went into Decatur to hear Bilbo speak. Bilbo spotted them sitting on the courthouse steps. "If we fail to hold high the wall of separation between the races, we will live to see the day when those two nigger boys right there will be asking for everything that is ours by right. You see these two little niggers sitting down here. If you don't keep them in their place, then someday they'll be in Washington trying to represent you."[17]

Medgar Evers dropped out of high school to join the army during World War II and served with the 325th Port Company, a segregated unit, in Europe. When he returned to Mississippi, he and Charles, who had served in the Pacific, tried to vote but were turned away by a white mob. In 1947 they did become the first black voters in Decatur. Medgar enrolled at Alcorn A&M College in southwestern Mississippi, met Myrlie Beasley there, and married her on Christmas Eve 1951.[18]

The Everses could have left the state as many other young black Mississippians of ambition did in the 1940s and 1950s. Thousands of black people from the Delta to the Gulf Coast headed north to St. Louis, Chicago, or Detroit to seek jobs and an end to the degrading discrimination of the South. Myrlie Evers wanted to go to Chicago. "I could not imagine a Negro with a college degree and any imagination at all planning to remain in Mississippi. It seemed inconceivable, despite Medgar's frequently professed love for the state, that he, of all people, would decide to stay, and in the last few weeks of college we had many discussions of these points."[19]

They stayed in Mississippi. Medgar, a trim, athletic-looking man (he ran track and played football at Alcorn) with a pencil-thin mustache, took a job with Magnolia Mutual Life Insurance Company in Mound Bayou, the state's only black-run town. His boss was Dr. T. R. M. Howard, an outspoken and today largely forgotten black civil rights advocate. Howard owned a plantation worked by sharecroppers, raised quail, drove a red Buick, founded a local hospital, and regularly drew crowds to meetings where black leaders spoke. Myrlie Evers described him as "that rare Negro in Mississippi who had somehow beaten the system."[20] And he was always willing to challenge that system. In 1952 he and Medgar Evers had bumper stickers printed that read "Don't Buy Gas Where You Can't Use the Restroom," and Evers put one on his car.

Evers drove around the Delta, seeing its poor, ragged black children and their unheated homes, then told his wife what he had seen. Children without shoes or proper clothing. Adults with nothing to eat. "Sanitary conditions no self-respecting farmer would permit in his pigpen," as Myrlie Evers recalled.[21] His resentment began to build about the conditions under which the Delta sharecroppers lived because they were totally at the mercy of the landowners for whom they worked. As he traveled to sell insurance, he also surreptitiously told sharecroppers what was going on in the world and signed them up for the NAACP. On one of these rides, Evers told his friend and fellow insurance salesman Thomas Moore about his dreams for himself and the state. "If everything got straight here, this would be the best place in the world to live."[22] He had started organizing NAACP chapters in 1952, and in 1954 he went to work for the NAACP full-time in Jackson.

The NAACP, organized in 1910, concentrated on litigation as opposed to direct action. Its attorneys filed cases against unequal public transportation, discrimination against black voters, and segregated public schools and universities. An interracial group of wealthy whites and educated blacks had established the organization, which had most of its strength in the North. By the 1960s student activists in Mississippi considered the NAACP overly conservative, but earlier it had been the first civil rights organization signing up sharecroppers at a time when it was dangerous to be either a recruiter or a member. The summer after Evers started working for the NAACP, he went into the Delta to investigate the Emmett Till murder and was often chased down the dark roads of the Delta as he sought witnesses to the crime.

Evers sometimes thought that the extremely hierarchical NAACP leadership, based in New York, was more concerned about his office expenses than the dangerous and frustrating realities of work in Mississippi. He reported monthly on his attempts to create a presence for the NAACP in Mississippi and to provide support for those local people who dared to sign their children up for white schools or who tried to register to vote. In September 1956 Evers reported to New York that he had gone to Yazoo City to check on the people who had petitioned to enroll their children in white schools. The day after the fifty-three parents signed up, the local Citizens' Council published their names and addresses in the *Yazoo Herald* "as a public service." As a result, Evers wrote to his bosses, "economic pressure is very much in evidence, with most of the persons remaining without steady employment, and in some instances where employment is rather consistent, threats of violence are meted out against the workers. Fear is so prevalent in the community the regular monthly meeting of the organization is non-existent." A carpenter who signed the petition received no more calls for work. A plumber whose clients were mostly white saw his income drop to $20 a week. The white wholesalers who supplied a black grocer and two other merchants stopped dealing with them. A lumber company fired the husband of a woman who signed the petition, and soon the couple left for Chicago. Fifty-one people removed their names from the petition, and the other two had already left the county.[23]

Intimidation and even murder were employed to keep blacks from the polls. In October 1956 the state NAACP wired President Eisenhower, reporting that in Humphreys County in central Mississippi the Reverend George Lee, an NAACP leader, had been killed and Gus Courts shot "because they tried to vote as Americans." In Jefferson Davis County, more than a thousand persons who had been qualified voters from three to ten years were disenfranchised because they were blacks. In Hattiesburg, there were fewer than 25 blacks registered out of 12,000 eligible.[24]

It was within this climate that Evers wrote his letter of protest to the FCC about WLBT's broadcast on the Little Rock crisis. Under what was known as the Fairness Doctrine, broadcasters had to provide "a reasonable amount of time for the presentation . . . of programs devoted to the discussion and consideration of public issues" while also encouraging and enabling broadcast of all sides of controversial issues. This Fairness Doctrine would play a central role in the fate of WLBT ownership.

The FCC had laid out the doctrine in 1949 in its "Report on Editorializing by Broadcasting Licensees" to clarify confusion that existed in the broadcasting world about how far stations could go in expressing their own views. Broadcasters had an affirmative duty to air controversial issues so long as they made available opportunities to express opposing views, the FCC said, adding that no one had the right to distort the news. The broadcasting industry, never happy with anyone trying to regulate its content, thought that the Fairness Doctrine violated the First Amendment guarantee of freedom of speech. This debate would continue into the 1980s. Congress did not write the Fairness Doctrine into law until 1959 when it amended Section 315(a) of the Communications Act.[25] Nonetheless, the Fairness Doctrine supposedly had the FCC's authority behind it when Medgar Evers watched the 1957 program that featured white Mississippi politicians talking about events surrounding enrollment of black students in Little Rock.

This WLBT broadcast expressed only the segregationists' point of view, Evers wrote, "and thereby did not express the views of Negroes on this very vital issue." Evers had asked station manager Beard to allow a group of blacks to appear in response. Beard replied that the station's board had turned down the request, and Evers appealed to the FCC.[26] The NAACP's Washington counsel reminded the commission in a separate letter of Beard's earlier statement after the "Sorry, Cable Trouble" incident, that he didn't schedule programs about integration. "His present activities indicate a violation of that self-imposed restriction," the NAACP lawyer stated.[27]

The commission's response was a masterpiece of artful dodging. The Communications Act prohibited censorship of broadcasts, the FCC secretary wrote Evers, and the commission interpreted that provision as also forbidding the commission to compel a licensee to carry a specific program. "It is true, of course, that the commission's policies regarding licensee responsibility require a licensee to be fair in its presentation of controversial issues." The manner in which a balance should be struck in achieving this fairness and who should be the spokesperson for opposing viewpoints was left to the discretion of individual licensees, the letter added. The commission would consider the presentations of the station as a whole, rather than any single program, in determining the broadcaster's fairness. "As you may know, the over-all operations of a broadcast licensee are reviewed by the commission when it passes on the licensee's application for renewal of license."[28]

Ask yourself, as this story unfolds, how carefully the FCC adhered to this stated responsibility to scrutinize the overall operations of WLBT as it considered renewing its license. The FCC routinely accepted a broadcaster's word when it questioned a station about its behavior. Not until nine years after Evers's letter—and as a direct result of the challenge of WLBT—were citizens allowed to participate in commission business. In the 1950s and into the 1960s the only people who could legitimately be involved in proceedings at the FCC were those seeking a license, and thus having an economic interest, or those who could claim that they suffered some electrical interference from a station. The public had no "standing," as lawyers would say. The FCC would refer a complaint to the broadcaster, who most often would claim it hadn't happened or, if it had, there was a logical explanation or even that it wasn't happening anymore. And the FCC would take no action. Little in the FCC's history would have reassured Evers that the commission would be responsive.

In a letter to the commission the following year concerning WLBT's adherence to the Fairness Doctrine, Beard noted that the station had never considered it necessary to provide reply time for speeches by the president, the governor, or other elected representatives. Concerning the broadcast that Evers criticized, Beard acknowledged that no reply time was given "as we did not consider the matters presented as being controversial but a report from our duly elected officials to the people of Mississippi." Many people had called this statewide telecast one of the greatest public service programs ever presented in Mississippi, Beard added. "What was said on that program was most helpful in preventing serious trouble in the state by urging the citizens of the state to remain calm and look to the elected representatives for leadership."[29] But, no, it was not controversial.

WLBT's license came up for renewal in 1958. The commission deferred its decision because of complaints but in 1959 renewed the license.

Resistance to racial change and violence against blacks were not abating in Mississippi. In 1959 Mack Parker, awaiting trial on charges that he had raped a white woman, was killed by a white mob that took him from his jail cell in Poplarville. A Federal Bureau of

Investigation (FBI) probe of the lynching identified some members of the white mob, but the local grand jury issued no indictments. That same year, Clyde Kennard, a black former paratrooper who had attended the University of Chicago, sought unsuccessfully to enroll at Mississippi Southern College in Hattiesburg. Arrested a year later on a flagrantly trumped-up charge of stealing chicken feed, Kennard was sentenced to seven years in Parchman penitentiary. Thurgood Marshall and the NAACP fought for his release, which was obtained in 1963 only because Kennard had cancer. He died that summer.[30]

Despite killings and reprisals, civil rights activity persisted. In Jackson in the spring of 1961, Tougaloo College students, inspired by lunch counter sit-in demonstrations in North Carolina, tried to use the downtown public library and were arrested. They were charged under a 1960 state law requiring groups to leave a public place when ordered to do so. Students at Jackson State, another black college in the capital, organized a sympathy protest, which was broken up by the school's president. The next day they marched toward the city jail. When police ordered them to break up their demonstration, they refused. The police fired tear gas and charged the students with clubs and police dogs. The next day the police also beat blacks who had gathered outside the trial of the Tougaloo students. Student protests mounted at the same time as one of the Freedom Riders' buses arrived in Jackson. These activists, testing the refusal of southern bus stations to provide unsegregated waiting rooms, restaurants, and restrooms as required by federal law, had been badly beaten in Montgomery, Alabama. Whites torched one of their buses outside Anniston, Alabama. In Jackson, they were quickly and quietly arrested, as were other Freedom Riders who poured into the state that summer.

WLBT covered the arrival of the "so-called Freedom Riders," as the station identified the first twelve protesters to arrive in Jackson. "From all reports," Richard Sanders told his audience, "the state reacted as authorities and civic leaders asked . . . no violence, with state and local authorities in complete control, and in sufficient numbers to have coped with any situation." In the script for a news special aired May 24, 1961, the station quoted the public safety commissioner, T. B. Birdsong, at length about the commendable behavior of Jacksonians. "You've got to hand it to the people of Mississippi. They were just as nice as they could be. They didn't jeer. They didn't yell. They didn't do anything. When we would tell them to move on, they would move on." There was no comment from any of those arrested or their supporters as to why they had conducted their protest.[31]

In a broadcast two days later about the trial of the Freedom Riders, WLBT reported that the protesters' defense attorney had argued that his clients had been arrested because of their race and that the arrest violated the U.S. Constitution and regulations of the Interstate Commerce Commission. Municipal Judge James Spencer found the defendants guilty of a breach of the peace. Rather than challenge the law through proper procedures, Spencer said, the defendants had chosen to take the law into their own hands. They were not "traveling for traveling but for enflaming the populace. . . . Their conduct had already led to violence," he added. "We are not going to let judicial questions be decided by mob violence."[32] Any violence, however, came not from the Freedom Riders but from those who tried to block their access to bus stations that under federal regulations were supposed to be desegregated. That was not noted in the newscast script.

WLBT continued to cover the trials of the Freedom Riders and other demonstrations in Jackson. For example, WLBT sent a reporter to cover the December 1961 meeting in Jackson of the Mississippi Civil Rights Advisory Committee, which heard complaints of voter discrimination and alleged police brutality. Early the next year, WLBT staffed another advisory committee meeting at which three Madison County blacks said they had been threatened because they appeared before the committee in December. WLBT sent a staff member to report on the annual meeting of the association representing the state's black teachers the following March. At that meeting, the retiring president, O. E. Jordan of Carthage, said, "For those of us who live in Mississippi it seems to me that if we do not find some avenue for peaceful coexistence, for mutual respect for the individual based on his ability, we are in great danger."[33]

Late in 1961 a fifty-nine-year-old Baptist minister, supermarket operator, and former letter carrier in Jackson, the Reverend R. L. T. Smith, decided to run for Congress, the first black person to do so since Reconstruction. "I wasn't silly enough to believe I could win the seat," said the soft-spoken NAACP activist, "but I could focus attention on the plight of blacks who could not register."[34] Mississippi still had a poll tax which, coupled with a registration test that questioned arcane knowledge of the state constitution, kept most blacks from voting. Smith wanted to buy airtime on WLBT well before the election to urge people to pay their poll tax so they could vote. Fred Beard turned him down, saying the election would not be held for many months.

Smith was able to buy time on WJTV, Jackson's other station. On that broadcast in December 1961, Smith urged voters to ignore "the screaming epithets of bigotry." Mississippians could not live in the past, he said. "The time is far spent when men of insight and ability can afford to remain silent when unscrupulous politicians get themselves elected by waving the red flag of hatred and bigotry, thus confusing the minds of people who are inherently good." If Mississippi did not solve its problems, Smith commented, "the blame will, in large part, be due to shortsighted planning by men holding high elective offices in our state government and by cunning men and predatory organizations who peddle hate with the use of our tax money." Although he didn't name the Citizens' Councils or the Sovereignty

Commission, a state-financed agency that spied on civil rights work-ers, it was clear whom he meant.[35]

Myrlie Evers recalled the impact of Smith's televised speech. "It was the first time in the memory of anyone that a Negro had been seen on Mississippi television giving a political speech. The blackout of tele-vision news on civil rights had gone so far that network news pro-grams originating in New York were systematically interrupted with signs indicating technical difficulties whenever the news turned to race. We had been denied all of the network documentaries on civil rights. We were cut off from news developments within our own state. The only news we received on race relations was the distorted news the local stations decided that we should have," she wrote in her 1967 book, *For Us, the Living.*[36]

"Against this background of suppression," Evers added, "the sight and sound of the Reverend Robert L. T. Smith . . . were like the lift-ing of a giant curtain. No one believed that he could win the Democratic nomination with Negroes largely excluded from voting, but he was a voice, and he was on television, and he was saying things that had never before been said by a Negro to whites in Mississippi."

What Smith said angered some white viewers. A station representa-tive told the FCC that he got so many phone calls threatening to blow up the transmitter or harm staff members that he told Smith that WJTV would not present him again on TV until he appeared on WLBT as well. Smith still wanted to appear on WLBT, but he contin-ued to face what he considered racial discrimination on the station's part. The time that he had requested, Smith told the FCC in January 1962, was necessary because blacks' interest in voting had been killed by threats and intimidation.[37] Smith also wrote Attorney General Robert Kennedy that WLBT had not only denied him airtime, it had run a ninety-minute program on December 29, 1961, on which former general Edwin Walker and Congressman John Bell Williams had lambasted the present administration in Washington. Williams was Smith's opponent in the upcoming primary election. Walker, a militant anti-Communist, had resigned from the army that November after being disciplined for insubordination.[38]

In response, Fred Beard wired the commission that WLBT would sell Smith time two months before the election (after the poll-tax deadline). "We felt that there is no public interest in what any candidate might say regarding the office six to eight months before the election." Beard said Smith had "told us what time he wanted two days before he wanted the time. He wanted to take half of the Sing Along with Mitch [Miller] time at 9 P.M. on Thursday night." In a subsequent letter to the FCC, Beard added that the station had assured Smith that no one would be able to buy more time than he could buy. "We have also made it clear to Rev. Smith that he cannot walk into our station on Tuesday and tell us that we are going to sell him a half-hour period on Thursday."[39]

The following day, Smith again requested to buy time. Again he was refused. Again he wrote the attorney general and wired the FCC.[40] Later in February Smith received a letter from the FCC outlining the equal-time rules under the Communications Act. Because WLBT had not sold airtime to any other candidates for the office Smith was seeking and because it had offered to sell him time two months before the election and spot announcements right away, the FCC said no further action seemed warranted.[41]

Smith's situation did not go unnoticed outside Mississippi. In March he traveled north to raise money for his campaign and to seek moral support. Visiting New York, he and his attorney, Bill Higgs, a young white man from Mississippi, had lunch with former first lady Eleanor Roosevelt. "Here were two Mississippians born and bred in communities deeply ingrained with the southern tradition," Roosevelt wrote in her weekly column. "One was black and he was trying to run for Congress, something unheard of since the days of the Civil War. Yet if his race was to have representation it certainly was eminently fair that he should be on the ballot and that his people should be allowed to qualify for voting if they complied with the legal requirements." He and his lawyer faced harassment and economic pressures condoned by public officials. "They do not even move to prevent violence in their states and this is a sorry spectacle that is not ignored in the rest of the world."[42]

New York Post columnist James A. Wechsler also wrote about Smith and his opponent, John Bell Williams, whom he described as "a raucous spokesman of white supremacy." He wondered why Smith, at age fifty-nine and the father of eleven children, a man who had won respectability within the limits of Mississippi's caste system, would have chosen this fight. "The answer is not really complicated," Wechsler concluded. "It involves only the dignity of man, which John Bell Williams will never understand."[43]

On Smith's return to Mississippi, he continued to write letters—to the FCC, the Commission on Civil Rights, and the Democratic National Committee—complaining about WLBT's unwillingness to sell him airtime. On April 12 Beard notified Smith and the commission that the station had decided it would not be in the public interest to sell airtime to any candidates in his congressional race.[44]

"By excluding both Rev. Smith and incumbent segregationist Williams from the air," Wechsler wrote in a second column about the issue, "the station has assumed a spurious position of aloofness that deceives no one in the state. As Rev. Smith points out, the action is a crude continuation of the effort to smother his candidacy." Wechsler quoted Smith: "Because of rigid customs and usages here, white citizens would hardly dare to come to any public meeting to hear me speak. Negro citizens, by the same token, fear to come because of the long-existing taboo on Negroes participating in political affairs.

I merely want a chance to reach these people by means of television in their own homes and reason with them. Beyond a doubt this would awaken many to the fact the disfranchisement of Negro citizens also penalizes white citizens and we all lose."

Calling Smith's battle to be heard "more than a local incident," Wechsler concluded: "Obviously this dispute involves a fateful precedent. It threatens the conspiracy of silence through which southern racists hope to convince Negroes that it is futile for them to seek office. [FCC chairman] Newton Minow and his colleagues have a historic chance to challenge that conspiracy in as clear-cut a case as they will ever get. . . . It is a big moment in the quest for a new political era in the south. Undoubtedly that is why the racists are engaged in such a variety of efforts to blot out the image of this quiet, earnest man."[45]

The FCC became somewhat more responsive as Smith gathered these influential supporters. Once again Lamar Life received a letter from the FCC. The commission reminded WLBT that the FCC considered carrying political broadcasts a public service criterion to be used in license renewal proceedings and that the U.S. Supreme Court had upheld this section of the law.[46] On April 23 Smith reported to Burke Marshall, the chief of the Justice Department's Civil Rights Division, that he had finally succeeded. "After calling on the President and through the efforts of many other fine people, including Mrs. Eleanor Roosevelt, the television black-out against my campaign has been broken." WLBT had agreed to sell him thirty minutes of airtime on May 4. But still there were problems.

"Today the manager, Mr. Fred Beard, told me and two members of my campaign committee that there was great danger for me. He said there had been many threats against WJTV—Channel 12, to blow it up. He said he would hire fifty policemen, put a fence all around the grounds of the studio and that he would pull all curtains down and barricade all windows. He said he would double all of his insurance.

He said that his body and mine, too, would likely be found in the river. Of course, Pearl River is right across the street from the studio." Smith didn't know whether Beard's assessment was correct, but he asked Marshall to investigate and to provide protection if necessary. "As you know, I am for the President and his administration straight down the line, and doubtless the Kluxers and such would gladly cooperate with any one who appears to wish to harm us. It is a fact that as of now, the States-Righters and the elements that wish to continue to disfranchise Negro citizens are definitely in control, and brutality, fear and even murder has [sic] sometimes been used heretofore."[47] Smith said later that he took Beard's words as a threat. Beard said it wasn't— it was a realistic description of what might happen.

News director Sanders vividly remembered Smith going through those boarded doors. "Fred Beard, with some justification, feared the rednecks in Rankin County just across the river from WLBT might bomb the station. So he had the windows facing the Pearl River and the front door covered with heavy plyboard and painted, as I recall, the blue that was the trim of most of the building."[48]

In his remarks aired on WLBT, Smith said that if elected he would vigorously support the Kennedy administration in both domestic and foreign policy. According to a UPI story, he delivered a blistering attack on his opponent in the upcoming primary, John Bell Williams, without mentioning him by name. "The short-sightedness of my opponent has caused him to consistently vote against many bills in Congress that would have helped Mississippi." Smith said that Mississippi was the poorest state in the Union, and the representation it was receiving would keep it at the bottom of all fifty states.

He added that he would work for more federal aid to schools. "We have the poorest schools. Nobody is helping you by voting against measures that would help you catch up with the rest of the nation." Smith pledged to support legislation to broaden the wage-and-hour law, to back a more comprehensive program of medical care for the aged (this was three years before Medicare was created), and to strengthen unemployment insurance.

If elected, Smith said, "I will do my every bit to help Mississippi get in step with the 20th century." Disenfranchisement of black voters in Mississippi, he added, "has contributed to no small degree in helping keep Mississippi on the bottom in practically all areas where human betterment" is the objective.[49]

Smith took care to thank Eleanor Roosevelt, citing her help in writing Newton Minow.[50] Smith had clearly been moved by his visit with the former first lady. "With her rich background of human relationships, she is keenly sensitive to the needs for the betterment of mankind the world over," he wrote later. "It was most rewarding to listen to her" and recognize her commitment to the teachings of Christ and to the aims of the U.S. Constitution.[51]

After Smith appeared twice on WLBT, he returned to the air on WJTV. The station received fewer than ten phone calls after this appearance, said WJTV's general manager, L. M. Sepaugh. He explained to the commission that Mississippians became violently upset over the first violations of precedent involving race relations and then gradually accepted at least some changes.[52]

As these events occurred in Jackson, elsewhere in the state young black activists were trying to persuade frightened black sharecroppers to register to vote. Police and local political leaders resisted their efforts at every step of the way, from McComb in the southwest to the Delta farther north. Landowners threw people off their farms who dared seek to vote. For example, Fannie Lou Hamer, a forty-four-year-old timekeeper on a plantation in Sunflower County, was fired and evicted in August 1962 because she and a busload of other black people had gone to the county seat to try to register.

In 1962 WLBT drew criticism again. On June 28 Medgar Evers wrote Fred Beard requesting time to respond to Citizens' Council programs on racial segregation. On July 12 Beard responded, saying that the race question had not been mentioned on any recent *Citizens' Council Forum*. He denied Evers's request.[53] The Citizens' Councils' very reason for existence, of course, was the race question. On July 16 Evers wrote the FCC in complaint; Beard again responded that he would not grant broadcast time. Beard was acting on advice of WLBT's local lawyer, who had consulted with Russell Rowell, a Washington, D.C., attorney. "I concur with you in recommending to station WLBT that the letter of July 16 from Medgar Evers should be ignored," Rowell wrote W. C. Wells Jr. "Undoubtedly, Evers will endeavor to have the Federal Communications Commission bring pressure to bear on the station to accept the program of the NAACP. However, I see no justification for the station to recognize the NAACP as being an authorized spokesman to oppose views expressed on the Forum program carried on occasion by WLBT which does not relate to matters which directly concern the NAACP."[54]

The biggest flare-up between WLBT and civil rights forces before the formal legal challenge to the station occurred after federal courts ordered that James Meredith be admitted to the University of Mississippi in the fall of 1962. The young crusaders at work in Jackson, in McComb, and in the Delta had drawn relatively little national attention up to that point. But riots surrounding Meredith's entry to the university put the focus on Mississippi.

Meredith, an Air Force veteran, had started college at Jackson State, then wanted to enroll at the University of Mississippi. Constance Baker Motley and Derrick Bell, his NAACP attorneys, fought court battle after court battle, winning admission for Meredith. Actual enrollment would be another matter—just as public school enrollment still was for black children. Governor Ross Barnett had pledged resistance.

WLBT in essence told the FCC later that it covered more elements of the Ole Miss–James Meredith crisis than any other television station. It covered meetings of the state college board, speeches by the governor, and events in Oxford. Both chief reporter-photographer Cliff Bingham and Richard Sanders traveled to New Orleans to cover a key federal court hearing, "the only Mississippi reporters to make the trip," as WLBT said in a filing to the FCC. On September 25, when Barnett stopped Meredith from entering the state college board offices in Jackson to register as ordered by a federal court, WLBT said, it was the only station there throughout the afternoon. It also shot the only film of the governor's refusal to submit to federal court orders.[55]

As the day approached for Meredith's arrival at the Oxford campus, Fred Beard editorialized on WLBT that Mississippi was facing "the final hour in its official fight to maintain segregation in all of its public schools. The showdown that has been building up since 1954 is here. Mississippi is fortunate in having men at its leadership who have vowed to prevent integration of our schools. The very sovereignty of our state is threatened." He pointed out that the U.S. Constitution reserved to the states those powers not specifically delegated to the federal government, and running the public school system was one of those powers. "We urge all Mississippians to again trust their elected officials to handle this problem as they so ably handled last year's Freedom Rides."[56]

The following day Barnett spoke on the air, saying, "No schools will be integrated while I am your governor." Calling Meredith's admission "our greatest crisis since the War Between the States," Barnett said that the federal government was "employing naked and arbitrary power." Even as he spoke, the governor added, "professional agitators, an unfriendly liberal press and other troublemakers are pouring across our borders, intent upon instigating strife among our people," and the Kennedy administration was lending its power to "the ruthless demands of these agitators." Barnett assured Mississippians that the university and other public schools would not be closed if that could possibly be avoided, "but they will not be integrated," he stressed. "If there be any official who is not prepared to suffer imprisonment for this righteous cause, I ask him now to submit his resignation."[57] He placed the sovereignty of the state of Mississippi against enforcement of the court decree. In a WLBT editorial, Beard declared that the governor had said, " 'Never' and he means 'Never.' . . . We can all stand with him and say 'Never!' "[58]

Beard hammered away. On September 17 he editorialized that Washington seemed "more concerned about placing a student in the University of Mississippi, for political purposes, than they are about removing thousands of Communist troops from Cuba. Why must the federal government continue to harass the loyal, patriotic southern states—states who are more responsible today for this great nation of ours than any other segment of our nation? If our nation is to survive the threats of socialism from within our country, it will survive through the efforts of the southern states."[59]

At one point, according to charges filed later by the AFL-CIO of Mississippi, Beard appealed over the air for Mississippians to surround the governor's mansion with a "wall of human flesh" to protect Barnett against federal troops who were rumored planning to arrest him there.[60] There was no such plan; the AFL-CIO said that Beard knew that the governor was considering capitulating to let Meredith into the university, and he wanted to produce a show of support to buck up his courage. Beard later denied that he made any such comments on the air.[61]

Beard also editorialized about the death from a heart attack of the city editor of the local newspaper, Gene Wirth. Beard called Wirth's death during this crisis "the first casualty in the fight to prevent integration in the public schools. Unfortunately, I am afraid that Gene will not be the last casualty of this fight to preserve segregation in the schools of Mississippi." Beard aimed some of his fire at newspapers, magazines, and broadcasters from outside the state. "You will hear little about the support we are receiving from thousands of people from every state in the Union. The liberal press, radio and television will only give coverage to those who will condemn us for the stand that Mississippi has taken."[62]

On September 30, 1962, federal marshals escorted James Meredith onto the Oxford campus. Governor Barnett had secretly promised President John F. Kennedy and his brother, Robert, the attorney general, to maintain order as Meredith enrolled. He did not keep his promise. The federal marshals were quickly outnumbered by several thousand students and others. In rioting that followed, a French journalist and an Oxford bystander were killed, and 160 federal marshals were wounded before army troops arrived to restore order. WLBT and its affiliated radio station sent five reporters to Oxford. When the journalists left Jackson, Sanders recalled in a commentary aired October 4, "We had no idea . . . that our crew and other reporters would be working under conditions that can be likened only to rebellions in South America or Asia. In wartime, the correspondents know at least the general direction from which the attack may come." But on the darkened campus, with demonstrators coming from all directions, the immediate danger was from all sides. Photographers were attacked and their equipment destroyed; turning on lights to film the action would have been dangerous, Sanders said.[63]

Events at the campus riveted the nation's attention. The FCC received complaints about citizens band radio operators whipping up anti-integration sentiment and about the performance of several television stations, including WLBT. The situation proved too intense to ignore. The FCC sent two investigators, William Ray and John O'Malley, to Mississippi, although it waited until mid-November to dispatch them. Their assignment was to look into charges that broadcasters and CBers had incited a riot and that some broadcasters had violated the Fairness Doctrine. In a rigorous investigation, the FCC staff members interviewed fifty-four people between November 14 and 24, 1962, visiting five radio stations and three television stations. They traveled to Oxford, Hickory Flat, Amory, Mathiston, Columbus, Jackson, and Tougaloo as well as to Memphis, Tennessee. The FCC reported later that many people were unwilling to have their identities revealed as complainants because of "fear of social or business repercussions or, in some cases, fear of physical violence."[64]

Ray, then fifty-four years old, had long experience in broadcasting and ended his career as head of the complaints and compliance division of the FCC Broadcast Bureau. Born in a small town in Arkansas, he had worked as a reporter at the *Louisville Courier-Journal* and received a bachelor's degree from the University of Chicago. He worked for NBC in Chicago, eventually becoming its Midwest news director before joining the FCC. He was on the Broadcast Bureau staff when he went to Mississippi.[65]

O'Malley, then thirty-eight, grew up in Reading, Massachusetts, around the corner from the police station. He had not given much thought to college. "Irish Catholics thought in terms of getting on the police department," he said. But after World War II, in which he served as an infantryman in the 84th Division in Europe, he was able to use the GI Bill to go to Boston College for bachelor's and master's degrees and then graduated third in his class from the Georgetown University law school. He began working at the FCC in 1955 and later served as liaison between the commission and the Department of Justice and the FBI. In that job, he read a lot of FBI reports. "I knew how to make an investigation," he later told me. "I had an idea what looked good and what didn't."[66] Before investigating the Mississippi stations, O'Malley had conducted an earlier FCC probe into the payola scandals. Thousands of disc jockeys had been accepting money from record companies for playing their recordings on the air, and some also held stock in record companies. O'Malley was on the staff of the FCC general counsel when he and Ray went to Mississippi.

When they arrived, "you could cut the tension," O'Malley said. Guns were everywhere. "You knew that in a moment of passion someone could simply blow people away." The federal government was held in such contempt that the only American flag O'Malley saw during his entire stay in the state was at the U.S. courthouse in Jackson. Bumper stickers read, "The Kennedy Brothers Are the Castro Brothers." At a motel where Ray and O'Malley stayed near Oxford, the owner asked the men for whom they worked. O'Malley replied, "The FCC." In ignorance that helped the FCC men, the owner said that that was okay. "If I thought you worked for the federal government, I would have thrown you out."

Medgar Evers gave the investigators a list of the times WLBT had allegedly broadcast messages urging people to join the Citizens' Council. These turned out to be one-minute and twenty-second spots that the Citizens' Council had paid for and were identified as such. The spots argued that Communists were behind integration moves in the state and that people should join the council to help fight integration. Even though the FCC staff later reported that the announcements complied with the law concerning sponsorship identification, it added that the announcements "definitely did advocate one side of a controversial public issue."[67] Beard could point to nothing that he had done to encourage broadcasting all sides of that issue, "unless his vague claim to having 'let it be known many times that time is available on our stations'" is considered as establishing compliance with the policy, the staff said.

O'Malley recalled sitting with Bill Ray in Medgar Evers's office in Jackson, "looking out the windows and seeing bullet holes [in the wall] and realizing that Medgar Evers had somehow decided he was locked into this for better or worse. He was going to keep up this fight with WLBT and the other stations until justice was done. He was very resolute. I would say he never showed any hate." Seeing Evers taught O'Malley that "you can pound a man, try to frighten him, but some people don't give up." Rev. Smith, who would later become one of the challengers of the WLBT license, was the same way. Both Evers and Smith had undoubtedly lost faith that the FCC would ever regulate the stations. "I felt sorry for them. They were both waging a fight, handling things quietly but firmly, and Washington wasn't paying any attention to them," O'Malley remarked.

WLBT really didn't have too many worries, O'Malley said. "They knew the FCC wasn't going to do anything." Before Ray and O'Malley left Washington, *Broadcasting* magazine, the industry bible with many sources within the commission, reported that the investigation had been postponed. "We sneaked down without *Broadcasting* knowing. Beard was appalled when we walked in."

Beard explained to the FCC investigators that WLBT had begun editorializing regularly after commission chairman Newton Minow had urged broadcasters to do so at a conference of the National Association of Broadcasters (NAB) that March. "The editorials are written or approved by me, read by a member of our staff and presented as the views of the management of the station," Beard said in a summary of information he had given to Ray and O'Malley. WLBT and its affiliated radio station also carried the *Citizens' Council Forum* but had aired no forums dealing with integration, he said.

"We never broadcast any advice, exhortation or message urging citizens either to go to Oxford during the crisis there, or to surround the Governor's mansion here in Jackson." Beard said that the station believed its overall treatment of the school integration question, especially involving Meredith's enrollment at Ole Miss, had been balanced. In fact, he thought it was strongly in favor of the federal government's position because "the network programs have been very top-heavy in favor of federal intervention and against state's [*sic*] rights."

The station had broadcast network interviews with Martin Luther King Jr., Thurgood Marshall, and other prominent blacks, he said, adding that WLBT had never refused to broadcast special network programs on race because they presented blacks or dealt with racial issues. No one had ever been refused time on WLBT in connection with one of its editorials, Beard went on. "As far as I know, no one down here is against state's [*sic*] rights, which is what we occasionally have editorialized about." Beard said that he previewed any network specials that touched on integration or race and did not broadcast them if they were likely to cause violence in the area.[68]

Fred Beard was "a sincere believer in segregation," O'Malley observed. "Blacks belonged with themselves and whites belonged with themselves. He was a believer in states' rights, that this was not a federal matter. And he had been getting away with it for so many years." As the FCC would later say in its driest legalese, "Persons interviewed in Mississippi by the commission's investigators generally agreed that Beard had been the most active of all broadcasters in the use of radio and television to promote segregation and to oppose federal intervention."[69] Beard insisted that the editorials that had drawn complaints to the commission concerned states' rights as guaranteed by the Tenth Amendment to the U.S. Constitution, "not school integration as such."[70]

The investigation involving the other Jackson television station—WJTV—and its affiliated radio station disclosed no evidence that these stations broadcast anything tending to incite to riot, said an

FCC report. "They did not even send a reporter to Oxford, lest he broadcast inflammatory material. On the whole, this licensee seems to have exhibited greater restraint and more sense of responsibility during the Ole Miss crisis than any other which was the subject of a complaint."[71] The principal violation that could be charged against WJTV, the report said, was its lack of effort to broadcast all sides of controversial issues presented on radio broadcasts by the *Citizens' Council Forum*.

O'Malley's investigation clearly had an impact on him, one that he remembered more than thirty-five years later when I interviewed him in his home in Fredericksburg, Texas, where he had retired. "It's one thing to see something on TV like the war in Kosovo when you're removed from it," O'Malley said of fighting that had just occurred. "You see the refugees and the bombing and you think, 'That's awful but what can I do about it?' I don't think there's any substitute for being on the scene, perceiving the smells and the horror." The WLBT case, he said, undoubtedly "made people more sensitive, more aware of the terrible evil that the case represented. All these problems had all simply stemmed from the color of a person's skin." In his mind, he could still see Medgar Evers. "He was a very calm individual. He was just trying to get whatever was coming to him."

As the commission staff worked on its report, protests against discrimination escalated in Jackson. College students picketed downtown stores during the 1962 Christmas buying season but received little support from the national NAACP leadership, always wary of direct action. In March 1963 Medgar Evers and a handful of other parents sued to try to desegregate Jackson's public schools. On May 12 the Mississippi NAACP adopted a resolution calling for fair employment practices as well as equal access to restrooms, restaurants, theaters, parks, schools, and libraries for blacks and whites. It urged the mayor to appoint a biracial committee to work toward these goals and vowed to continue selective buying campaigns and other demonstrations if he did not. Mayor Allen Thompson turned them down, saying, "The only thing that can come of such an arrangement is compliance with the demands of racial agitators from outside. The agitators decide who will represent them on such committees, not the local Negroes."[72]

That night Thompson broadcast a message over WLBT and other local stations that, despite "terrible trouble in some of our neighboring states," the people of Jackson would continue their way of doing things. He directed much of his talk to blacks in the audience. "When all the agitation is over," he said, "Jackson will still be prosperous, people will still be happy, and the races will live side by side in peace and harmony." The city had some of the best facilities anywhere, the mayor added. "Beautiful, wonderful schools, parks, playgrounds, libraries, and so many, many other things. Next, there are no slums. Have you ever thought about it?"[73]

During May, the previously cautious NAACP national leadership started demonstrating its support for the Jackson movement. It was spurred on, historian John Dittmer wrote, by the international attention the organization's civil rights rival, Martin Luther King Jr. and the Southern Christian Leadership Conference (SCLC), had been drawing with demonstrations in Birmingham.[74] Police there turned fire hoses and dogs on protesters. Photos of men, women, and children blasted against walls by streams of water or chased by snarling dogs flashed around the world. Gloster B. Current, the director of NAACP branches, traveled to Jackson with several other leaders for conferences with community leaders, while Clarence Mitchell, the NAACP's Washington, D.C., bureau director, spoke at a public meeting in Jackson on May 12.

Even more surprising than the arrival in Jackson of NAACP leaders was the announcement that local television stations would give Medgar Evers airtime on May 20 to respond to Mayor Thompson,

as Evers had requested. The civil rights leader worked especially hard
preparing this speech, his wife remembered, reading parts of it aloud
to her, returning to his desk to rewrite it. "He had always taken
speeches in his stride, usually speaking just from notes, but we both
knew this was different. This time he would be speaking not just for
the NAACP but for all of the Negroes of Jackson, of Mississippi, and
in a way, everywhere."

Myrlie Evers was nervous. "Thousands of Mississippi whites who
had never seen a picture of him would now be seeing Medgar on television. They would have time to become familiar with his appearance. When it was over, he would be recognized everywhere: at a stop
light in the city, on a lonely road in the Delta, in the light from the
fuel pump at a gas station."[75]

Viewers expected to see their regular programming, and some
called the WLBT in protest. "Will you please get the damn nigger
off the air?" one woman insisted.[76]

Using a moderate tone, Evers gave a seventeen-minute speech. He
taped it at WLBT, then watched himself on television later in the
evening in a home near the Masonic Temple, one of Jackson's longtime civil rights meeting places. "I speak as a native Mississippian," he
began. "I was educated in Mississippi schools, and served overseas in
our nation's armed forces in the war against Hitlerism and Fascism."
He went on to refute the mayor's contention that the NAACP was
an outside group. Half its membership was southern, he said. There
had been a branch of the NAACP in Mississippi since 1918 and in
Jackson since 1926.

Evers rejected the idea that, left alone, Mississippi would change.
It was the Supreme Court, he said, that had opened the way for blacks
to vote, attend public schools, travel, and use nonsegregated public
facilities. The American tradition recognized the right to demonstrate,
to assemble peacefully, and to petition the government for a redress of

grievances. "Such a petition may legitimately take the form of picket-ing, although in Jackson, Negroes are immediately arrested when they attempt to exercise this constitutional right." Evers urged the mayor to appoint the biracial committee that blacks were requesting.

Blacks were discontent, he said, because they could see change occurring throughout the world but not at home. "Tonight the Negro plantation worker in the Delta knows from his radio and television what happened today all over the world. He knows what black people are doing and he knows what white people are doing. He can see on the 6:00 o'clock news screen the picture of a 3:00 o'clock bite by a police dog. He knows that Willie Mays, a Birmingham Negro, is the highest paid baseball player in the nation. He knows that Leontyne Price, a native of Laurel, Mississippi, is a star with the Metropolitan Opera in New York. He knows about the new free nations in Africa and knows that a Congo native can be a locomotive engineer but in Jackson he cannot even drive a garbage truck. He can see black prime ministers and ambassadors, financiers and technicians."

When a black man looked at Jackson, what, Evers asked rhetori-cally, did he see, "to quote our mayor, in this 'progressive, beautiful, friendly, prosperous city with an exciting future'? He sees a city where Negro citizens are refused admittance to the City Auditorium and the Coliseum; his children refused a ticket to a good movie in a downtown theater; his wife and children refused service at a lunch counter in a downtown store where they trade; students refused the use of the main public libraries, parks, playgrounds and other tax-supported recre-ational facilities. He sees Negro lawyers, physicians, dentists, teachers and other professionals prevented from attending meetings of profes-sional organizations. He sees a city of over 150,000, of which 40 per-cent is Negro, in which there is not a single black police officer, school crossing guard, fireman, clerk, stenographer or supervisor employed in any city department or in the mayor's office in other than menial capacities, except those employed in segregated facilities—the College Park Auditorium, Carver Library and the segregated schools. He sees local hospitals which segregate Negro patients and deny staff privileges to Negro family physicians.

"The mayor spoke of the twenty-four-hour police protection we have," Evers added. "There are questions in the minds of many Negroes whether we have twenty-four hours of protection, or twenty-four hours of harassment." Evers enumerated what blacks in Jackson wanted and what they did not have, such as voting rights, jobs above a menial level in stores where they spent their money, and integrated public schools and universities. He asked the white population: "If you suffered these deprivations, were often called by your first name, 'boy,' 'girl,' 'auntie,' and 'uncle,' would you not be discontent?

". . . The NAACP believes that Jackson can change if it wills to do so. If there should be resistance, how much better to have turbulence to effect improvement, rather than turbulence to maintain a stand-pat policy. We believe there are white Mississippians who want to go forward on the race question. Their religion tells them there is something wrong with the old system. Their sense of justice and fair play sends the same message. But whether Jackson and the state choose change or not, the years of change are upon us. In the racial picture things will never be as they once were. History has reached a turning point, here and over the world.

"Here in Jackson, we can recognize the situation and make an honest effort to bring fresh ideas and new methods to bear, or we can have what Mayor Thompson called 'turbulent times.' If we choose this latter course, the turbulence will come, not because of so-called agitators or presence or absence of the NAACP, but because the time has come for a change and certain citizens refuse to accept the inevitable.

"Negro citizens want to help all other good citizens bring about a meaningful improvement in an orderly fashion . . . the two races have lived here together. The Negro has been in America since 1619, a total of 344 years. He is not going anywhere else; this country is his home. He wants to do his part to help make his city, state and nation a better place for everyone regardless of color and race.

"Let me appeal to the consciences of many silent, responsible citizens of the white community who know that a victory for democracy in Jackson will be a victory for democracy everywhere."[77]

After Evers's speech, the phone rang at his home with complimentary phone calls, many of them from whites, none of whom gave their names. Myrlie Evers said whites seemed more polite in the shops over the next few days, and people in the black community were calm and proud.[78] But she was correct in her fears. Although Evers's work had previously threatened white domination of Mississippi, he himself had not been a visible figure. His TV appearance put him in the crosshairs, as did the escalating protests in Jackson over the next few weeks. People now had a face to match his name in the papers.

On May 28 Tougaloo students sat in at the Woolworth's lunch counter to seek service. One student was beaten, then arrested for disturbing the peace. A white mob poured ketchup and mustard and salt and pepper on the students. The next night a firebomb was thrown into the Everses' carport. Myrlie Evers, home with the couple's children, put the flames out with a garden hose. When her husband reached home later, she told him angrily that the investigating police had virtually accused her of setting off the bomb with gas that the Everses used for their lawnmower.[79]

In early June the national NAACP leaders announced that there would be no more mass marches. Medgar Evers was caught in the middle between his bosses and the students. Threats continued, and his friends wanted him to have a full-time bodyguard. They were willing to pay part of the cost and asked the NAACP's Gloster Current if the national organization would match their funds. Myrlie Evers recalled that Current denied the request, saying, "The NAACP has more important things to do with its money."

"It's okay," Evers told his wife. "When my time comes, I'm going to go regardless of the protection I have. Besides, I don't want anyone to get hurt trying to save me."[80]

On June 11 President Kennedy spoke on national television about events at the University of Alabama, where two black students had just been admitted. Kennedy said that it should be anyone's right, no matter what color, to receive equal service in restaurants and hotels without having to demonstrate in the streets. People should also be able to vote without interference or fear of reprisal. It was time for Congress to act, he said, and he proposed a civil rights bill to open public accommodations to all, to speed school desegregation, and to protect the right to vote. Kennedy's action represented his firmest commitment to date in the field of civil rights.

Medgar Evers had attended a meeting at a local church the evening of the speech, while Myrlie stayed with the children at home where they watched the president's message. Later they heard Evers's car pulling into the driveway, then they heard a shot. Evers had trained his children to stay away from windows and to fall onto the floor if they heard gunfire. They did as they had been taught. Myrlie Evers ran to the door and saw her husband lying in the driveway. He had dropped some NAACP sweatshirts that said, "Jim Crow Must Go." Blood was everywhere. Medgar Evers was taken to the University of Mississippi Hospital, where he died.

Street demonstrations followed Evers's funeral in Jackson and threatened to lead to violence until Justice Department official John Doar stepped in and persuaded people to go home. At the same time that Evers was killed, police in Winona, Mississippi, arrested and beat a group of civil rights workers returning from voter education training in South Carolina. When they were finally released, Fannie Lou

Hamer, Annelle Ponder, Lawrence Guyot, June Johnson, and the others learned that Evers had been killed.

The next month, following Bill Ray and John O'Malley's investigation, the FCC announced its decision. The commission accepted its staff's recommendation that the Mississippi stations—chief among them WLBT—be put on notice that the commission's inquiry into incidents surrounding James Meredith's entry into Ole Miss had "revealed serious public interest questions which are likely to arise again as racial integration becomes an ever more acute problem, not only in the South but in other areas of the country."[81] For example, the FCC told WLBT that its *Comment* program, broadcast five times a week, apparently had never included any spokespersons for favoring or expediting integration.

The FCC investigation had raised serious questions about whether WLBT had complied with the requirement that stations offer reasonable opportunities for the discussion of opposing views. As the commission wrote Lamar Life Broadcasting, WLBT's owner, on July 25, 1963, there were also serious questions "whether you have operated your station in the public interest, rather than for your own private interest." The commission did not mean to question the station's judgment for editorializing from the segregation viewpoint, its letter said. But its investigation showed that the station had apparently not consulted with representative black leaders to learn the views of their large community on this issue. WLBT was told it could not dodge its obligations by saying the broadcasts concerned states' rights, not school integration as such. The station's editorials also raised a serious question because "a licensee cannot properly permit his facilities to be used to incite a riot . . . or to prevent, by unlawful means, implementation of a court order." The FCC asked WLBT to respond within forty days.[82]

In October P. K. Lutken, president of Lamar Life Broadcasting, sent a thirty-six-page letter to the FCC, saying that the station had "always made a conscientious and sincere effort to serve the public interest" of its community. Jackson was still a small community, Lutken said, and the station management believed that it and its staff were in continual contact with and had knowledge of that community's problems. Management shared the feelings, desires, mores, and customs of the local people and made what it considered informed and intelligent decisions in the light of the climate of the community. Lest he be misunderstood, Lutken added: "The vast majority of the community leaders and the citizens of Jackson are pro-segregationist. The management believes that the majority of the Negroes in the community, although openly favoring integration, fully realize that there are many ways to achieve this objective. The management also believes that the majority of the Negro citizens are as concerned as the white citizens with the prevention of violence."

As early as 1955, Lutken noted, the station management had told the FCC that it did not provide program time to either the Citizens' Council or the NAACP to discuss integration. In keeping with that policy, the station still did not present local programs "that are inflammatory in any way." The station's rare departures from that policy, either at the urging of the FCC or on the advice of its lawyers, led to trouble, Lutken wrote. One such time was the May 4, 1962, talk by R. L. T. Smith described earlier in this chapter. "An announcement was made that Mr. Smith was not at the studio but was being presented by video tape. After the program was completed, the station's phone lines were tied up for over three hours while complaints and threatening calls were received." After Medgar Evers's presentation earlier in 1963, Lutken wrote, "threatening calls and complaints tied up the station's phone lines for over two hours." Station management therefore held "the honest opinion that these two cases give substantial support to its decision to avoid presenting any local shows dealing with this very inflammatory issue."

As for Beard himself, Lutken said that "despite his known pro-segregationist personal views, he has received many complaints and threats because of the pro-integration programming of the network. Other members of the staff have experienced the same consequences."

Addressing specifically the editorials that WLBT broadcast during the crisis over Meredith's admission to the University of Mississippi, Lutken said that despite the emotional and explosive circumstances of the times, the management sincerely believed that "it was not presenting any local programs for or against integration, was not doing anything unlawful, and was adhering to its policy of offering reasonable opportunity for opposing viewpoints to appear." The editorials dealt with "a far more important subject than the enrollment of one Negro in the University. The elected officials, the prominent civic, educational and religious leaders of the community almost unanimously felt that the real issue involved was the constitutional rights of a state."

WLBT once again complained that NBC network programs dealing with race relations had generally presented the prointegrationist viewpoint in the most favorable light. "The management does not doubt that NBC, from its viewpoint in New York, sincerely and honestly believes that it is presenting a 'fair' coverage of this controversial issue." Even though the station's leadership considered these programs heavily prointegration, the station had not only carried them but also aided producers of many network television news shows, which were then shown in Jackson.[83]

NBC took great offense at WLBT's characterization of its programming as prointegrationist. Howard Monderer, the network's Washington attorney, wrote the FCC disagreeing with WLBT's allegation: "The racial issue has many aspects and manifestations.

Frequently, these are news events which must be covered as such. Riots in Birmingham and the March on Washington are reported on as they occur; such reports are not susceptible of being treated on a 'pro' or a 'con' basis."

WLBT had listed programs under headings such as "favorable to integration," "favorable to segregation," "both sides presented that could be considered fair," and "both sides presented but which are heavily weighted for integration." NBC responded that it did not believe its programming on such a complex subject could be so easily categorized. For example, WLBT had listed under "favorable to integration" two presidential addresses and seven segments from the *Today* show concerning civil rights legislation.

Beard had written to NBC in October 1963 inquiring whether the network would run any programming to offset the time given to the March on Washington, which had just occurred. NBC had replied that the network did not try to achieve mathematical equality in its treatment of a controversial public issue. "We believe that such a course would be impossible and any attempt to follow it would be destructive of responsible news coverage . . . . Civil unrest in Birmingham is an on-the-spot news story; it cannot be handled in the same manner as a discussion of the pros and cons of foreign aid."[84]

In its letter culminating its investigation of the Mississippi stations, the FCC had spoken sternly to WLBT. It did not, however, make its letter public because it was part of an investigation. The question remained what the commission would do to follow up and whether it would even tell the public anything about its investigation. The next year, 1964, the commission's resolve and the muscle behind its warnings would be tested when members of the public demanded action.

2. SERVING WHOSE PUBLIC INTEREST?

Television was coming of age as America's prime source of entertainment and news in the 1950s and early 1960s. But black actors could play only limited roles in television series—usually maids or chauffeurs. When they appeared on other programs, it was frequently as singers, dancers, or musicians. Local or network broadcasters rarely covered news about the black community until civil rights protests began.[1] The 1968 *Report of the National Advisory Commission on Civil Disorders* chastened the media for failing to communicate "to a majority of their audience—which is white . . . a feeling for the difficulties and frustrations of being a Negro in the United States."[2] Civil rights protests that began with the 1955 Montgomery, Alabama, bus boycott and escalated after the 1960 student sit-ins offered a natural news focus. However, southern TV stations, like their newspaper counterparts, could report on the demonstrations with whatever slant they chose and not present any black point of view.

Civil rights leaders wanted this medium, which could influence many Americans, to provide more and fairer information on the issues they were raising. They began a deliberate, sustained effort in the early 1960s to challenge the rules governing television and the inertia of the agency charged with enforcing them, the Federal Communications Commission. Much as Martin Luther King Jr. and attorney Thurgood Marshall challenged systems across the South to illustrate the injustice of segregation, the new challengers would focus attention on WLBT to highlight the unfairness of local television's treatment of and service to black Americans. Just as the efforts of King and Marshall led to an expansion of the civil rights of all Americans, so did the challenge of one station lead to an expansion of the television news content for all Americans. It gave citizens the opportunity to participate in decisions not just on how America's television stations were run but on who would run them as well. And it buttressed the rules of fairness governing presentation of controversial issues on local stations. Those on the other side of the challenge, however, viewed the case as a complete miscarriage of justice. They believed that the judges—the ultimate decision makers in this case, not the FCC—acted out of political concerns, not on the evidence presented. They considered themselves random victims for practices prevalent at many southern stations. As usual in complex tales of this sort, each group had elements of truth on its side.

The Reverend Everett Parker, head of the Office of Communication of the United Church of Christ, was the man behind this landmark case. Parker said that he began to think in earnest about the connection between the civil rights movement and television at a meeting with Martin Luther King Jr., Andrew Young, and Truman B. Douglas of the church's Board of Home Missions in New York City in the late 1950s or early 1960s.

King, still a young minister at the time, was already famous after rising to leadership during the lengthy Montgomery bus boycott in the 1950s—although hardly the icon he would later become. The son of a minister, King had grown up in Atlanta, pastored his first church in Montgomery, then moved back to Atlanta. In 1957 he had helped establish the Southern Christian Leadership Conference (SCLC), a group of black church leaders, to work in the civil rights arena. While the older NAACP focused on litigation, King saw voting rights as critical if southern blacks were to achieve gains. Working with the Highlander Folk School in Tennessee, where movement activists had long trained in an integrated setting, the SCLC developed a citizenship education program. Local leaders like Fannie Lou Hamer traveled to participate in the program at Dorchester, Georgia, to learn techniques for teaching their neighbors the value of registering to vote and how to do it.[3]

Young, the son of a New Orleans dentist and a former school-teacher, was three years younger than King. A graduate of Hartford Seminary, he had his first full-time job pastoring two small churches around Thomasville in southwestern Georgia. In 1961 he started working at the Dorchester program. As civil rights efforts accelerated in Albany, Georgia, about sixty miles north of Thomasville, and later in Birmingham, Alabama, Young found himself working more and more directly with King, while Dorothy Cotton, SCLC's education director, took on the responsibility of the citizenship education program. Eventually, Young would become SCLC's executive director.[4]

At their meeting with Parker and Douglas in New York, King complained about southern television stations' coverage of civil rights demonstrations, saying that local news coverage was distorting their message. Parker asked King what the church could do to help his efforts. "Please do something about the TV stations," King replied.[5]

Parker had been fascinated with broadcasting since his high school days on the South Side of Chicago in 1931. One of his first projects in radio involved producing programs about Chicago's teachers, who were not being paid because of a city financial crisis. They were offered free time on WCFL, owned by the Chicago Federation of Labor, to explain their position. Parker undertook that work even though he said he'd never seen a microphone until then.

The only child of the manufacturer of hotel and restaurant kitchen equipment and a former department store buyer, Parker was born in Chicago on January 17, 1913. He attended Catholic school even though his family was Congregationalist. His mother died when he was sixteen after his father had spent "every cent he could get his hands on trying to save her," and then lost his business in the Depression. When Parker graduated from college, he washed windows the last week to pay his $25 graduation fee, things were so bad.[6]

Parker enjoyed his studies at the University of Chicago and had in mind working for a Ph.D. He planned to do his dissertation on the FCC, which he believed was totally controlled by the industries it regulated: AT&T, broadcasters, and telegraph companies. Despite this interest, the university wanted him to examine the effects of drainage into the Mississippi River.[7] That wasn't for him, so he left for Washington the day after graduation in 1935. He landed with the Works Progress Administration, one of the Depression-era agencies created to provide jobs. On visits home, his father, a strong Republican, would introduce him by saying: "This is my son, he's down in Washington on relief."

Later Parker ran radio stations in New Orleans and Hammond, Indiana; produced radio programs for several churches in Chicago; worked for NBC's war program section during World War II; and did key research about the potential for educational television. He brought a variety of skills to bear when he became head of the Office of Communication of the United Church of Christ, formed in 1954 to provide accurate information about the union of the Congregational Christian Churches and the Evangelical and Reformed Church, which was stirring internal controversy in some of the congregations. Parker saw it as part of the church's mission of social justice to advocate for the public in the broadcasting arena. "If you really believe in what the Bible says, and I do, you have to, if you have any ground to stand on or any resources to use that you can help people that are voiceless, you have to do it if you want to act as a Christian. And I think that's what drives me," he said. A graduate of the Chicago Theological Seminary in 1943, Parker could discuss Calvinism and communications with equal authority. If you try to think which actor might have portrayed him in his heyday, think E. G. Marshall.

The world of communications was changing radically. The advent of broadcasting in the United States had changed Americans' access to information in the 1920s much the same way as the Internet has changed access today. No longer did it take hours or days for the public to find out about election results or the outcome of a championship boxing match. The World Series could come into people's homes. Seeking to sell more radio receivers by providing regular broadcasts, Westinghouse launched station KDKA in 1920. In just a few years, several hundred stations were on the air; many tried to broadcast in the same area and suffered interference from other stations' signals. Commerce Secretary Herbert Hoover called several conferences to try to impose order, which the industry itself wanted, but the courts said he had no authority to regulate radio frequencies.

In 1927 Congress passed the Radio Act, creating the Federal Radio Commission, with five members subject to congressional confirmation. This commission was never really independent and shared its regulatory responsibilities with the secretary of commerce. After President Franklin D. Roosevelt was inaugurated in 1933, he initiated a study of radio regulation that recommended consolidating the activities of several agencies in this arena into one. Congress then passed the Communications Act of 1934, establishing the FCC, which would oversee the telephone and telegraph industries as well as serve as traffic cop over the airwaves by issuing licenses to broadcasters.[8]

With the advent of broadcasting, the nature of the freedom envisioned in the First Amendment to the Constitution changed. Former CBS News president Fred W. Friendly pointed this out most clearly: "The drafters of the First Amendment assumed that all citizens speak with equal tongues at reasonably equal decibels. The pamphlets of Tom Paine, beyond their biting eloquence, afforded him no strong advantage over Alexander Hamilton. In turn, Hamilton wielded great power, but he could not drown out the iconoclastic Paine by amplifying his own words through an exclusive bullhorn. Similarly, Daniel Webster and John Calhoun faced the states' rights issue with the same equipment and opportunity. One could outwit or outdebate the other, as Abraham Lincoln and Stephen Douglas did, but neither of them had access to the one soapbox or the only printing plant in town.

"The advent of radio forever eliminated this equality, and whatever radio did to the speakers' platform, television has done to radio. Politics, civil rights and war have not been the same since KDKA, Pittsburgh, went on the air in 1920. To deny the implications of this new revolution is akin to misreading the atomic bomb as a new variety of gunpowder."9

Regulation of this revolution—broadcasting—occurs, of course, in a political world. FCC members are appointed by the president (often on the recommendation of key members of Congress who need to be courted or appeased) and confirmed by the Senate. They must deal with the White House and Congress about the FCC budget and about their own reappointment. At the time the WLBT license was challenged, the commission had seven members (later reduced to five). The commissioners were, and still are, subject to the same push and pull on broadcasting questions as members of Congress—how many media voices there should be, what constitutes obscenity on the airwaves, what can be done about violent cartoons on children's television.

Into the 1960s virtually all the commissioners were male. To that point, all were white. Half had legal backgrounds, and half had some previous experience with broadcasting.[10] Their agenda, as former FCC member Nicholas Johnson has written, was "the product of industry pressures, staff idiosyncrasies, and political judgments."[11] The commission has a huge workload because it both makes the rules for the industries it regulates and enforces them. Because of that workload, the turnover in commission membership, and the complexity of many of the issues, FCC staff members and industry representatives have enormous impact on the information the commission members receive and thus the decisions they make. As a result of the WLBT case, public interest lawyers gained an impact for a time as well.

The Communications Act of 1934 required broadcasters to operate in the "public interest, convenience and necessity." Interpretation of that phrase has been the subject of lawsuits, hours of congressional testimony, and a flood of articles in law journals and other publications. Lawyers, lawmakers, and broadcasters debated what public was to be served and how far the government could go in monitoring that service without imposing censorship. In the 1960s the FCC could not have told WLBT and other southern stations that they could not editorially advocate segregation. But it could tell WLBT, and in fact *did* tell WLBT, that it had an obligation to let others present their opposing points of view on the issue under the Fairness Doctrine. WLBT's disregard of that warning contributed to the license challenge in 1964.

During this period, many broadcasters bristled at the Fairness Doctrine, but the Supreme Court would uphold its constitutionality in 1969.[12] The court found that the FCC regulations were constitutional and necessary, given the advantages conferred on broadcasters. Broadcasting frequencies were still relatively scarce, and people could legitimately claim that they could not express their views on the air without government assistance.[13] The United Church of Christ's action against WLBT, based as it was in part on charges of Fairness Doctrine violations, would show the strength of that doctrine before the courts at that time.

After meeting with King and hearing his plea, Parker swung into action. He and Ray Gibbons, who headed the church's Council for Social Action, took a trip through the South. While Gibbons made connections with local church groups, Parker watched television. In Atlanta. In Nashville. In Memphis. In Jackson. In New Orleans. In Birmingham. Parker said that Truman Douglas allotted him $10,000 for this work, without which he could never have accomplished what he did. "I wavered back and forth: should we do Birmingham or should we do Jackson?" Parker said. "But Jackson was so much worse in its effects on the black community (and of course we did have our college there), that we decided to do Jackson," challenging both WLBT, an NBC affiliate, and WJTV, the CBS affiliate. WLBT also had the strongest signal in the South, meaning that its programming reached a broad audience.

Parker and his allies in several other church denominations went to Washington to see the president of the National Association of Broadcasters (NAB), the industry's influential trade group. LeRoy Collins had become NAB president in 1961 when his term of governor of Florida ended. Elected governor in 1954, Collins was considered one of the founders of the "New South," recruiting businesses to the state and trying to head off the most militant segregationists from extreme action. He was governor when the Supreme Court's school desegregation decision was handed down; historians write that although Collins supported segregation, he allowed integration to go forward slowly without the upheavals in other southern states. His somewhat moderate civil rights stance led to his being named to chair the 1960 Democratic National Convention.[14]

Thus Parker had reason to hope that Collins might support the efforts of the Office of Communication. He asked Collins to send a letter to every station to try to get them to change their practices regarding race. Specifically, Parker suggested that stations give equal time to blacks to present their views, integrate their children's programs, and always address blacks with courtesy titles, such as "Mr." The NAB president thought it was a great idea, Parker said, but his board of broadcasting representatives, looking to their own interests, rejected it unanimously. "It's an interesting fact that all the troubles the broadcasters have with their license renewals came about because the directors of the NAB were such reactionaries," Parker said. "If they'd given us our statement, we probably wouldn't have gone further."[15]

Mississippi's television licenses were up for renewal in 1964. Having struck out trying to win voluntary change, Parker decided to gather evidence about the Jackson stations' programming. The Office of Communication would present the FCC with a "bill of particulars" about the stations' failure to serve the interest of their entire public, black as well as white. Parker had to take that course because the public could not participate in FCC matters. Only people with an economic interest at stake or who suffered electrical interference from stations could participate. Parker reasoned that as a regulatory agency, the FCC functioned on the same level as a federal district court for hearing cases. He wanted to catch WLBT in a lie, then present to the FCC documentation of that lie and ask it to hold a hearing. "We also determined that it was important to hit, wherever we did hit, a powerful group that would feel it because we were hitting them in their pocketbooks."[16]

Parker knew that what he was doing in Mississippi could be dangerous. Medgar Evers had been killed the previous June in Jackson. Civil rights workers were routinely jailed for encouraging blacks to register to vote, and potential black voters were intimidated through physical or economic force. In the summer of 1964, white college students from around the country would join black civil rights workers teaching people about voter registration and setting up Freedom Schools for their children. Many Mississippians considered their activities a hostile invasion. At the beginning of that summer, civil rights workers James Chaney, Michael Schwerner, and Andrew Goodman disappeared while investigating the burning of a black church. Their bodies were found in August, just before the Democratic National Convention at which the Mississippi Freedom Democratic Party challenged the all-white regular Democratic Party delegation for its seats.

Once in Jackson, Parker sought allies. He went first to Tougaloo, the church-affiliated college, where some faculty members, black and white, were active in or at least sympathetic to the civil rights efforts of the black students. One of them referred Parker to Gordon Henderson, a political science professor and department chair at Millsaps College, and his wife, Mary Ann. Millsaps, a Methodist-affiliated college in a comfortable section of Jackson not far from the home of famed writer Eudora Welty, had no black students then. But Henderson argued that the school should enroll some, especially since it was a church-related college. "That got me noticed by the Citizens' Council, which among other things at one point tacked a flyer detailing my traitorous activities on telephone poles around the campus." The Hendersons agreed to help Parker monitor WLBT and WJTV so there would be an exact record of their programming. "The television was terrible. It was so slanted, so biased. Especially during the Ole Miss crisis—it was unbelievable how much they stirred things up," Gordon Henderson said years later, explaining why he and his wife were willing to get involved.[17]

The Hendersons had met in New York City as undergraduates— he at Columbia College, she at Barnard College. While working on his doctorate in political science, Henderson, a Canadian by birth, taught at Middlebury College in Vermont. The couple married in 1953 and spent each summer in Jackson, Mary Ann's hometown. Her family had come to Mississippi from South Carolina in 1803. "That made her a member of one of Mississippi's oldest families and gave her strength," her husband said, "because there was absolutely no way the Citizens' Council could label her an outside agitator the way they could others who were not born in Mississippi."

Even before he began to teach American government and other political science courses at Millsaps in 1962, Gordon Henderson was learning about Mississippi customs during his summer visits. Once he was doing research on voting patterns using records in the state archives downtown. The old files were dusty. He grew thirsty. He bent down over the water fountain and wondered why everyone was looking at him. "Then I realized I was drinking from the colored water fountain. There were a lot of things to get used to."

When Henderson accepted the job at Millsaps, his wife made him promise not to make trouble for her parents by getting heavily involved in civil rights activities. "Ha!" he said, recalling those days. "The Sunday after we moved to Jackson, we attended a lecture at Millsaps by an officer and chief publicist for the Citizens' Council and he and Mary Ann had a very sharp argument, which made it clear (to me at least) that she was from this moment on up to her eyeballs in civil rights."

Parker told the Hendersons that he wanted to challenge the TV stations' licenses. He planned to monitor what they broadcast so that there would be prima facie evidence about the stations' practices and the FCC would have to hold a hearing to determine whether their renewal applications were accurate. Parker had previously done monitoring when he and Dallas Smythe, an economist, checked programs in New Haven, Connecticut, to demonstrate the need for an educational television channel. "He was very aboveboard about everything he was doing," Gordon Henderson said. "He told me a lot about his background and I thought it would work."

Henderson rented television sets and radios and found a local businessman who let the monitoring group use his home. "Something that has gotten lost in the history is that we not only monitored WLBT and WJTV but also their associated radio stations. What a huge job that was," Henderson recalled, because the time had passed when stations aired soap operas in half-hour segments in the afternoon. Radio was by then into "drive time," and so it was more difficult to monitor.

In those truly perilous times, even watching television with a political purpose was risky business. "It was something progressive white people could do," said the Reverend Edwin King, who at the time was pastor of the United Church of Christ church at Tougaloo and its college chaplain. He was one of the few white Mississippians willing to demonstrate for civil rights and was badly injured when another car sideswiped his in 1963. Some did not consider it an accident. He worked with the church on its case against WLBT. Everett Parker called those who did the monitoring "people of real substance in the Jackson community," to which King added: "If they had been found out, they would have been run out of town. That was very risky, very courageous, and just as important as those of us who were demonstrating."[18]

The Office of Communication of the United Church of Christ paid the monitors whom Henderson hired. There were about twenty, five of whom were college students. Several had Ph.D.'s, some were professional people, some were housewives. The Hendersons and Parker promised they would never reveal any of the monitors' names. They had also decided that there would be no blacks on the monitoring team so that no one could say there was any conflict of interest.

The monitors received about eight to twelve hours of training, which Parker led. "Each program, each station break, each commercial or promotional announcement will be entered on the program log," the monitors' instruction sheet said. "One of the most important functions of the monitor is to determine accurately how programs should be typed and the significance of content, i.e., what is distorted or untruthful, what may influence program content or the way content is treated." The information sheets included brief descriptions of program types—such as news, drama, sports, or religion—for the monitors' guidance. If there was any mention of race on a program, the monitors were to fill out a separate form to indicate whether anyone black participated and what was discussed. That form also called for the monitor to note whether any inflammatory language or a sarcastic tone was used and whether network and local reports on the same item agreed.[19] Once the team members had talked about how to record the information, they were told to go home and practice by watching one of the channels for several hours. Then they met again with Henderson to go over any questions they might have. On Sunday, March 1, 1964, the monitoring began.

The monitors used two rooms of the house. Each end of the larger room had a television set, a tape recorder for the sound portion of the broadcasts (the monitoring occurred before VCRs were in use), a table and a chair, a clock next to the television, the log forms, a stopwatch, and pencils. There was a similar setup in the other room for monitoring the two radio stations. The monitors worked in shifts from sign-on in the morning to sign off at night (stations often were not on the air around the clock in those days). They would watch the television stations for two hours and then take a break. Each shift had a supervisor, one of whom was Mary Ann Henderson. By week's end, the monitors had compiled a stack of forms about four inches high.[20]

"I took all this very seriously," said one of the monitors, Winifred Green. "We had to log everything. We were trying to be very precise."

Parker and the Hendersons had kept their pledge never to reveal the names of the monitors. But when I told Patricia Derian, who had been active in the 1960s trying to keep the public schools open and reforming the Democratic Party in Mississippi, about my book, she volunteered the information that she and Winifred Green had been among the monitors. Years earlier, Derian had told a reporter that the monitors "weren't to tell anyone about it, only the most trusted people were to do it. . . . None of us knew anything about television. All we knew was that this local station was terrible."[21]

At the time of the monitoring, Winifred Green was married to a masonry contractor in Jackson. Like Patricia Derian and Mary Ann Henderson, she had become involved with Mississippians for Public Education, a group of white women seeking to keep the public schools open when the governor and legislature threatened to close them rather than desegregate. Green remained active in education reform.

"It is very hard for people to think back to those days," she said. "Memories are selective. I think all the women in Mississippians for Public Education were realizing for the first time in our lives that we were not going to be housewives all our lives." There was no middle ground on the school issue or other controversies that spring. To be involved or not was a major decision. Looking back on the WLBT case thirty-five years later, Green told me that "having the TV station change, having the newspaper change [as it did over time], meant that never again could we be the closed society we once were. That's the big picture point of view. For the black community, I think a major gain was not to have your children walk in front of the TV and worry about them hearing racial slurs or someone calling them apes."[22]

Blacks made up 40 percent of the population of Hinds County, in which WLBT was located, and 45 percent of its five-county service area. The Channel 3 monitoring report concluded that despite this huge potential audience and despite the station's responsibility as a license holder to serve the public, WLBT failed to give a fair presentation of controversial issues, especially in the field of race relations. The station carried news about official attempts by the state of Mississippi to maintain segregation but did not present any balanced statement of activities by blacks to obtain freedom. Nor did it discuss the basis of their grievances. A check of the monitors' reports shows that the news broadcasts, although straightforwardly reported, focused mainly on those who supported segregation and denial of voting rights to blacks.[23]

For example, *Dick Sanders, Sunday Report*, airing on March 1, included a segment about a young black civil rights leader who was trying to win admission to the University of Southern Mississippi. The monitoring indicated that the report said nothing about the university's policies about admitting black students, nor did it quote the young man about why he wanted to attend the university.[24]

A segment the next day, Monday, March 2, on Sanders's program contained these two reports:

- The Mississippi Supreme Court had upheld the conviction of a group of Freedom Riders arrested in Jackson in 1961, including James Farmer, national director of the Congress of Racial Equality. The court ruled that the Jackson police had, in the words of the WLBT newscaster, "acted in good faith in an effort to keep the peace by ordering Farmer, a Negro, and his bi-racial group to leave the traditionally white waiting room of the Trailways Bus station. Farmer and his group were arrested when they refused to move on. The court said it was significant that Farmer did not claim he had any further business in the terminal." The report did not indicate that segregated waiting rooms were illegal in 1961.
- A local circuit court judge had told the Hinds County grand jury that the civil rights movement was "born of violence." In a broadcast segment, the judge said that the movement was

"heralded by the swirling mobs tramping through the streets, lanes and highways, demanding, threatening and terrorizing." The report did not question the judge's claims or include any comments from civil rights spokespersons.

On Tuesday, March 3, the monitors recorded a segment of *John Stennis Reports* in which the United States senator from Mississippi reported on the debate over what he called "the misnamed civil rights bill." The legislation, "under the guise of trying to give rights to some people," he said, "destroys certain civil rights of all people." The station presented no civil rights spokesperson to balance these comments.

That evening, the news carried a report that Governor Paul Johnson had urged the Mississippi legislature to enact a program to help the state maintain order. Johnson told the lawmakers that Mississippi had not chosen to become the focal point in the civil rights issue. He asked for creation of a police academy to train more law enforcement units, for legislation to expand the Mississippi Highway Patrol, and for authority for any jurisdiction that filled its jail to send its overflow prisoners to Parchman state penitentiary in the Delta, where inmates often labored in neighboring cotton fields. The station aired film of Johnson telling the legislators that at Parchman "there is plenty of healthy, rehabilitative work, too, for persons so idle that they can travel around the country stirring up strife." Laughter and applause greeted his words. The legislators laughed again when he said, "And in that other world that is Parchman, there is ample time for the trouble-maker to contemplate the error of his ways. And without interruption by reporters and cameramen." The monitoring indicated that WLBT included no comments from civil rights leaders on Johnson's proposals.

The next day, Wednesday, March 4, federal district judge Sidney Mize ordered the integration of schools in Jackson, Biloxi, and Leake County. He directed the school boards in each district to file plans by July 15 that would include complete desegregation of at least one grade that September and at least one grade each year thereafter. The station carried a straight news bulletin at 10 A.M. On the 6 P.M. news, this was the lead on the report: "Three Mississippi school districts have been ordered to begin desegregation in September. The school districts are Jackson, Biloxi and Leake County. The Jackson School Board has issued a statement saying, 'With the continued support of the mayor and commissioners of the city of Jackson and the superintendent of schools of the district, the trustees of the district will continue to resist and oppose this litigation by every legal and constitutional means available.'" During the rest of the report, which lasted for several minutes, there was no comment from the NAACP, which brought the case.

The *Mid-day News* on Thursday, March 5, reported that Mayor Allen Thompson said that he and the city commissioners would maintain their unqualified support of school officials in their "splendid efforts" to resist the school desegregation litigation. There were no comments from the NAACP included in the newscast.

On Saturday, March 7, the station carried several items during the day about a federal court dismissing a Justice Department suit attacking Mississippi's voting laws. Judges Ben Cameron of Meridian and Harold Cox of Jackson held that no provision of Mississippi law deprived any citizen of the right to vote because of race. There were also reports during the day of a hearing into a request that the Madison County registrar be ordered to speed up processing of black voter applications. A voter registration drive was under way in that county just north of Jackson, and the registrar was allowing only one person at a time to take the voter test. The registrar's attorneys were quoted as saying he acted as quickly as possible in processing applications when 200 blacks converged on the courthouse in a mass demonstration.

Judge Cox, who was conducting the hearing, questioned the motives of those who took part in the demonstration. "Were they more interested in citizenship or in publicity?" he asked. "They're just grandstanding in my opinion." Cox, appointed to the bench at the urging of his college roommate, Senator James O. Eastland, "soon developed a reputation as the most openly racist of the federal jurists," according to historian John Dittmer.[25] Cox said he was firmly against discrimination but thought that mass demonstrations were not the way to accomplish the goals of the protesters. His statement became the lead on the item on the evening news. In this case, the station reported one rebuttal comment, from Justice Department attorney John Doar, who said the registrar's delaying tactics were simply another form of racial discrimination.

Armed with this monitoring survey, Parker made the rounds of Washington attorneys familiar with broadcast law. None of them would touch the case, telling him that he would be wasting the church's time and money. Parker turned to Orrin Judd, a Baptist layman he had known through church affairs and a member of a Republican-connected law firm in New York City. Judd, then fifty-seven years old, was a Colgate University and Harvard Law School graduate who had been law secretary for Judge Learned Hand in 1930–1931. He served as solicitor general of New York under Governor Thomas E. Dewey from 1943 to 1946 and represented Governor Nelson Rockefeller in constitutional cases during his administration.[26] Judd later became a federal judge. While he knew no communications law, he had worked with Parker during controversies over the merger of the Congregational Christian Churches and the Evangelical and Reformed Church, creating the United Church of Christ, in 1957. Earle K. "Dick" Moore, a junior partner in Judd's firm whose father had been lieutenant governor in the Dewey administration, soon worked on the case as well. He later figured in many of the license challenges and other negotiations that resulted from the WLBT case.

In March 1964 WLBT filed its license renewal application. The next month, the United Church of Christ filed what in FCC terminology is called a "Petition to Intervene and to Deny Application for Renewal" against both WLBT's and WJTV's licenses. The petition claimed that these broadcasters failed to serve the interests of their large black audience or to give a fair presentation of controversial issues, especially in the field of race relations.[27] A modest ten pages, this document would generate twenty-five hefty boxes of files at the FCC alone over the next sixteen years.

To strengthen the church's case, Parker had lined up as fellow challengers the Reverend R. L. T. Smith, the Jackson minister and grocer who had sought to buy time on WLBT in 1962, and Aaron Henry, a Clarksdale druggist who was statewide NAACP president. Henry had also tried to buy airtime on WLBT when he ran for governor in a mock Freedom Vote election in 1963. Smith eventually did get on the air, but Henry did not.

Smith may have been soft-spoken, but he was not afraid to speak up. In 1959 he had filed suit against the Mississippi Sovereignty Commission, which would later spy on civil rights workers, to try to stop it from subsidizing the Citizens' Council. He did not have the money to carry the suit forward when he lost in court.[28] In January 1962, not long after he had declared his candidacy for Congress, Smith was one of seven blacks who sat in the Mississippi House gallery to hear a speech by Governor Ross Barnett. This simply wasn't done. The next day the House voted to require that all visitors obtain passes from legislators, the idea being that no legislator would give anyone black a pass. (There were no black legislators in Mississippi after Reconstruction until 1967.) Smith commented that the legislators were "piling stupidity on top of injustice" in an effort to keep blacks from watching their government in action. "I cannot conceive of intelligent men elected to make laws for all of the people wishing to hide their deliberations from citizens who pay the taxes to operate our government," Smith said. Such an action had "too much in common with the tactics used by a dictator." The state senate held up action on the House proposal when one member said that Mississippi citizens should have the right to see their legislature in action.[29] In the WLBT case, Smith would be asking that citizens' voices be heard at the federal regulatory level as well.

Smith was born December 9, 1902, in Utica, Mississippi. He finished high school—a rarity in those days in Mississippi for black or white—and married in 1922. He and his wife, Annie Louise, had eleven children, so Smith worked three jobs—mail carrier, grocery store operator, and minister—much of his life. He registered to vote when few other black voters were on the books. He described how that happened to visiting writer Arthur Whitman.

"The post office where I worked was on the same block with the courthouse," Smith recalled, "and I went there twice a day to deliver the mail. Every time I was in the building, I'd stop and try to register. Naturally, I'd keep getting turned away just as regular as dew in the morning. One day the forms wouldn't be in, the next day the clerk would be suffering a cramp. Some days it was too hot, others too cold. Many days it was somebody's birthday or funeral, and the clerk just couldn't work at a time like that.

"I just kept going back, twice every day, till it became a big joke for all parties concerned, and finally the man told me one day, 'Well, Robert, I guess you just mean to get your name in the book,' and he put it down. There weren't too many colored people trying to register in those days, and a man could win out if he just kept at it."[30]

At fifty-nine, Smith was "a tall, broad man, grown paunchy and gray-haired," Whitman wrote of him in 1962. "His skin is the little-coffee-lots-of-cream product of mixed Indian, white and Negro ancestry. He chews constantly on a half-smoked cigar, and faces the world from behind a screen of wordy, slow-talking geniality. He doesn't say, 'Hello,' to someone he sees on the street. He says, 'Hello, Mister Jones, my very good and true friend. How are you this fine, sunny day?' And then he pauses to chat."

He hadn't been the first choice of a group looking for a black candidate for Congress. But many younger men were economically vulnerable or didn't care about politics. Once the group considered Smith, it found his qualifications excellent, Whitman wrote. "He was clearly an intelligent man of enormous energy, and a gifted speaker. He had the time to devote to a campaign. His standing as a stable, responsible family man would go a long way with the woman's vote in the Negro community. . . . As a minister, he would be difficult to smear on moral grounds, or to be dismissed by whites as an illiterate field hand." And he was economically independent. Besides, as he told Whitman, "'My children are all grown, and my small affairs are pretty much in order.' What he meant, of course, is that he was ready to take on the role of sacrificial lamb, not just in the sense of fighting a hopeless fight, but in the more literal sense of perhaps not living through it."

Smith felt insulted by the way local members of Congress treated black postal employees, he later testified at an FCC hearing. Various congressmen would come around and shake hands with all of the white employees. "Very conveniently they didn't see a single Negro. And I'd say, 'By God A-mighty, if I ever get a chance, I'm gonna try to run for Congress. If I can't get it, maybe I'll inspire some decent person to run for it that will recognize all citizens as men.' And basically that's why I ran for Congress."[31]

Lining up Smith to sign the petition to the FCC against WLBT was like a scene out of the movies, only this was real life. Gordon Henderson knew Smith, who trusted him, so he suggested to Parker that they go to see him. After his television appearances, Smith had received so many threats that he was vigilant against drive-by shooters or other violence. "We called a pay phone and somebody answered and said to go to another pay phone and they would call and so we did," Parker recalled, "and Smith agreed to meet us at his home. They gave us instructions on what to do, and Gordon and I went out there about 9 o'clock at night and the Smith home was lighted with spotlights and there were guards because ever since he had run for Congress, he'd been threatened constantly. And of course you know Medgar Evers had been killed." Henderson and Parker drove by Smith's house. "They knew what kind of car it was and what the license plate was and then we went down the road a ways and we turned around. We unscrewed the light in the car, which came on automatically, so that we wouldn't be targets as we were getting out of the car. And we turned off the headlights and drove back into the yard. As we drove into the yard, they turned off the searchlights and we got out of the car and ran into the house. And they turned the searchlights back on." They spent about half an hour with Smith, and he signed the petition.[32]

Of the two Mississippians who joined the WLBT challenge, Aaron Henry became better known, statewide and nationally. Elected state NAACP president in 1959, Henry headed the integrated Mississippi Freedom Democratic Party delegation that challenged seating the all-white party regulars at the dramatic 1964 Democratic National Convention in Atlantic City. He later became a Democratic Party national committeeman and served in the Mississippi House of Representatives from 1980 to 1996.

Aaron Henry was born July 2, 1922, and grew up on the Flowers plantation in Coahoma County in the Mississippi Delta. His mother died when he was three years old and his father two years later. He was brought up by his uncle Ed Henry and his aunt Mattie, whom he considered his parents. Early on, Henry knew he had no intention of becoming a field hand. In his memoir, Henry wrote that as far back as he could remember, he "detested everything about growing cotton. When we would pick, I was one of the slowest workers. . . . I would start down my row picking that cotton and stuffing it into my sack and never looking up." When he thought he was halfway down the row, he would look up and see that he was about twenty yards from where he began, was behind everybody else, and had a sack only about half as full as the others.

Young Aaron became best friends with Randolph Smithers, son of a white sharecropper on the plantation. Smithers's family moved into the small town of Webb about the same time the Henrys did. Aaron's father ran a shoemaking shop, and Randolph's father delivered wood and coal. During that spring and summer the boys shot marbles, picked berries, swam in the creek, and hunted hickory nuts. "We had a great time talking about when we would start school in September and we looked forward to enjoying it together," Henry said. "But when the time came, we were told that we would have to go to separate schools. That was one of the greatest heartbreaks of my life." The school for whites was in Webb. It was brick and sat directly across the road from where the Henrys lived. School for black children was located in a Baptist church on a nearby plantation, with two teachers in charge of all grades.

"Randolph and I never discussed it," Henry recalled, "but it was then I began to realize that my family and I were considered something less than our white counterparts. I was considered inferior to Randolph simply because his skin was white and mine was black. In every other respect we were the same—our cultural background, our economic status, and even our social status were all about the same. In fact, I think probably Father's business gave us a financial independence that the Smithers family did not enjoy."

Henry's parents were eager that their children receive an education, so they moved twenty-five miles away, into Clarksdale, famous for its blues musicians. Henry went to school across the street from his home. He had a separate teacher for each grade, an improvement over the school near Webb. But most of the teachers had not finished high school.

When Henry was ten years old, he hired out during the summers as a day laborer, picking cotton again. Once he started attending the Coahoma County Agricultural High School, Henry worked part-time as a delivery boy at the Henderson Drug Store, his first brush with pharmacy as a profession. Henry described his high school as a gigantic farm operation. His freshman class had five acres of cotton as its project, "and I was returned to those damn fields again and hated them as much as ever. But I could at least tell myself that at last there was a useful reason for my labors."

Henry's English and economics teacher, Thelma K. Shelby, played a pivotal role in his life. Unbeknownst to the local board of education, she had joined the NAACP while at Dillard University in New Orleans and talked to her students about civil rights. Her entire class joined the youth division of the NAACP, and Henry remained a member the rest of his life.

Finishing high school in 1941, Henry worked as a night clerk at a local motel, then was drafted into the army in 1943. "Three years in the army taught me that racial segregation and discrimination were not unique to Mississippi but confirmed my feeling that the situation was worse in my home state." He served in a segregated quartermaster trucking unit in Hawaii and joined NAACP branches outside every base where he was stationed. Returning to Clarksdale after the war, he tried unsuccessfully to register to vote. White veterans had no such trouble. Henry went back to the registrar's office and, after some rigmarole, passed the qualifying test and was registered. He had decided to go to pharmacy school under the GI Bill and attended Xavier University in New Orleans. He hadn't learned much at his agricultural high school, he soon discovered, so he was kept busy studying. He returned to Clarksdale in 1950, married, and opened a drugstore in partnership with a local white man. Later he bought out the other man's interest. His drugstore became a stopping-off point for civil rights activists and journalists for several decades.

Long known as "Doc," Henry led voter registration activities in the 1950s. After the Supreme Court decision outlawing school segregation, he organized a group that requested that its children attend the all-white schools, a group that suffered the same reprisals as other black parents faced around the state. In 1961, under Henry's leadership, blacks began boycotting Clarksdale's white merchants. The dispute had begun over the city's exclusion of the bands from the black high school and Coahoma Junior College from the annual Christmas parade, then spread to demands that black clerks be hired and black customers be addressed by courtesy titles. Police arrested Henry on charges of organizing an illegal boycott. His wife lost her teaching job.[33]

By 1963 civil rights forces in Mississippi had grown tired of hearing that blacks wouldn't vote even if they could register—and precious few were registered even then. They decided to hold a Freedom Vote with an integrated ticket, Aaron Henry for governor and the Reverend Ed King for lieutenant governor; balloting would be conducted at black churches, beauty parlors, barbershops, wherever people congregated. To gain some attention for their campaign, Henry sought to buy airtime on WLBT. The station manager told him, "We don't sell niggers airtime," one of Henry's longtime allies, Dr. Robert Smith, recalled.[34] Aaron Henry never forgot that snub and told the story with some glee years later when he became chairman of the board at WLBT.

When he met the Reverend Everett Parker, Henry was beginning preparations for the Mississippi civil rights drive known as Freedom Summer. Civil rights workers had formed the Council of Federated Organizations (COFO) to bring together the activities of the NAACP, the Student Non-Violent Coordinating Committee, the SCLC, and the Congress of Racial Equality. Henry headed COFO.

Parker and Gordon Henderson wanted Henry to join them in the action against WLBT. They met him at the NAACP office on Farish Street, then the heart of Jackson's black business district. An older man, presumably an NAACP lawyer, accompanied Henry. "He said, 'Aaron, you're not going to sign this man's petition,'" Parker recalled. "'You don't know anything about him. And you don't know what he's going to do—I won't let you sign it.' We talked to him a little longer, and he said, 'Aaron, if you sign that thing, your life won't be worth a penny.' Aaron says, 'Not worth that now,' and he signed it."[35]

The church's move against WLBT's license was particularly audacious because of the FCC's narrow concept about who might challenge licenses or otherwise be involved in its proceedings. The commission considered itself the only guarantor of the public interest necessary. Broadcasters rarely faced hearings in front of the commission, arguing that if they had to do so, it would hurt their business. It would be a signal to advertisers and potential aspirants for the license that they were in trouble even if they ultimately were vindicated. The power of the broadcasting industry and the FCC's limited view of its mission put WLBT in a seemingly commanding position on the eve of commission consideration of the challenge by the Office of Communication, Aaron Henry, and R. L. T. Smith.

3. ENTER WARREN BURGER

WLBT won the first round. The challengers lost at the Federal Communications Commission on a 4-2 vote on May 19, 1965. The FCC renewed WLBT's license, albeit for only one year. Although the commission found that WLBT had violated the Fairness Doctrine and had ignored the needs of its black audience, it would not go as far as revoking its license.[1] The station was still in business.

No one should have expected otherwise. The commission was emerging from an era in which it had been "notorious for being the handmaiden of the industry," as E. William "Bill" Henry, then chairman of the commission, put it many years later.[2] In 1958 Commissioner Richard A. Mack resigned because of charges that he had received "loans" that he never repaid and other financial considerations from the lawyer for a company seeking a Miami television license. Another commissioner, John C. Doerfer, who had been FCC chairman from 1957 to 1960, resigned after taking rides on a broadcaster's yacht. He was also accused during a congressional investigation of receiving honoraria even as the government was reimbursing him for his expenses. Storer Broadcasting, the company cited during the investigation for having entertained Doerfer, hired him when he left the FCC.[3]

Jackson station WJTV, which had also been challenged, did not receive the same treatment as WLBT because the FCC believed its management had shown signs of improvement and had pledged even more changes. WLBT, in contrast, dug in its heels. It argued that the challengers apparently thought that "forty-five percent of the programming on Station WLBT should be Negro programming, simply because it is their understanding that this is the population percentage in the area. It appears immaterial to them that many of these Negroes may not desire to appear on the station, may not have anything to say, may not have any talent, and, to date, have not been able to take advantage of the offers of time made to them by the station."

WLBT's management said it had concluded that the best way to serve the black population was to work with the educational and religious leaders of the community. The station's legal brief included supportive statements from several local black leaders, including Jacob Reddix, who, as president of Jackson State College, had clamped down on student demonstrations for civil rights at his publicly funded college, and Percy Greene, editor and publisher of the *Jackson Advocate*. Greene had been active in the NAACP in drives for the vote in the 1940s but later argued against wider integration efforts and informed the State Sovereignty Commission about civil rights activities, which it opposed.

The station said it sought to serve all the people in the community and in doing so had aired NBC programs on civil rights. It had presented those programs over objections of many in the area because it believed that such programs were in the public interest. It was not, however, in the public interest to present local programs on this very inflammatory issue, the station had decided. Nonetheless, the station thought that the views of the petitioners had received more than a fair share of airtime.[4]

As a rationale for its decision to renew WLBT's license, the FCC majority observed that the Jackson area was "entering a critical period in race relations" and needed the contribution to understanding that a responsible broadcaster could make. The majority believed that WLBT could make this contribution if it operated under the conditions the FCC laid down. One of those conditions was that the station observe the Fairness Doctrine. "The practice of asserting ignorance of the doctrine's applicability"—that is, to appearances of elected officials or to spot announcements—"is over," the commission said.[5]

The commission took action without holding a hearing on the charges, a hearing the challengers wanted and the two FCC dissenters, Bill Henry and Kenneth Cox, insisted should have been held. *Broadcasting* magazine reported that some commissioners believed that a hearing held in Jackson "would inflame the racial issue there and make progress in civil rights all the more difficult."[6] This was a pivotal point: had the FCC been willing to break precedent and hear from the public at this stage, it might have avoided two stinging court defeats.

The irony was that most of the majority opinion read as though the commission was going to act harshly, Henry observed, but all it did was "give WLBT a slap on the wrist, put broadly worded conditions on the station's performance no greater than the law already required." The station said that it should be free to make improvements and wouldn't have that freedom if there were hearings, he added, calling that argument "completely phony."

"Nothing would have motivated them like putting them in a hearing," Henry commented. The majority opinion was really just a burden on the station, not a true motivator. It was written so that the majority couldn't be criticized for overlooking the conditions that the challengers had raised, Henry said, adding that the majority would have been flirting with reversal by the federal appeals court if it had ignored those issues.[7]

There was a good reason the FCC opinion read as it did: the man who wrote it—general counsel Henry Geller—didn't agree with it. He thought WLBT's record was bad enough to warrant a much closer look. "We went in there and argued very strongly that you must designate this for a hearing. The statute says [there should be a hearing if there are] 'substantial material issues of fact.' You have very serious issues of fact here. You have issues of fact about the Fairness Doctrine because they put on all these editorials saying, 'Never, never,' calling it states' rights, that they don't deal with integration. . . . You had issues of misrepresentation. They say they don't cover the issue because it's inflammatory and they cover the issue like mad in editorials, calling it states' rights."

Geller, a lanky, smart, loquacious midwesterner who graduated from Northwestern University law school, held what he called "the three-outhouse theory." The FCC will come down hard on any broadcaster in a jerkwater town with fewer than three outhouses—that is, a small-time operator—but let the bigger stations off the hook. It had been clear to him, Geller said, that WLBT had discriminated. It used only white ministers and white children on its programs even though half the churches in the area were black and 40 to 45 percent of the population was black. Likewise, WLBT never included Tougaloo in its programming about colleges. "What you've got are people who are lying, people who are violating the Fairness Doctrine, and people who are engaged in discriminatory programming practices, very clearly not serving the needs and interests" of the entire community.

When the general counsel's office lost before the commission, one of Geller's deputies was furious. He slammed his books together, said to Geller that the decision was "evil," and stalked out. Geller stayed because, as general counsel, he had to write something. "So I sat down and wrote what was utter nonsense, and we knew we were writing utter nonsense."

All Geller could think to write was that Mississippi needed proper broadcasting immediately because it was entering a dicey racial situation. "They'll be under the gun, and we'll get an immediate contribution which is urgently needed because of this burning issue," ran Geller's argument for the majority opinion. "Which is poppycock. The reason that it's poppycock is that people have to run on their record. The worst thing you can do is let a guy really screw up and then say, 'But that's all right. If you promise to reform, we will let you go.' Because that means you've lost control over the industry. It means that everybody out there can screw up totally" and then promise to reform. "We tried to make it a purple cow by saying that the situation there was so dicey with integration being so important, the South being a raging inferno with this chasm, that if we could get immediate compliance, it was worth it in the public interest. It was really totally wrong."

Geller, who had been general counsel since 1964, said that when one feels as he did about that decision, "either you resign or on balance you think that you're getting more done" so you stay. "I thought I could get a lot done. Maybe I was wrong on that."[8]

The four commissioners who voted to renew the WLBT license were Lee Loevinger, Robert Bartley, Robert E. Lee, and Rosel Hyde, two Democrats and two Republicans. One other commissioner, James Wadsworth, did not participate in the decision for reasons that today are not recalled. Loevinger, born in St. Paul and a summa cum laude graduate of the University of Minnesota, had left the Minnesota Supreme Court to become assistant attorney general in charge of the antitrust division in the Kennedy administration. In 1963 he was named to fill Newton Minow's slot on the FCC, where he served until 1968. Despite having been named to the commission by Kennedy, the same president who appointed dissenters Henry and Cox, Loevinger voted to renew the license. As Les Brown, longtime television writer for the *New York Times*, has said, Loevinger "held to the conservative view that the commission may not undertake regulation of program content in any form in broadcasting. He subscribed to the belief that broadcasters give the public what it wants and on the whole serve the public well."[9]

The other Democrat in the majority was Robert Bartley. Born in Ladonia, Texas, he had served on the FCC staff and worked at the Securities and Exchange Commission (SEC) before becoming a broadcast executive and later director of government relations for the National Association of Broadcasters (NAB). He worked for House Speaker Sam Rayburn for four years and had been appointed to the FCC by President Truman in 1952. Robert E. Lee, a Republican, was named to the commission in 1953 by President Eisenhower. He was its staunchest advocate of developing the UHF channels of television, that is, those above the basic VHF channels two to thirteen in precable days. Lee had been an FBI agent for three years, then a fiscal assistant to FBI director J. Edgar Hoover for six years. Rosel H. Hyde, born in Idaho, joined the staff of the Radio Commission in 1928 and moved in 1934 to the newly created FCC, where he worked in a variety of positions, including general counsel. A Republican, he was named a commissioner by President Truman in 1946. He had chaired the commission in 1953 and 1954 and would again, starting in 1966.[10]

The dissenters in the case came from separate regions of the country and different backgrounds, but they shared much the same political outlook. A Tennessean, Bill Henry had roomed at Vanderbilt law school with John Jay Hooker, who later ran for governor. Through Hooker's connections, Henry met Robert F. Kennedy and signed on for John F. Kennedy's 1960 presidential campaign. After the election, he went home to Memphis.

Later, an impasse over an appointment to the FCC developed between the chairs of the House and Senate committees that oversaw the commission. Each was recommending a different man for the job, and the president sought a way out of the dilemma. As Henry told it, Bobby Kennedy asked, "Why not that young lawyer from Memphis?" Henry was offered the job in August 1962 and arrived in Washington just as the president was ordering the missiles out of Cuba in the fall of 1962. He fully expected to be simply a commissioner but became chairman eight months later when Minow quit. Henry was thirty-four years old.[11]

Kenneth Cox, the other dissenter in the first WLBT decision, was the child of "rock-ribbed Kansas Republicans." His family had moved to Seattle when he was in high school, and Cox remembered giving a speech in his debate club favoring the reelection of Herbert Hoover. At the University of Washington he encountered students and professors with far more liberal attitudes and interests; that helped alter his political outlook. In addition, he was influenced by his wife and her mother, liberal Democrats from Butte, Montana, and he often listened to discussions about the work their relatives had done as miners. In 1955 Cox started working with Warren Magnuson, the influential Senate Commerce Committee chairman and Democrat from Washington State. In 1961 Cox became head of the FCC's Broadcast Bureau, then was named to the commission by President Kennedy in 1963. He served on the FCC until 1970.[12] Cox had a prodigious appetite for work, knew all the details of commission agenda items, and was known within the FCC as a formidable debater. Henry described his fellow dissenter in the WLBT case as "smart, no-nonsense, intellectually aggressive."[13]

In their dissent, Henry and Cox took note of the serious allegations made by WLBT's challengers "which, if true, would indicate that the station has made misrepresentations to the Commission, deceived the public, violated Commission policy, broken federal and state laws, and ignored the needs of a substantial portion of the community it has pledged to serve." The commission should have held an evidentiary hearing to resolve these issues, they wrote. On the question of misrepresentation, Henry and Cox said that WLBT several times assured the FCC that it did not sell or give time locally for programs dealing with racial integration. Yet the existence of WLBT's alleged policy was open to serious question because of its editorials opposing the enrollment of James Meredith at the University of Mississippi, its *Comment* programs dealing with racial integration, and paid spot announcements in 1962 made by the Jackson Citizens' Council. The commission had glossed over too many unresolved questions, the dissenters argued, and should hold a hearing.

WLBT's renewal signaled to broadcasters that they could follow a questionable course of conduct over several license periods, the dissenters said. When eventually called to account, these broadcasters could obtain a renewal by simply agreeing that they would cease all operations the FCC found contrary to the public interest. That ability to dodge punishment, they added, was not the intent of the Communications Act.[14]

Henry, a white southerner, dissented because, as he put it, "I knew what Mississippi was like. I knew what Memphis was like. I had a lifelong interest in civil rights. In my day, there were problems with [blacks] not voting, not sitting at lunch counters, sitting at the back of the bus, not getting equal pay. I'm sure that's the thing that made me a Democrat." Henry thought there were substantial questions that needed to be resolved at a hearing. "Ordering a hearing was not tantamount to license revocation. We wouldn't have been sentencing them to a death penalty, perhaps only to a prolonged hearing. It depends on what comes out at the hearing. You never really know. The fact that they had to come back in a year gave the commission far weaker leverage than if they had had a hearing hanging over their head."[15]

When the FCC decision was announced, much of the press played the story as a slap at the station: "FCC Tells Southern Stations to Halt Radio-TV Racial Bias," headlined the *New York Times*, while the

New York Herald Tribune's shorthand labeled the story "Mississippi TV Station—Bias Rap."[16] However, Walter Pincus, writing in the liberal *New Republic*, pointed out the dichotomy in the FCC decision. To be sure, he wrote, "other stations across the South must take into account the Commission's general feeling that broadcasters 'can make a most worthwhile contribution to the resolution of [race relations] problems. . . . That contribution is needed now—and should not be put off for the future.' " Those were good words, Pincus added, "but unless the Commission is willing to use its licensing power to back them up, they are meaningless."[17]

The commission majority dismissed any suggestion of the public's participation in broadcasting—called in legal terms "standing"—in a footnote to its opinion. The commission had consistently held that members of the public not directly related to the action being protested and without some tangible injury had no standing. The FCC majority did not think Aaron Henry and R. L. T. Smith, as members of a minority group, had any more claim to interest or injury than other people among the general public.[18]

But the times, as Bob Dylan was singing, they were a-changin'. The public was insisting on being heard, inside government and out, about the war in Vietnam, race relations, women's rights, the environment, and consumer complaints. The days in which only people with direct economic interests in a case could participate in discussing its issues were rapidly fading.

On June 10, 1965, three weeks after the FCC decision was announced, the Office of Communication filed an appeal at the U.S. Court of Appeals, District of Columbia Circuit. Most federal cases start at the district court level. However, federal regulatory agencies such as the FCC or Federal Trade Commission function essentially as district courts to decide the issues before them. Appeals from their decisions go to the U.S. Court of Appeals, District of Columbia

Circuit. That jurisdiction has allowed this court to emerge "as a contemporary leader in regulatory legal and political change among the family of federal courts," a legal scholar has written.[19] Because of its presence in the nation's capital and because of the nature of many of the issues it hears, the D.C. Circuit Court has gained considerable attention in the last several decades. Its members have been leaders in the judiciary and have frequently been tapped to move to the Supreme Court. Warren Burger, who figures in this story, went from the D.C. Circuit to the Supreme Court, as did Antonin Scalia, Clarence Thomas, and Ruth Bader Ginsburg more recently.

In their appeal, Parker and his allies argued that the commission had erred in denying them standing. They labeled as false the FCC's statement that the challengers could assert no greater interest or claim of injury than members of the general public. As blacks, Henry and Smith "are more seriously injured by discrimination against Negroes than are viewers of other races," the Office of Communication said. In addition, the United Church of Christ at Tougaloo suffered discrimination because WLBT excluded black churches from religious programming while white churches were allowed several hours for services on Sundays and ten minutes every day at noon. Tougaloo College, which was integrated, also suffered because it had been excluded from educational programming.

Furthermore, the Office of Communication argued, the FCC should have conducted a hearing. Its majority found on several points that the challengers had raised serious questions about whether WLBT met the public interest standard of the Communications Act and therefore granted only a conditional one-year renewal. Holding a hearing, the challengers said, would have helped the commission reach an informed judgment.[20]

In its more detailed appeals brief, filed August 24, 1965, the church elaborated on its arguments. Concerning standing, the challengers contended that the appeals court had held in a 1961 case that a customer or consumer is affected by an administrative order regulating a public utility. The Supreme Court had also held that customers of public utilities had standing to challenge discriminatory practices. Nor had that rule been limited to public utilities. People who bought oleomargarine had standing in one case as persons affected by orders regarding its ingredients, and an association of coal consumers had been held to have standing to review a minimum price order. "Nothing in the language of the Communications Act suggests any reason for a more restrictive rule governing proceedings before the Federal Communications Commission."

Regulators should recognize that, although broadcasting had widespread effects, viewers had few means to be heard, the challengers contended. When a railroad or trucking company seeks to raise rates, they added, "shippers have a direct economic interest and unquestioned standing to oppose the carrier before the Interstate Commerce Commission. The public interest is protected by the inter-play between the carrier and the shipper. In hearings on a radio or television broadcasting license, in contrast, there is normally no one to speak in behalf of the public interest." A station seeking a license can interpret as it chooses the kind of programming it carries. Unless representatives of the listening or viewing public—the consumers of the broadcaster's product—are considered to have an interest, "there is no likelihood of an adversary procedure under which the public interest can be protected."

Here the FCC stubbornly resisted, with costly results. If these challengers were given standing, the FCC argued, any group could be, perhaps without having substantial interest in the matter. The FCC implied that allowing television viewers to make public interest arguments would be administratively inconvenient, but the Office of Communication saw no reason "why it should be less convenient to hear television viewers than to hear bus passengers or oleomargarine consumers." The law protected the FCC from irresponsible groups, the challengers said, by requiring specific allegations of fact to show that the petitioner was an interested party and that renewing a broadcaster's license would be inconsistent with the public interest.

The Office of Communication's brief noted that "WLBT is one of the most important means of mass communication in Mississippi. By maintaining policies of racial discrimination, under Federal license, it can influence the whole temper of the state adversely." Not only was Jackson the state capital and Mississippi's largest city, the station also had the strongest signal of any television outlet in the state. "WLBT should have a responsibility commensurate with its influence."

In addition, the Office of Communication said that the Communications Act allowed the FCC to grant a license renewal without holding a hearing only if it found that no substantial and material questions of fact were at issue. If there were such questions, the Communications Act provided that the FCC "shall formally designate the application for hearing"—"shall," not "may." The challengers argued for holding that hearing in Jackson because Congress had stressed the importance of holding local hearings.[21]

In response, the FCC was dismissive of the challengers' claims, to its ultimate detriment. Citing legislative history, FCC lawyers wrote that each time Congress took up the question of standing, it was considered in terms of applicants, licensees, or competitors who would be subject to economic injury—that is, broadcasters, not members of the public. The commission warned that the agency's hearing processes would become clogged if listeners representing many diverse interests received standing merely because they were upset by some FCC action. This did not mean that the public could not participate in FCC matters, the commission said. The FCC required that stations maintain local files that the public might inspect and had created the complaints and compliance division of its Broadcast Bureau to evaluate complaints from the public as well as industry.

As to the issues the challengers raised, the FCC asserted that it had accepted the substance of their charges regarding the station's failure to comply with the Fairness Doctrine and its discriminatory programming, had ordered that those practices stop, and had granted only a short-term renewal because of those considerations. Thus, it said in a leap of logic, no hearing was necessary because there were no significant factual issues. "The Commission fully recognized that the station's operations, based on its investigation and appellants' submissions, fell short of operation consistent with the public interest," the FCC brief tellingly admitted. But the commission had decided that if the station in effect cleaned up its act, it could remain on the air and needed to do so because of heightened tensions over race relations.[22]

As the case moved to the U.S. Court of Appeals, changes were occurring in Jackson. On June 18, 1965, the law firm of Fletcher, Heald, Rowell, Kenehan and Hildreth stepped aside as WLBT's attorneys; Russell Rowell had been the principal attorney handling the case. Later that year, Fred Beard was asked to resign from WLBT and went back to his hometown of Columbus, where for the next twenty-five years he ran a Coca-Cola bottling plant. WLBT's leaders at Lamar Life Broadcasting still firmly believed that they would retain the station's license, but Beard's career in broadcasting was over. Five years later, Lamar would no longer be running WLBT either.

"I gave birth to a television station," Beard reflected years later. "I got the channel assigned to Mississippi. I trained all the people that I was capable of training. I hired engineers that were trained in radio and had a background in engineering. We learned how to do it by going to the other stations. There were very few stations on the air anywhere. We were one of the first. And I gave birth to it. And then I had somebody kill it right in front of me—not because I was guilty of anything but being there. I was guilty of political activity that took the station away from us. We were tried, found innocent and lost the station. Just like finding somebody not guilty and executing them. That's what happened."[23]

Beard believed that the station's news coverage had been fair even in the midst of civil rights controversies and that WLBT had upheld its responsibilities to the public. He recalled that the station's original law firm advised WLBT to give the FCC a thorough accounting of its programming—turn over all the records—and that that in effect would satisfy the commission. As I talked with Beard, his wife, Susanne, and son, John, at their home in Columbus more than thirty-five years after the challenge, Susanne Beard said she remembered the lawyer very well. "He said, 'Oh, you have done such a great job and given everybody an opportunity to express themselves. . . . What we want you to do is highlight your history of what you all have done—you've done such a great job.' Of course, him being a lawyer, I'm sure he knew that would be money in his pocket. . . . Then, as Fred later said, what happened was that the other stations kind of just turned it off" by not making much of a response. "What we did, we supplied all the ammunition, all of the records of what had been done, for them to pick at us about, to shoot holes in us." Susanne Beard said that she and her husband thought that the lawyers gave them bad advice, made them defensive. "We should have done what WJTV did," she added, that is, not give a detailed response to the challengers.[24]

Whatever the Beards and others may have thought about WLBT's original attorneys, the station purchased excellent lawyering when it hired Arnold & Porter. The firm had been established in the mid-1940s by Thurman Arnold, former head of the antitrust division of the Justice Department. Abe Fortas, a former student of Arnold's at Yale University and an expert in regulatory law and labor relations, joined the firm from his post as undersecretary of the Department of Interior. Paul A. Porter, who had been chairman of the FCC and head of the Office of Price Administration, was the third founding partner. The firm was known as Arnold, Fortas & Porter until Fortas left in 1965 when named to the Supreme Court by his friend, President Lyndon Johnson. It was among the first Washington law firms that specialized in using the information gained from its members' government service to help corporations and others weave their way through a growing number of federal agencies and regulations. In short, its attorneys were insiders, and they took that experience to the bank.

Porter, who headed the team representing WLBT, was a tall, white-haired, gregarious man, a raconteur brimming with bonhomie. He was an imposing speaker, famed for his anecdotes and in demand as a toastmaster at Washington dinners. Born in Joplin, Missouri, in 1904, Porter moved to Kentucky with his family when he was a child. Originally, he seemed destined for a career in journalism. At fourteen, he became a part-time reporter at the *Winchester (Kentucky) Sun* to help support his mother and seven other children after his father, a Baptist minister, died. Later he was city editor of the *Lexington Herald* while earning the money to pay his way through the University of Kentucky law school, from which he received his law degree in 1929. By 1931 he was the editor of the *News* in LaGrange, Georgia. The story goes that he showed such a grasp of farm problems that Secretary of Agriculture Henry Wallace gave him his first federal job in Washington in 1933 as a special legal assistant. It was the beginning of the New Deal, and Porter never left.[25] He got to know a young congressman named Lyndon Johnson and, through him, occasionally attended the "Board of Education" sessions that House Speaker Sam Rayburn of Texas held in his office. There, as Porter said with a laugh, "we would have a little bit of branch water and a cup of iced Postum."[26]

Most of Porter's early Washington career was spent in government service, although he did work as counsel for CBS in the late 1930s. After serving as publicity chairman for Roosevelt's campaign for a fourth term in 1944, Porter was named head of the FCC. He and the Johnsons lived in the same area of Chevy Chase, and Johnson frequently gave Porter a ride to the FCC as he headed for Capitol Hill. "Many is the night that I have come home and my wife has said, 'We are going over to Lyndon's and Lady Bird's for supper.'" The Johnsons' cook, Zephyr Wright, fixed hearty meals, and then their guests sat around discussing the universe.[27] President Truman soon named Porter head of the Office of Price Administration and then gave him the rank of ambassador to lead the U.S. economic mission to Greece after World War II. He left government service in 1947 to help found the firm now known as Arnold & Porter. By the time Porter took on the WLBT case, Johnson was in the White House and Porter on White House guest lists.

In Arnold & Porter, WLBT had one of the most prestigious law firms money could buy, one with some of the best lawyers in Washington and vast resources. When the church filed its appeal, Porter said to Everett Parker, "Everett, if you file this thing, I'm going to make this run at least ten years, and I will bankrupt the United Church of Christ and I will force you out of the broadcasting field." To which Parker said he replied: "Well, Paul, if it runs ten years or fifteen years and if you're dead and I'm dead, the United Church of Christ will still be in there."[28] Porter died a decade later in 1975, well before the license was awarded to a new owner. At age seventy-one, he choked on a piece of lobster at the Palm Restaurant and died five days later.

As the court case opened, the odds seemed to be with WLBT. It had solid legal counsel. It had an affirmative FCC decision in an area—license renewals—in which the courts had never overruled the commission. And it had a three-judge panel that on the surface might not have looked as though it would ripple those waters. Warren Burger, who headed the panel, was a Minnesotan named to the court of appeals by President Eisenhower in 1955. The other judges were

Edward A. Tamm, a former FBI special agent, and Carl McGowan, who had taught law at Northwestern University.

But their unanimous opinions would surprise people. Tamm, whose qualifications had been questioned when he moved to the U.S. District Court bench from a post as assistant to FBI director J. Edgar Hoover, by all accounts conducted his cases there fairly and firmly. Once he moved to the court of appeals in 1965, he did not always agree with the court's liberal wing, but news accounts said that he "was seemingly guided by a common-sense approach to the case at hand." For example, in 1977 he would set aside an FCC ruling that a George Carlin record could not be aired on the radio because it contained seven words that referred to various sexual activities and parts of a woman's anatomy. That was censorship, he said, and was a ban that would also prohibit broadcast of certain Shakespearean plays, parts of the Bible, and the Nixon tapes that contained presidential profanity.[29] McGowan, named to the court of appeals by President Kennedy, was described in his *Washington Post* obituary as "a man of powerful and persuasive intellect who often played the role of peacemaker among the feuding liberal and conservative factions on the court. He was said to have been a man of gentle demeanor whose written opinions reflected an attention to clarity and common sense," and he had a reputation "for balancing individual and state interests in such a way that it was impossible to label him either liberal or conservative."[30]

Perhaps the biggest surprise to the public were Warren Burger's strong words on the case when, on March 25, 1966, the court of appeals ruled that the FCC had indeed erred in not holding a hearing. Burger, who later became chief justice of the United States, did not come from the kind of political background that might lead one to think he would upset established practices within a regulatory agency and a key industry. Nonetheless, he considered this opinion one of his most important.[31]

Burger's grandparents on his father's side came from Switzerland and on his mother's side from Germany. His paternal grandfather, who joined the Union Army at fourteen, was severely wounded and awarded the Medal of Honor. Burger's father was a rail-cargo inspector and sometimes a traveling salesman. The family lived on a twenty-acre truck farm. One of seven children, Burger was born September 17, 1907, in St. Paul, Minnesota. His parents could not help him much with his education—he had to turn down a scholarship to Princeton because it wasn't enough to live on. He sold insurance while attending the University of Minnesota for two years, then took night law school courses at St. Paul College of Law. He received his law degree with high honors in 1931. Within five years of joining the firm of Boyesen, Otis and Faricy, he had made partner. He handled corporate cases, probate and trusts, and real estate at the firm for twenty-two years. During twelve of those years he also taught law. He argued cases before the Supreme Court more than a dozen times.

The president of the St. Paul Junior Chamber of Commerce, Burger became active in the campaigns of Harold E. Stassen, who in 1938 was elected governor. Stassen perennially attempted to win the Republican presidential nomination, with Burger a strong ally. At the Republican conventions of 1948 and 1952 Burger met Richard Nixon and Herbert Brownell. In 1952 the Minnesota delegation put Eisenhower over the top to clinch the nomination when it switched its votes from Stassen to Eisenhower, and Burger proved impressive in the fight. Eisenhower named Brownell as his attorney general. Brownell in turn named Burger assistant attorney general for the claims division, which became the civil division. Burger argued the government's case against John F. Peters, a federal health consultant dismissed on loyalty grounds in an era when hunting supposed Communists was rampant. (Peters was defended by Arnold & Porter.) The solicitor general had refused to argue the case, annoying Brownell, so Burger's stock within the administration went up when he took it on. Not long afterward, Eisenhower named Burger to the appeals court, and he was sworn in on April 13, 1956. During his tenure on the court of appeals, he often wrote and spoke about the need for federal judges to work more efficiently, thus eliminating the need for new judgeships. Burger criticized liberal colleagues on the appeals court, led by Chief Judge David L. Bazelon, for broadening the standards that judged insanity in criminal cases. He came to President Richard M. Nixon's attention, in fact, because of his developing reputation as a "law and order" judge.[32]

Today Burger is largely remembered as the justice who presided over a Supreme Court of increasing conservatism. But the court under his stewardship decided that school busing could be used as a remedy for segregation, affirmative action programs were acceptable, and women could legally obtain abortions. Concerning the WLBT case, perhaps an even better clue to Burger's mind-set was the fact that in Minnesota he had been a leader of "good government" campaigns. A tribute in his hometown newspaper, the *St. Paul Pioneer Press*, when he died described his brand of Republicanism as "progressive and compassionate, the creative center of national politics."[33] In Minnesota, Burger helped organize and was the first president of the St. Paul Council on Human Relations. That group sponsored training programs for the police to improve relations with minority groups. Burger was also a member of the Minnesota Governor's Interracial Commission for many years.

Once he became chief justice, it was clear that he didn't think much of television itself. Burger refused to allow televised coverage of oral arguments at the Supreme Court, and in 1981 he shoved a network television cameraman who followed him toward an elevator.[34] What this attitude had contributed to the WLBT decisions, if anything, one cannot say.

During their arguments before Burger and his fellow appeals court judges, the FCC attorneys had mainly discussed the question of standing. Henry Geller, then the FCC general counsel, said that his office wrote as good a brief as it could. "We couldn't gild the lily. We said there's no standing because we had to make that argument. It was the only argument that made any sense. We had some precedents on that. We lost on that, and once we lost on that, we knew would lose" on the issues that the commission had brushed aside. Believing that the commission should have held a hearing, Geller thought he couldn't argue the case before the appeals court. "People would say no wonder we lost—you were down here telling us you're going to lose."[35] John Conlin, assistant general counsel in charge of litigation, presented the FCC's case.

The challengers argued that they did have a right to be involved and were seeking to correct an obvious imbalance. On one hand, viewers, no matter how meritorious their case, could not present evidence to the FCC unless the commission wished to hear it, and they could not appeal any decisions, however arbitrary. On the other hand, licensees had a right to a hearing and to appeal. Such an unequal contest did not invite public participation.[36]

Burger and his fellow judges agreed. Unanimously. The court ruled in March 1966 that the challengers did have standing and that the FCC should hold a hearing on their charges. Writing for the court, Burger said there was no reason to believe that Congress had "any thought that electrical interference and economic injury were to be the exclusive grounds for standing or that it intended to limit participation of the listening public to writing letters to the Complaints Division of the Commission." That line of thinking would give an electronics manufacturer standing while denying it to listeners, "who are the most directly concerned with and intimately affected" by a station's performance. The judges had clearly been influenced by the challengers' arguments when they cited the case of oleomargarine users having standing to complain about orders affecting its ingredients.

The theory that the FCC can always effectively represent listeners in a renewal proceeding without the aid of legitimate public representatives "is one of those assumptions we collectively try to work with so long as they are adequate," the court stated. But neither the commission nor the court should continue to rely on that assumption when it no longer stands up to the reality of experience, the court said.

The FCC wanted to limit the public to writing letters, but the long history of complaints against WLBT beginning in 1955 "had left the Commission virtually unmoved." It was likely, the court added, that WLBT's license would have been routinely renewed had not the Office of Communication challenged it. "Such beneficial contribution as these Appellants, or some of them, can make must not be left to the grace of the Commission." Unless broadcast consumers can be heard, there may be no one to bring a station's deficiencies to the commission's attention. "In order to safeguard the public interest in broadcasting . . . we hold that some 'audience participation' must be allowed in license renewal proceedings."

With this landmark ruling, the appeals court profoundly altered the way the FCC would operate over the next several decades. The court had given the public the right to participate in commission business, a right it would exercise to seek equal employment opportunity rules, to try to improve children's television, and to affect the outcome of other license renewal proceedings and sales of television stations.

The court also ordered the FCC to conduct a hearing on WLBT's fitness to hold a broadcasting license and to allow public intervention in that hearing. The conditions the FCC set for future performance by WLBT should be implicit in every license grant, and WLBT should have already been doing what the FCC ordered it to do. The station should have been required to run on its record at a hearing, the court said.

"We recognize that the Commission was confronted with a difficult problem and difficult choices, but it would perhaps not go too far to say it elected to post the Wolf to guard the Sheep in the hope that the Wolf would mend his ways because some protection was needed at once and none but the Wolf was handy," Burger wrote. "This is not a case, however," Burger added, "where the Wolf had either promised or demonstrated any capacity and willingness to change," for WLBT had stoutly denied the charges of programming misconduct. "In these circumstances, a pious hope on the Commission's part for better things from WLBT is not a substitute for evidence and findings."[37]

What stirred such strong words from Burger and his fellow judges? Burger may have remembered his human relations work in Minnesota and been swayed by the charges of racial discrimination. Or as a judge knowledgeable in administrative law, he may not have liked the way the FCC flouted the requirement for a hearing when substantial issues had been raised. It is also possible that the climate of the times affected the judges, as people awakened from the gray Eisenhower years and sought to be heard on issues ranging from Vietnam to civil rights to environmental questions. Burger, never a big fan of the influence of television, may have also thought that the station had abused its public trust by not covering issues of concern to the black as well as the white community. Burger is no longer alive to respond to these suppositions.

Burger, McGowan, and Tamm were moderate Americans who had served their country in a variety of capacities. Burger especially had been active in politics and civic affairs, part of an American's birthright. His was not a passive concept of citizenship. He and his fellow judges were in effect allowing a case to continue in which a group of individuals had spoken up when they saw something wrong, when they believed a station licensed by the federal government was violating the rules governing that license. The decision would have a sweeping impact, not only on the property of one TV station owner but also on the political dialog in Jackson and in Mississippi and on broadcast reform efforts across the country. It is significant in this context that the court opinion quoted New York University law professor Edmond Cahn's article "Law in the Consumer Perspective": "Some consumers need bread; others need Shakespeare; others need their rightful place in the national society—what they all need is processors of law who will consider the people's needs more significant than administrative convenience."[38]

The court's decision put citizens into the process, said Albert Kramer, one of the attorneys who became active in the public interest communications law movement spawned by the WLBT case. "It opened up the floodgates to citizen intervention. The public got a role to play in how the public airwaves were handed out, as well as the media barons."[39]

The case galvanized the nonprofit world, including foundations, into exploring the media's impact. Because of this court decision, groups interested in fostering First Amendment rights, improving the environment, combating racism and sexism, and balancing commercial messages had leverage to meet with stations and negotiate changes in their programming and personnel practices. In Jackson, WLBT would reach out more to the black community, with all the altered perceptions that would involve. The FCC still had not resolved the status of WLBT itself, but the entire broadcasting industry was put on notice that it could no longer rely on a cozy relationship with the commission as it conducted business. The public would not only be watching but could now act. This first WLBT decision had given citizens a direct legal avenue for addressing issues concerning the nation's medium with the highest impact, television.

4. THE FCC HEARS NO EVIL

The Reverend Everett Parker and attorney Earle K. Moore met a mixed reaction when they arrived in Jackson in May 1967 for the hearing the appeals court had ordered. A white federal judge refused to allow use of his courtroom. At first, only challenger R. L. T. Smith had the nerve to sit at the table with Moore and his associates. Gradually, more blacks attended the hearing. But when black elevator operators at Parker's and Moore's hotel saw the pair lugging briefcases bulging with legal files, they whisked them to their floors.[1]

Political and social change had started to occur in Mississippi, but only glacially. The state's white power structure was trying wherever possible to slow down the advancement of the black population; some black people were willing to push forward while others hesitated. James Meredith undertook a "march against fear" along Mississippi highways to encourage blacks to register and vote and on June 6, 1966, was shot from ambush. Civil rights leaders from around the country took up his march. At an encampment in Greenwood, Stokely Carmichael, long active in the Mississippi movement, urged "black power." His cry reverberated across a country torn by race-related riots in the Watts section of Los Angeles in 1965 and in numerous cities in

1966. His words drove a wedge between some blacks and whites allied in the civil rights cause.

WLBT was also changing. Robert Hearin, a powerful local businessman, replaced P. K. Lutken as president of Lamar Life Broadcasting. Fred Beard had left, too, as the station management sought to retain its license. Beard's former assistant, Robert "Bob" McRaney Jr., was the new station manager. McRaney, thirty-one at the time, had grown up in broadcasting. He was born in Hattiesburg. His family moved to Columbus, Mississippi, where his father put WCBI radio on the air. He graduated from nearby Mississippi State University with a degree in business administration and spent three years in the army, serving at Fort Slocum, New York, and doing radio and television work for the U.S. Army Air Defense Command in Colorado Springs, Colorado. The year McRaney graduated from college, his father had started WCBI television. McRaney went to cities around the South to see how other stations were organized. He started at WLBT in 1959 as assistant to the general manager.[2]

Some radio stations still played "Dixie" at all hours of the day and urged people to carry guns, McRaney recalled. "Those were volatile times. I stepped into that situation as general manager." He considered that he brought a sense of moderation to the prevalent states' rights attitude. McRaney had gotten along well with Beard, he said, believing that Beard enjoyed the intellectual stimulation their talks gave him. He agreed that Beard had been the lightning rod in the case. "The United Church of Christ attorney tried to make him out to be an evil person, and he wasn't. Stubborn, hard-headed, argumentative, yes, but he was always willing to listen to my point of view and he never refused to meet with any of the black leaders. He'd try to preach at them, but he met with them."[3]

Parker and Moore would match Arnold & Porter's legal team point by point, but the case tested their staying power and that of the church. The lawyers had already spent almost a year debating how the hearing should be conducted, delaying its start until May 1967. For all the importance of the case to the people of Jackson, the hearing marked their only chance to be heard directly by anyone from the FCC during the challenge.

In its order of May 26, 1966, the FCC had directed its examiner to hear testimony regarding several facets of WLBT's practices: whether the station provided opportunities for discussions of conflicting views, whether it provided all significant groups in its area the chance to use its facilities, whether it acted in good faith on racial matters or misrepresented such matters to the public or the FCC, and whether granting a new license to the station's current owners would serve the public interest. The FCC ruled that the burden of proof on the first two issues lay with the challengers, that is, the Office of Communication, Aaron Henry, and Rev. R. L. T. Smith, and with the commission's own Broadcast Bureau for the third. On the fourth point, the station would have to prove whether, in light of all the evidence, renewing its license would serve the public interest. This was important because the weight of proving the merits of the challenge rested on those who brought it, not on the station against which it was brought, except on the last point. If the challengers and the Broadcast Bureau couldn't prove their case to an examiner and the commission, then the station had an easier task proving it had served the public.[4]

Kenneth Cox, who had disagreed with his colleagues on the 1965 license renewal, agreed with the decision to hold a hearing but dissented on several points. He believed that the FCC majority should not permit the promise of reform under the spur of the one-year renewal to obscure the station's record over the past eleven years. He cited the court's language that past performance should be the FCC's best criterion, and he also disagreed with the commission majority over who should have the burden of proof on each of the issues.[5]

Legal papers streamed into the FCC in response to its order about issues at the hearing. On June 16, 1966, the Office of Communication asked the FCC to reconsider its decision about the burden of proof. It should have placed that burden on all issues on the applicant, the church said, adding that the commission should forbid evidence on the station's operation since the case began.[6] On July 12 WLBT opposed the church's request.[7] This was no small issue, and both sides knew that it was critical to their case.

In September the commission denied the Office of Communication petition, saying that when a petition to deny a license was involved, the burden of proof should rest on the party making the charges of misconduct. The commission's logic seemed at times worthy of Lewis Carroll. The majority held that the issues involved in this case "relate largely to acts of omission rather than commission. The failure to present particular viewpoints and the failure to provide the opportunity for expression by significant community groups may be better known to those claiming to represent the viewpoints or groups denied access to broadcast facilities than to the broadcaster who keeps records of what he has presented rather than of what he has not presented."[8]

Once again, Cox disagreed. "Certainly the refusal to present a point of view is an affirmative act of commission—even though it can be turned around and described as an omission of the desired programming." Calling the commission's argument "nonsense," Cox asked: "How can the man who is denied access to WLBT know more about his unsuccessful effort to present his viewpoint than the representative of the station who denied him time to discuss the issue?" Someone who has heard a segregationist point of view broadcast can testify that he sought time to answer and was denied that opportunity, but he cannot demonstrate conclusively that, at some time when he wasn't watching the station, his view was not broadcast. With its records, a station could report what had aired.

Cox then went to the heart of the question—should WLBT be given a new license because it might show improvement or should it, as the court had said, have to prove its merit based on its record before the challenge was filed? "Let us assume that a station has been operated in complete disregard for the public interest, so that the commission sets its renewal for hearing," Cox wrote. "The licensee, faced with the loss of a valuable franchise, discharges the people in direct charge of the day-to-day operations of the station, hires new, competent and respected broadcasters to take their place, and begins to conduct a highly praiseworthy broadcast operation. When the renewal hearing gets underway, it concedes its past derelictions but points to its present high quality service, and paints in glowing terms the fine things it proposes to do in the future," Cox wrote, in essence describing WLBT's legal strategy. Cox thought that if the license were renewed on that basis, the station might operate properly until pressure from the commission stopped. Then it "would revert to its former bad habits."

Those who seriously disregarded FCC rules should lose their licenses, Cox warned. "If broadcasters learn that they can abuse their franchise, but earn renewals anyway on the basis of promised reform, then a certain element in the industry will ignore the public interest until caught." Evidence of reform under pressure was irrelevant to him.[9]

In the midst of the legal maneuvering, FCC general counsel Henry Geller spoke with Paul Porter. He recalled telling Porter that if matters stayed as they were and the commission renewed the license again, "we'll be looking at a howitzer in the court of appeals. Tell your client the jig is up—put blacks on all over the place, hire more, do everything he can for the black community. Call in Parker, Aaron Henry, bring them on board." He urged a settlement. "I don't really care about your jeopardizing your investment but I do care about the FCC," Geller told Porter.[10]

Earle K. Moore's calendars from early 1967 showed that he conferred several times with Everett Parker about a possible settlement.[11] On March 17, 1967, Moore sent Parker a memo about proposed terms for a settlement. The United Church of Christ wanted WLBT to make what the old management would have considered sweeping changes: hire a black news announcer who would appear regularly; air in prime time each week a half-hour program on which an integrated panel discussed a controversial issue; develop a series on race relations and black history aimed at the junior high level; and include spot announcements for black groups on such matters as voter registration. The station should also agree to omit mention of race in crime news except where necessary to help catch a suspect or when the alleged crime was related to race relations; broadcast a religious service from a black church once a month during normal Sunday worship hours; continue equal use of courtesy titles; and permit black colleges to participate in the *Our Colleges* program. Two people nominated by the challengers would sit on the Lamar Life Broadcasting Company board and on a committee to consult with management about programming. All the groups, including the FCC, would announce that WLBT would try to set an example for the industry in improving television service to the black community. WLBT would also pay the church's legal fees.[12]

Should there be settlement negotiations, Parker told Moore in a memo, the challengers should make it clear their unshakeable objective was an airtight procedure that would make WLBT a model for all stations in the South in serving the black community. He wanted WLBT to state publicly that it would show the way in serving the interests of minority groups in accordance with the Communications Act. The challengers in turn would make it clear that they considered the agreement of WLBT to become a model operation to be a major victory in behalf of civil rights.[13]

On April 11 Moore sent Orrin Judd, senior member of the legal team, a memo saying that Reed Miller of Arnold & Porter had asked what legal fees the challengers would want paid in any settlement.[14] Years later, Moore didn't remember the amount but thought that it was certainly no more than $200,000. In light of the value of the station, Moore added, the amount was "a bagatelle," but the station refused and the case continued. Paul Porter said of his client's decision: "Some of these Mississippians said they wouldn't traffic with the devil. They felt this was a bunch of carpetbaggers."[15]

The FCC named Jay Kyle as the hearing examiner for the case. Kyle, sixty-one, was from Kansas and had received his undergraduate degree from the College of Emporia and law degrees from Washburn Law School in Topeka—an LL.B. in 1931 and a J.D. degree in 1938.[16] He held a conference with the attorneys on December 13, 1966, in Washington. Reed Miller, representing WLBT for Arnold & Porter, objected to the first two issues that were to be raised at the hearing— that is, whether WLBT provided opportunities for discussions of views other than its own and whether it provided blacks the opportunity to use its facilities. Such inquiries violated the broadcaster's First Amendment rights, and therefore the FCC could not deny the license renewal on those grounds, Miller argued.[17] This question has always been a fundamental one for the FCC—how far could it go to enforce fairness without imposing censorship?

WLBT asked that the hearing be held in Washington. It said it had complied with the FCC's conditions and felt that "harmonious relations between the station and the Negro community have been cemented" and racial tensions "substantially diminished." However, it added, holding the hearing in Jackson would revive what it considered old charges of racial discrimination, arousing possibly irresponsible elements of both the black and white communities.[18] Many black leaders in Mississippi, however, doubted that progress in race relations was sufficient. Vernon Dahmer, a farmer in the Hattiesburg area who was leading voter registration activities for the NAACP, had died in a fire set by Ku Klux Klansmen attacking his home in January 1966. The following February, just weeks before the FCC hearing began, a car bomb killed Wharlest Jackson in Natchez not long after he was promoted to a job previously held by whites.

The Office of Communication preferred that the hearing be in Jackson. Its lawyers told the FCC that many people involved could not afford to travel to Washington. Congress had also placed great emphasis on holding local hearings. The church did not believe the broadcaster's claim of noteworthy strides, adding that "the best answer to the extremists is to demonstrate publicly that racial injustices can be remedied by lawful means."[19]

On December 27, 1966, chief examiner James D. Cunningham ruled that the hearings should be held in Jackson and later in Washington, if necessary. They were to begin February 27, 1967.[20] Prehearing maneuvering continued.

"Spin doctoring" was not a phrase in use then, but each side framed the issues involved in the hearings as best it could. WLBT's general manager Bob McRaney said he thought the public was conscious of the station's efforts to operate fairly. "A television license is a public trust. We believe we have been operating consistent with that trust and will continue to do so." McRaney, whom *Newsweek* described as "a bright salesman tuned in to local white moderates," said that the station had worked hard to establish a dialogue between the station and the black community.[21]

For its part, the Office of Communication called the hearings a "historic event in communications law. We are concerned lest WLBT's minimal, inadequate gestures to present Negroes in segregated programs and information about Negroes in segregated time periods be mistaken for genuine compliance with the public interest requirements of the Communications Act. The needs of Negroes can be fulfilled only on the basis of true equality with whites. WLBT still maintains the arrogant stand that the Negro is different and separate from the white man. We are, therefore, forced to continue our demand that the license of this station not be renewed." Church leaders acknowledged that WLBT had improved but added that the station should still be punished. "Once you've committed a crime," said Everett Parker, "you're punished for it, even if you've reformed."[22]

Finally, on May 1, 1967, the hearing got under way at the U.S. Post Office and Courthouse in downtown Jackson. Attorneys Harry Huge and Reed Miller appeared for WLBT; William A. Kehoe Jr. and Leo I. George, both Georgetown University law school graduates, for the FCC's Broadcast Bureau; and Earle K. Moore and Ann Aldrich for the Office of Communication.

Paul Porter had earlier dispatched Huge, a young associate at Arnold & Porter, to Jackson to work with the station to prepare for the hearing. Huge had grown up in Superior, Nebraska, a small town on the Kansas-Nebraska border. "There were no blacks there," he told me. "The first time I came into contact with blacks was when I played college basketball." That was at Nebraska Wesleyan University, from which he graduated in 1959. Then he served in the U.S. Army with blacks and Puerto Ricans and "never thought anything about it." He graduated from Georgetown University Law Center in 1963 and in 1965 became an associate at Arnold & Porter.

Porter told Huge that the firm was representing the Murchison brothers, who owned Lamar Life Insurance Company. He wanted to know if Huge would work on the license challenge case, which Huge did not want to do. The prospect of going to Mississippi to represent what newspapers depicted as a racist television station did not appeal to him. Porter asked him at least to go to Mississippi and talk to people about WLBT, which Huge did.

NAACP activist Charles Evers told Huge that the station wasn't as bad as it was portrayed in the North. Huge met with political and business people and educators, some of whom he contacted through Evers, and decided that he could work on the case. "For a while I moved my wife and six-months-old son down and we lived in Jackson, before the hearings and afterwards."[23] Huge worked closely with McRaney. Both had infants at the time, and their families became good friends. It was not the calmest time to be in Mississippi. While the Huges were there, a young black man was killed by police who fired into a group of Jackson State students and bystanders. The climate was such in the state, Huge would write later, that "one measures time in Mississippi by when this or that killing took place."[24]

WLBT's management had already launched a plan of reform "that did not include Beard," Huge said. "The strategy that we evolved was that you couldn't defend the station's past. You had to defend the station in the present and the future. To do that, you had to take far-reaching steps."[25] The steps ranged from putting a well-known black disc jockey on the air to setting up a new program featuring commentaries by respected state leaders and newsmen.[26] The law firm and Robert Hearin were very much involved in the strategy, Huge said, adding that the station's efforts were "going a long way for Jackson, Mississippi, in 1967."[27]

The other station in Jackson did little local coverage, "perhaps feeling that the less said the better," McRaney recalled, while WLBT did. WLBT also cooperated with network reporters. "There was a great deal of pride in what we as a station and individuals as journalists" were doing, McRaney noted. "We felt that we were in fact holding a mirror up to the community instead of turning our backs on it."[28]

Opposing the Arnold & Porter attorneys in Jackson were Earle K. Moore and Ann Aldrich for the Office of Communication. Orrin Judd was tied up on other issues and wanted Moore to handle the hearing. (Judd was named to the federal bench the next year and thereafter was not connected with the case.) Moore, an amiable, mild-mannered man who would become what Henry Geller described as "the backbone of the public interest movement in the communications field," was born in 1921 and grew up in Kenmore, New York, a suburb of Buffalo.[29] He graduated from Harvard University in 1943. After serving in the army, he graduated from Harvard Law School in 1948 and started working for the well-connected law firm of Goldstein, Judd & Gurfein.[30]

The other member of the challengers' legal team, Ann Aldrich, had received her bachelor's degree from Columbia University and her law degree from New York University (NYU). She also had a doctorate in law from NYU, where she wrote her thesis on law for outer space. She had done research for NYU law professor Edmond Cahn and for Arthur Vanderbilt, the New Jersey chief justice. From 1953 to 1960 she was on the FCC general counsel's staff. Everett Parker had been trying to find communications lawyers to work on the case, but they would have nothing to do with challenging the FCC's authority. Aldrich thought that since she had worked at the FCC, she could be helpful. She later taught law at Cleveland State University in Ohio and was named a U.S. District Court judge in Ohio in 1980.[31]

The Office of Communication presented its case first, with the Reverend Everett Parker as the first witness. By way of background, Parker said that he and colleagues had worked on a weeklong monitoring study of New York City and New Haven, Connecticut, television stations to show the need for educational television. He said he drew on this experience to develop categories for describing programs during the WLBT monitoring.[32] The value of this monitoring proved a key point of contention between the two sides.

Next, both Gordon Henderson, then working for a Phoenix, Arizona, research firm, and his wife, Mary Ann, testified about the monitoring. Mary Ann Henderson was a native of Jackson and a graduate of Millsaps College, making her, as her husband had said, clearly a person at home in Mississippi. She had also worked for five years in New York for the A. C. Nielsen Company, which compiled ratings on the popularity of television programs. She was thus familiar with monitoring techniques and gave the challengers an air of authority concerning their survey, which she described.[33] Her husband's testimony covered the background of the monitors, the layout of the monitoring equipment, and the forms on which information was recorded.

The hearing examiner and the attorneys often sparred on points that may have seemed minor at the time, but the pattern of treatment that the challengers received later played a key role in the appeals court's second decision. For example, on cross-examination, Henderson was asked whether he had the names of the monitors.

"I do."[34]

Moore contended that the names of the monitors were not relevant. "In order to make this study, we have morally committed ourselves not to disclose the names of the individual monitors, because of the fear, on their part, that harassment would result if their identities became known."

WLBT's attorney, Reed Miller objected, and the hearing examiner said that Henderson had to give the monitors' names. "I want them in the record."

Moore then asked for a short recess. The examiner granted the request, adding, "This witness is testifying about monitors, and I want to know who they are. Counsel has asked the question, and he's entitled to know. So am I." Kyle threatened to subpoena them.

"Sir," said Moore, "this has really presented us with a serious decision and we would like to confer about it."

"Mr. Moore," the examiner replied, "the whole thing's a serious matter, this whole hearing's a serious matter, and we're not going to eliminate a thing from this record. Now, we're down here to hear this case, and I want to know who those monitors are, or I'll strike all of his testimony."

After a conference among themselves, the WLBT attorneys decided not to require disclosure of the monitors' names, provided that further testimony on the monitoring study dealt only with material found in the logs and monitoring sheets, not with any opinions about the programming. The examiner and the commission could draw their own conclusions.[35]

The next day the Reverend R. L. T. Smith took the stand. Smith repeated his complaint that when WLBT finally agreed to let him appear on the air while he was running for Congress, Beard had said that people who disagreed with his message probably "would blow up my house and his house and blow up my business."

"Now what do you think about that?" Smith said that Beard asked him.

"I told him to give me the contract and let's sign it."

Smith added that he had the idea that Beard "tried everything in the book to frighten us," which didn't work.[36]

Smith also mentioned the presence of the conservative Freedom Bookstore in the WLBT lobby, another point that became contentious between the WLBT attorneys, the challengers' lawyers, and Kyle. The challengers thought the bookstore bore on the case because it sold what Moore described as "extreme right-wing literature" in a TV station licensed to serve the public interest, one that ran announcements for right-wing causes without presenting other viewpoints. WLBT's lawyers argued that the bookstore was irrelevant. The hearing examiner sided with WLBT, saying, "I don't see any issue that has anything to do with what any bookstore sells in Jackson, Mississippi."[37]

Trying to show that the station had changed, WLBT attorney Miller elicited from Smith on cross-examination that in 1966 he had sent a complimentary letter to station manager McRaney about a program called "Mississippi: A Self-Portrait." He also got into the record the information that Smith and the station management had conferred about using black ministers on midday devotional programs beginning in 1965.[38] The church's attorneys continued to object to testimony regarding improvements since their petition had been filed in 1964. Kyle overruled them, saying the FCC order directed him to consider anything up to the current date involving the station.[39] At least that was how he interpreted the commission's order.

Some viewers had taken offense at WLBT programming and editorials, and the Office of Communication attorneys brought in witnesses to testify about practices that troubled them. For example, A. D. Beittel, who had been president of Tougaloo College from 1960 to 1964 and who was white, said that the station could have helped educate the community during the controversy over James Meredith's entry into the University of Mississippi. Instead, he thought that it was used to aggravate the situation.

Asked if the station had improved, Beittel replied: "I think it has improved substantially in this direction. Matters of this kind are relative, to be sure. If one compares it to the depths of which it sank during the previous period, it has improved considerably. If you compared it to what I think they should be doing, I still think they have further improvement to make."[40]

George Owens, a Columbia University graduate and Tougaloo's business manager (later its president), testified about a regular WLBT contributor who customarily referred to "niggers."

"Did he say n-i-g-g-e-r or n-e-g-r-a-s?" Owens, a black man, was asked.

"Both of those terms are objectionable to us when an educated person can't pronounce a simple word," Owens replied. "I personally found it greatly to my discomfort and I didn't like it." He had not complained to the station, but his wife had called.[41]

The lawyers for the Office of Communication were attempting to show elements of discrimination and lack of service to WLBT's total viewing audience, that is, blacks as well as whites. Their witnesses, like George Owens and his wife, Ruth, who also testified, often could not cite exact dates and times of programs or comments that they found discriminatory or offensive because they doubtless never dreamed they would need to record that information. When Ruth Owens said that she had called the station to complain about use of the word "nigger," for example, FCC attorney William Kehoe hammered at her lack of precision. When, he asked, had she called the station? Had she called from home or from her office? What time of day did she call? Was it after 5 P.M.? Did she know to whom she spoke at the station? Did she make note of every time she listened to a WLBT newscast? Did she make note of every time black women were or were not referred to by courtesy titles? This failure of recollection was a weakness in the challengers' case that the WLBT attorneys sought to exploit. WLBT wanted to paint much of the testimony of the challengers' witnesses as hearsay—and therefore legally flawed. As the questioning of Ruth Owens showed, FCC lawyers helped in the effort, wittingly or not.[42]

The testimony of Andrew Young, then an assistant to Martin Luther King Jr. and executive director of the Southern Christian Leadership Conference (SCLC), went to the core of the challengers' complaints about distorted news coverage. While Young was directing the SCLC's citizenship education program in Georgia, he traveled often to Mississippi to recruit local leaders for the training. While in Cleveland, Mississippi, Young recalled watching a television news report about three civil rights workers—the Reverend James Bevel; his wife, Diane; and Bob Moses—"which strongly implied that they were communists and that the voter registration effort was being influenced by communists." Reed Miller objected because Young couldn't pin down on which station he had seen this report. The examiner sustained Miller's motion.

Said Moore: "I think we can establish beyond question the only station that can be seen in Cleveland is WLBT."

Then Young talked about a report on a march to the courthouse in Greenwood during a voter registration drive in March 1963. Young, watching television in Jackson, saw that police with dogs had stopped the march. "The news was reported by WLBT—this time I am sure of it—as though people were going down to start trouble." The police beat several people, Young said, yet the local television news story was "that there was an assault on the courthouse, that Negroes attempted to charge the courthouse." The national network story said that police interrupted a voter registration march. Both the network and the local news show used virtually the same pictures, Young said.[43]

Moore's next witness was the Reverend Wendell P. Taylor, who since 1963 had been pastor of the Central Methodist Church in Jackson. Earlier, he had served as the church's district superintendent in Hattiesburg. Although he had bachelor's and master's degrees from Columbia University, Taylor, a black man, had been unsuccessful in an attempt to register in Forrest County and had filed an affidavit against the registrar. He testified in federal court in that case concerning the difficulty black applicants had in trying to register. At the FCC hearing, he said he had complained to WLBT when a sermon that he had given was inaccurately reported as condemning Martin Luther King Jr.

Taylor also testified that his daughter watched *Teen Tempo* on WLBT, adding, "Kids just like the music. I think the rhythm of it is what she enjoyed but she did wonder why there were no Negro kids on it." Taylor stated that as far as he could tell at the time, WLBT had a general policy "to eliminate these network programs where Negroes were involved."

Huge asked that Taylor's comment be struck. "He does not know the policy of WLBT." The examiner sustained his motion. Taylor replied that from June 1963 to April 1964 when a black person was to be interviewed on the *Today* show, there were interruptions by local announcements over WLBT. "It was not the same as with white people. It was not normal as I saw it."[44]

Returning to the issue of distorted coverage of civil rights demonstrations, the Reverend Edwin King testified about witnessing a group of black students trying to obtain service at the Woolworth's lunch counter in Jackson. A mob began crowding them, throwing ketchup and mustard and salt and pepper at them. "Then they began picking up deodorants, shouting, 'Niggers stink,' and breaking bottles of deodorant near them. Then they began getting insecticides and bug spray and sprayed it in the faces of the people at the counter." John Salter, a white professor who had joined them, was hit in the head with a glass canister. A black man who had been seated at the counter was hit in the head and stomped on by a white man.

WLBT carried a report on the incident that night, King testified. "When the news came on of the demonstration, 'Violence at Woolworth's,' the television station, Channel 3, showed pictures of white people leaving the lunch counter. It showed empty seats at the lunch counter. It showed the Negroes sitting in at the lunch counter. It did not show the white mob attacking the Negroes. It did not show the Negro student who was knocked from the chair and kicked unconscious by the white man. It showed a very seemingly peaceful scene with no trouble going on. . . . The behavior of the white mob was not shown."

"Let me understand this," examiner Kyle said. "What you are saying is your criticism of WLBT is that they didn't carry more of this incident?"

"Yes," King said. "May I say more?"

"No," Kyle said. "That answers my question."[45]

Then the examiner added that he did not consider this incident had any bearing on the hearing, but he was "trying to be reasonable and leaning over backwards to be fair to the intervenors. As I said yesterday, this is not a civil rights forum. This is an evidentiary hearing for the purpose of determining the issues laid down by the commission under the mandate of the circuit court of appeals. I want to give everyone an opportunity to be heard but only on the issues."[46] WLBT's coverage of civil rights activities was, however, one of the issues in the case because the challengers were charging the station with failing to deal fairly with racial matters.

Asked many years later how they felt about Kyle's handling of the hearing, the attorneys for each side held decidedly opposite views. Everett Parker and Earle K. Moore felt the examiner was prejudiced against them. "The hearing examiner was doing everything that he could do to exonerate the station," Parker said.[47] Harry Huge, in contrast, had a sense that Kyle was evenhanded. "You have to remember that this was a public hearing. The parties were contentious. The lawyers [for the church] and I clashed." Everett Parker "had the fire of self-righteousness about him," Huge added, recalling that meetings to try to settle issues in the case failed. "At breaks in the hearing Everett would be lecturing me and I'd get mad. Their lawyer was calmer." But that carried over into the hearing room. "With some witnesses, you'd ask a question and you'd get a speech."[48]

The hearing progressed. Hodding Carter, editor of the *Delta Democrat-Times* in Greenville, testified that he often listened to WLBT's program *Comment* and had heard Tom Ellis say "negras" or "niggers" on the air. And he heard Fred Beard editorialize that Mississippians should resist the ruling opening the university to James Meredith. "We should stand fast, that the rest of the nation would join us, and in the context of what he said meant a physical resistance to the court rulings."

Miller objected that Carter was speculating about what Beard meant. Sustained.

Carter was asked whether WLBT newsman Richard Sanders had ever said he was under intense pressure? Yes.

Sanders told Carter that on several occasions he had been within an inch of losing his job because of news decisions he had made; only the intervention of someone above the station manager level could save him from losing that job.[49] (Sanders said in an interview that after Robert Hearin became involved with station operations, he reported to him. Beard didn't always "like it that I was kind of in the middle. I was trying to cover it so everybody got a fair shake." Sanders turned to Hearin occasionally. "He told me, 'You do what you think is right. Go ahead.' It was a weird last year," Sanders said of the period before he left the station in 1965 because he wanted to work for ABC in Washington.)[50]

Ed King testified again, this time about programming the morning after Medgar Evers was killed. He said he turned on the television set just before 7 A.M. for the *Today* show. A voice announced, "What you are about to see is an example of biased, managed northern news. Stay tuned at 7:25 for your Mississippi news." The national news came on, leading with Evers's killing in Jackson.

Once again, King spoke about what he considered biased news coverage. The day after Evers's death, police swinging clubs had moved in on demonstrators outraged by the slaying. They grabbed Tougaloo professor John Salter, pulled him from the porch where he had been standing, clubbed him, then dragged him to a police car, King stated. "His clothing was torn, he was bleeding profusely."

That night WLBT showed pictures of police rushing toward Salter. "Then the newsreel stopped, the newscaster was suddenly seen," King said. No film was shown as the announcer reported, "At this point, Mr. Salter stumbled and fell from the porch, injuring himself." Then the newsreel came back on. "We saw none of the pictures of the police beating Mr. Salter, only the pictures of a man with his clothing ripped to shreds, bleeding terribly, being led to a police car." King also testified that WLBT cut a section from a network documentary that featured the Woolworth's lunch counter sit-in demonstration.[51]

Just before the hearing recessed that day, there was one note of levity as the FCC's Kehoe said: "After listening to what these people in Mississippi have been doing to each other, I think they must be all of Irish descent."

"You ought to know," the examiner replied, "with a name like yours."[52]

The following Monday, May 8, the Broadcast Bureau called Fred Beard to the stand. Kehoe handled the questioning for the FCC. Beard acknowledged that he had been a member of the Citizens' Council between roughly 1956 and 1961 or 1962. He was asked its intent. As he understood it, the Citizens' Council was "a moderate segregational group that would allow people, law-abiding, and people who believed in segregation, to become a member of an organization who would work against integration through lawful, legal means and to in turn prevent violence." To his knowledge, he added, the Citizens' Council had sought out elements of the community that might have committed violence and prevented them from doing so.[53]

WLBT broadcast the *Citizens' Council Forum*, which discussed important news issues, for about five years, Beard said. "We did not carry any of the programs that dealt with integration or segregation," only those that dealt with national issues. He added that the station received few complaints about carrying the program. One group asked for time to discuss integration but was turned down on the advice of the station's attorneys in Washington.

"The Citizens' Council was more unhappy with me in running my station than was the NAACP," Beard said. Ed King had testified that

Beard had received an award from the Citizens' Council, but Beard said neither he nor the station had received any such award. "I doublechecked with the Citizens' Council after I heard of that and I am sure I have not gotten so senile I would not remember it. . . . As a matter of fact, they are very cool to me and have been for many years."[54]

Asked whether WLBT carried the network interview of Thurgood Marshall on the *Home* show, Beard replied: "We did not." He didn't want to have to fight Bill Simmons of the Citizens' Council all the next day and give them half an hour to oppose Marshall. Beard insisted that WLBT substituted another program for that segment. "The alleged deal that we would throw up [a sign saying] 'Sorry, Cable Trouble,' is ridiculous."[55]

"Mr. Beard," Kehoe asked, "do you recall ever making a statement at a Citizens' Council meeting either in Jackson, Mississippi, or anyplace else to the effect that you kept Negroes from appearing on WLBT by posting a sign, 'Sorry, Cable Trouble'?"

"We did not."

Beard added that the station did not want to incite violence or pit one group against another. He added that he frequently criticized the *Jackson Daily News* and its fiery editor, Fred Sullens, for "always blowing up out of proportion any small incidents that took place that involved white or Negro. . . . We have had a fine climate between the races here in Mississippi. There were no problems, no race instances, no Detroit, Chicago, the problems that were taking place in other sections of the country, and we wanted to keep it that way."

At a Citizens' Council meeting, Beard had said that his station "would not give headline coverage to such incidents and blow them up. We carried Negro programs, we carried Negro entertainment and such as that but we didn't go out deliberately and cover any news story and blow it out of proportion."[56]

Next Beard was questioned about giving the Reverend R. L. T. Smith airtime. He acknowledged that he had been influenced by a letter from the FCC, although many times its directives were too vague.[57] Furthermore, WLBT's attorneys also received a call from Senator James O. Eastland about the matter, Beard said. The FCC had contacted Eastland and told him that "if we didn't sell time [to Smith] that we would regret it and that they would in turn come up with other charges against us and harass us to the point where we would be better off to sell the time."

"Before you sold him time, did you indicate there might be any problems of violence if he was put on WLBT?"

"I certainly did."

Asked what he told Smith, Beard replied: "Reverend Smith and I had visited by this time quite a number of times and we were on a very friendly, cordial basis." Beard told Smith the station would take precautions to see that nothing happened to him or the station. "We wanted him to make a fine speech and a speech that was not inflammatory in any way that would cause any problems by either race, one towards the other." He cautioned Smith: "If you make an inflammatory speech, you are going to end up in the Pearl River with me alongside you, floating down it, because they are going to blame me as much as they are you, for what you say.

"So I said, 'Use tact and diplomacy and you can do a good selling job without going off the deep end.'" Beard told Smith that they would give him a teleprompter to read from so he could make a better appearance. "So, we were most cooperative in working with him in every way and gave him his television image. In other words, I was a Robert Montgomery [a TV actor/coach] to him like Montgomery was to Eisenhower."

After Smith appeared, the station received about sixty telephone calls, including some threats. Smith's statement had been mild mannered, Beard said. "He did a fine job and received compliments that he did a good job."[58]

As for Aaron Henry's request for airtime, Beard testified that the Mississippi attorney general had ruled he was not a legally qualified candidate for governor, so his request was turned down. "We offered Negroes time to appear on television from time to time and very few of them would ever appear."[59]

Beard was asked whether WLBT had broadcast editorials in 1962 concerning the admission of James Meredith to the University of Mississippi. Yes, Beard replied. He explained that in February 1962 he had attended a meeting at which the FCC told broadcasters "in no uncertain terms that we had a responsibility to editorialize, and that when license renewals came up that they would be reviewed in the light of whether you were editorializing or not." WLBT's attorneys told the station that an editorial "was not against sin and for motherhood and the church. It had to be an editorial with meat in it and we had to take stands." The station started editorializing soon after the conference and continued to do so until late September 1962. It stopped then because its officials could see that confrontation was imminent between the federal government and the state over the Meredith situation.[60]

Asked why national news was specifically identified as such, Beard said that the average person who watched a newscast did not know whether it came from the network or local station unless it had someone on it like Chet Huntley or David Brinkley. WLBT received complaints about the network news, so the station wanted to clarify that national, not local, news was coming up. Beard said he let NBC know what he intended to do. His announcement would say, "The following news is network news and represents the views of the northern press. Stay tuned for the local news which will follow immediately—words to that effect."

"Did you use 'biased, managed northern news'?"

"It could have been. It would please our audience because that is what most of us felt. Even the NBC reporters who were down here agreed. There was no argument about it."[61]

Asked then about the interruption to the network program "The American Revolution, 1963" that Ed King had mentioned, Beard testified that he had asked AT&T to give him a statement to the fact that the station had lost its feed then. He did that "because every time we had a failure from the telephone company, somebody would accuse you of cutting off something we didn't want to see. You could have a tornado or blackout and they would call and say, 'You cut off something you didn't want us to see.' That was constant harassment."[62]

What, Kehoe asked, was the station's general policy about editorials on racial discrimination in Mississippi?

"Our policy generally was to try to stay away from that particular subject. Of course, every time it came up you ran into circumstances on one side or the other where nobody was ever happy with what you did." In terms of news, the station covered it as it happened. "Many times we were the only group—no other radio, TV or news media—there covering the pro-integration group, but we knocked ourselves out trying to cover them."

Did WLBT have any policy about editing news programs that dealt with racial discrimination in Mississippi?

"Our news editor was Dick Sanders," Beard responded. "He was born and raised in Chicago, Illinois. He was very liberal. He was an integrationist, he believed in integration and he was on the liberal side of every question that came about. We knew that when we hired him. He was in charge of the news department and he at all times tried to be fair, but in many instances we received criticisms about Dick because of his left leanings. He is an integrationist, and as a result I tried to balance him from the other side to keep the media down the middle."

Sanders was a fair man, Beard said, one who had weekly or daily contact with NAACP leaders Medgar Evers and Charles Evers and Pulitzer Prize–winning journalist Hazel Brannon Smith. "His close associates outside were on the liberal camp and yet we kept him and did business with him in every way. But I didn't let my personal feelings reflect into the operation of the station."[63]

Moore asked Beard why he considered WLBT's editorials on Meredith's admission to the university as being about states' rights rather than about segregation or integration. Moore read part of one editorial: "Mississippi is facing the final hour in its official fight to maintain segregation in all of its public schools. The showdown that has been building up since 1954 is here. Mississippi is fortunate in having men at its leadership who have vowed to prevent integration of our schools." Then he asked Beard: "Would you say that dealt with integration or segregation?"

Beard: "You didn't read 'The very sovereignty of our state is threatened. We have every confidence that our elected and appointed officials will prevent the integration of our schools.'" The problem "of putting one Negro into the University of Mississippi was not the issue involved here. That made no difference one way or the other. The issue was whether a state could continue to control its schools or whether the Federal Government could come and dictate; whether the registrar could no longer make the decision or whether the federal government was going to make that decision."[64]

Beard and other Mississippians were voicing an idea that had been at issue since the founding of the Republic—whether states had the right to decide what federal laws they would obey. Most people outside the South thought that the question had been resolved in the federal government's favor by the Civil War.

Race remained a highly volatile issue in the South, however, and the WLBT license would in part fall victim to the difficulty Beard and his philosophical soul mates had in recognizing that the country had changed around them.

The next day, May 9, 1967, Richard Sanders, then forty-one years old, testified as the first witness that Lamar Life, WLBT's owner, called. Sanders had been news director at WLBT from 1954 to 1965 and worked for ABC's news bureau in Washington at the time of the hearing. He discussed WLBT's coverage of political events involving the black community, saying, for example, that his had been the only Jackson TV station covering the news conference at which Aaron Henry and Ed King announced their candidacies for governor and lieutenant governor during the Freedom Vote of 1963. WLBT covered their campaign but not as inclusively as it covered the regular candidates because the courts had ruled that they could not be on the ballot. "So, what they actually had was a side story to the regular election. It was an important story but it was not the same as an election because they could not be elected."[65]

Harry Huge asked Sanders about a meeting he had with Rev. Smith and Rev. Parker during the summer of 1964 after the Office of Communication had challenged WLBT's license. "Did Dr. Parker say what the aim of the church was in filing this complaint?"

"Yes, he said they hoped to effect changes in the programming of the stations in Jackson and that by causing those changes here that they could bring about a change throughout the country. He said that Jackson was chosen because it was the focal point for civil rights at that particular time but that the same charges could have been made against most other stations in the south and some in the north." Parker had also said the challengers were not interested in applying for the license or trying necessarily to change the ownership, Sanders added.[66]

During a discussion of WLBT's *Comment* program, Moore asked Sanders: "Do you consider yourself an integrationist?"

"No."

"Did you ever deliver any comment in which you advocated integration of any institution in Mississippi?"

"I wouldn't phrase it that way. I had comments that pointed out the inevitability of the court decisions and that it would certainly be to the best interests of the state if they could accept that and start working with the Negro community so that that transition could be made to the best interests of both communities."[67]

Asked whether Beard ever gave him any instructions on what civil rights news would or would not be covered, Sanders said no. "My instructions were to use my judgment as a newsman." He had based that judgment on the Journalist's Creed that Walter Williams, former dean of journalism at the University of Missouri, created. "I believe the first line is, 'The public journal is a public trust.' That was my yardstick—what news was significant, what news was important for people to know about their community whether they liked seeing it, whether they would believe what they saw after they saw it or heard it." He tempered his judgment with the belief that at times one must be careful in writing a story "or you will damage and completely ruin that which you were trying to accomplish, which is good public information."[68]

Sanders then asked if he could amplify an answer. "I did not want to leave the impression on the record that covering racial news in Mississippi through this period, particularly the period you covered, was routine coverage. There was tremendous pressure because there was the pressure of the community itself. There was the pressure of your friends, at times colleagues at the station differing with your news judgment on whether you should cover this, and there were personal threats telephoned to my home and to my wife. These made reporting a difficult task. That does not change my answers but this was a factor. This was not just routine coverage. In fact, I doubt if there is anything quite like it."[69]

Journalists Wilson F. "Bill" Minor and Hazel Brannon Smith, both whites, testified about Sanders's professionalism in covering the news. Smith, editor of the *Lexington Advertiser* in Holmes County, Mississippi, stated that she never saw Sanders present the news in any biased manner, that he did a thoroughly professional job under great stress. People needed to know the Mississippi political climate, Smith said, and she summed it up for the hearing. "We were living in a time where all that Mississippians heard were reports of politicians crying loud defiance of the U.S. government, of the Supreme Court decision, the desegregation decision, and of course these politicians naturally got into the news. When the U.S. Senator—when Jim Eastland gets on the floor and makes a speech about the United States Supreme Court not being the law of the land and all that sort of thing, well, naturally that is reported—that is reported in big headlines in your newspapers and by the same token it gets a lot of time on the air."[70]

Sanders did not seek rebuttals to these presentations, Smith said, but "as a straight newscaster Dick Sanders could not be beat, and his fairness and objectivity were as great as any one person could be living in Mississippi at that time and working under the circumstances under which he worked." To her, Sanders was "the one sane voice on the air." There was "so much wild stuff" being said in editorials and elsewhere, Smith added.

Newspapers and politicians in Mississippi brainwashed people into believing that they would not have to integrate, she said. "That was the line on the Citizens' Council program on WLBT and by the leading politicians of the state, including our men in Congress and in the Senate, so if the people hear something like that often enough, they will believe it, especially when they want to believe it in the first place."[71]

When she said "wild stuff," Smith was asked, to what was she referring? To the station's editorials, she replied. Sanders was ordinarily the one that read the editorials "and the ones that he read were not that way. I do know this for a fact, that Dick Sanders never had to read anything from that station that he didn't agree with himself. . . . What I remember is Mr. Beard reading those editorials. Mr. Beard, in fact, is the only one I remember reading what I call the wild editorials."[72]

Community representatives and various WLBT staff members appeared at the hearing as witnesses for WLBT. "We were just trying to say how the station had changed and it shouldn't be punished for what happened under the previous management," said Harry Huge years later. Among the things that had changed at the station: "We had the first black training program. We had black college students where the station hadn't hired any blacks, and they did camera work" and other jobs. "We put the first black news announcer on the air at a time when there were no black news announcers on any network." Some black ministers were appearing on devotional programs, and local black leaders were consulted on programming. Every station in the South could have been looked at in terms of adherence to the Fairness Doctrine, Huge said. "There were a lot of politics involved here. And if you wanted to pick on this station or that station because you didn't like it, where does it end?"[73]

The station's witnesses included many local people testifying about help their organizations had been given. For example, Jane M. Schutt, who had helped establish the Mississippi Advisory Committee to the U.S. Advisory Committee on Civil Rights, testified about constructive criticism she felt that her committee had received from Dick Sanders of WLBT. In October 1963 she had written to Sanders that, "in contrast to the treatment afforded me by other local newsmen, you and the wire service reporters were always courteous and fair, and even more than that seemed genuinely interested in getting all the facts in any given situation."[74]

Several witnesses testified about programming aimed at the black audience. Dr. L. H. Newsome, pastor of two churches in Jackson, appeared on a fifteen-minute Saturday morning program called *Civic Calendar*. He often broadcast announcements concerning local organizations and interviews with people of interest to the black community. Rev. Newsome also broadcast a religious program on Sunday called *Faith for Life*. He testified that no one ever directed him about whom he could or could not have on the program, and the station never placed any restrictions on the development of either program.[75]

Cecil J. Jaquith, a longtime Jackson resident, testified about the help that WLBT had given both the March of Dimes and the American Red Cross on their campaigns. Others spoke of assistance in raising money to replace the Jackson Little Theatre and other support for the arts, coverage of Millsaps College and the Mississippi bar association, reports on job programs offered through the Mississippi Employment Service, and substantial coverage about people's rights and responsibilities concerning Social Security benefits and Medicare coverage. Others from Jackson and Greenville spoke of assistance the station had given with drives for the Shriners' programs for crippled children, for college fund-raising campaigns, for films on state history, and for Chamber of Commerce activities, as well as about their regular coverage of Jackson and Greenville city issues.[76]

Kenneth L. Dean, executive director of the Mississippi Council on Human Relations, told the hearing that WLBT had covered the first meeting of his organization, which sought to promote better race relations. A WLBT cameraman and newsman had ridden with him on a tour of the Delta following poverty hearings that WLBT covered. Dean, who would figure again prominently in this case, said that progress toward better relations "is very limited and very slow until the public news media at a given city or region becomes involved with a type of news coverage, programming and editorializing that is favorable to law and order and justice." He thought that WLBT was giving considerable publicity to the work of his organization.[77]

Bob McRaney testified on several different days, discussing WLBT programming and attempts to maintain liaison with different segments of community. At one point he said there were some unpaid announcements for the Freedom Bookstore. Kyle said: "Didn't I rule out any evidence concerning the Freedom Bookstore from the beginning?" Yes, Miller replied. "Then," said Kyle, "I don't want to hear anything about it."[78]

Asked when blacks first appeared on *Teen Tempo*, McRaney replied that it was during the fall of 1965. When students were from a black high school, the program had a black announcer; when they were from a white high school, there was a white announcer. And there wasn't just dancing—there was also a French class, a Spanish class, and a range of school activities.[79]

The church's attorneys wanted Charles Evers, who had returned to Mississippi after his brother, Medgar, was killed, to testify but were uncertain whether he would because he was unpredictable. Earle K. Moore thought that Evers might be most receptive to a request to testify coming from a white woman, so Ann Aldrich headed off to Fayette, Mississippi, in the southwestern part of the state, to find Evers. "We did not subpoena anybody to testify. We wanted them to testify voluntarily," Aldrich said. A black faculty member from Tougaloo drove her through the country to the small town, and it was, because of the racial climate, like a scene out of *Driving Miss Daisy*. The man took off his suit jacket and tie and placed them on the seat beside him and had Aldrich ride in the backseat. When they reached the country church where they had been told Evers was conducting a meeting, Evers came out, and he and Aldrich sat in the backseat. "I was talking about how much we needed him. He lived in the service area. I don't know what I said that got to him. I just know I didn't shut up." When a police car passed by, she was shoved below window level so the officers wouldn't see her.[80]

Evers agreed to testify and did so on May 15, 1967. He told the hearing that he had contacted WLBT in 1964 about having Ralph Bunche, the first black person to win the Nobel Prize in 1950 for his diplomatic work, appear on the station. "I noticed on the station practically every prominent racist who came through the state would somehow be able to get on and voice his opinion about the progress of, or his dissatisfaction with, the civil rights movement." But WLBT did not interview Bunche. Nor did it interview basketball star Bill Russell when he was in the state because the station management said he was there for civil rights activity, not as an athlete.[81]

During his testimony, Evers spoke about the way his late brother's appearance was handled on WLBT in May 1963. WLBT had contributed to the buildup of hate in the community, Evers said. If a person requests time, the station should not allow its employees to say that there was a black person asking for rebuttal time to "make out our mayor is a liar," as he implied WLBT had done. "These types of things we just cannot have. This is personal but I hope that our stations will never do this anymore because I personally feel this is part of the hate that was built up through this particular station at this time that may possibly have contributed to the death of my brother."[82]

Two days after Evers testified, the hearing ended. Kyle thanked the lawyers for their cooperation during the lengthy proceeding. "If anyone would have been particularly stubborn," Kyle said, "we would have had some problems getting this show on the road. The big thing now is to get it off the road."[83]

Looking back, Harry Huge said that despite the testimony about WLBT's news coverage and editorializing and its overall treatment of the black community, he believed that the station's strategy would work. He couldn't defend the past—"we had already lost on that"—but he thought reform from the inside would work and that the FCC would accept that argument.[84] It did, but Henry Geller had been correct in predicting hostility from the appeals court.

5. ONCE AGAIN, A VERDICT

The South was not alone in facing racial tensions. By the summer of 1967 dozens of American cities had already seen pent-up frustrations erupt into riots in poor black neighborhoods. Early in July 1967 it was Newark, New Jersey's turn. Forty-three people died later that month in rioting in Detroit. Roger Wilkins, a nephew of NAACP leader Roy Wilkins and at the time a Justice Department official, described the rioting as "an extension of the civil rights movement, not something different." It was a jagged plea to the government, he said, from people whose lives of poverty had not changed despite new laws and new programs.[1] In this context, talking about lawyers trying to influence the outcome of a case about a television station might seem remote from the realities of the day. But ultimately the law, not street violence, would reclaim the arena to reshape the national debate. These lawyers were laying the foundation for a major court decision that would jolt the broadcasting industry. That decision would end the first segment of this saga and start the next—with continued high stakes for whoever won.

On July 28, 1967, the lawyers for all parties in the WLBT case submitted their "proposed findings and conclusions"—their take on the hearings concluded ten weeks earlier in Jackson. Their positions mirrored their presentations in those hearings. Examining their arguments shows how they not only sought to influence the decision that examiner Jay Kyle would make but also, especially in the case of the challengers, to lay the groundwork for any potential appeal.

The Office of Communication reviewed its charges of discrimination in programming. With Jackson's large black population segregated from the rest of Jackson through separate churches, separate schools, and separate cultural organizations, a broadcaster needed to make particular efforts to communicate with black leaders to learn what programs would interest the black community, lawyers Earle K. Moore and Ann Aldrich said. WLBT clearly had not made that good faith effort in the 1961 to 1964 license period.

The church's lawyers contended that WLBT had not provided reasonable opportunities for presentation of opposing points of view on controversial issues. The commission had based its 1959 renewal of WLBT's license on the conclusion that earlier complaints about the station's performance were isolated instances. The station was warned about its failures but during the 1961 to 1964 period remained "consistently myopic" where the controversy regarding race was concerned, the church's lawyers said. WLBT had also sought to avoid the application of the Fairness Doctrine to its editorials opposing James Meredith's entry into the University of Mississippi by contending that no one in the service area was opposed to states' rights, which was the subject of the editorials, the church said. "The statement is untrue."

WLBT's record, taken as a whole, "demonstrates that its programming on racial issues was designed to serve primarily the extremist fringe of the white population with which its general manager was associated. It failed completely to meet the intent of the Communications Act," which did not allow stations to be used for the private interest of those granted licenses, the church maintained.

The church's lawyers accused WLBT of misrepresentation when it told the FCC it avoided discussing racial integration so as not to encourage violence. That policy neither prevented the station from broadcasting a series of inflammatory editorials shortly before the riots at Oxford, nor from broadcasting Citizens' Council programs that carried the line that "you don't have to integrate," nor from carrying spot commercials during the Ole Miss crisis alleging that Communists were behind racial agitation, nor from airing offensive references to blacks.

In general, the church argued, the station had shown resentment against the commission and defied its rules. Even when called to account, it made little or no change in its practices "but simply altered its devices for evading compliance." WLBT should not be allowed off the hook because it had made some changes since the challenge was filed, the church's lawyers said—predictably arguing against the Arnold & Porter attorneys' view that credence should be given to those changes in operations and philosophy. Human experience showed that institutions might reform while they were in litigation or under the scrutiny of an enforcement officer, the church said, but those changes furnished no reliable basis for predicting how the institutions would conduct themselves when the close scrutiny ended. WLBT simply had failed to show that renewing its license would serve the public interest, the church concluded.[2]

Just as predictably, Lamar disagreed. One had to look at the station's context—that is, Jackson, Mississippi. "WLBT was not and is not located in New York—or Washington—or Denver—or Los Angeles," wrote attorneys Paul Porter, Reed Miller, and Harry Huge. "Rather it was broadcasting in probably the most trying conditions any television station has yet to operate—and not for one week—or one month—or one year—but essentially daily from its very inception. The turmoil, the change, the violence, the pressure from all sides in this focal point of the civil rights movement cannot be overlooked or discounted." No evidence was submitted that WLBT ever denied a request for equal time, its lawyers said.

WLBT disputed one allegation about "Sorry, Cable Trouble" signs appearing on the station and sought to explain another. Its lawyers said that Fred Beard had denied ever saying he substituted such a sign during the 1955 Thurgood Marshall interview. In the other case, an NBC documentary, "The American Revolution, 1963," was interrupted on September 2, 1963, as a sit-in at the Jackson Woolworth's lunch counter was being shown. Atmospheric conditions had interfered with the signal, according to a letter to WLBT from a Southern Bell transmission supervisor.

As for Beard's editorials about James Meredith's entry into the University of Mississippi, the lawyers denied that they were incendiary, using language that would appear again in the hearing examiner's opinion: "These editorials did not call for open defiance of the United States government—these editorials did not call for disobedience to law and order—these editorials did not constitute a call to arms—these editorials did not urge people to go to Oxford, Mississippi, to oppose federal forces—these editorials did not advocate violence or unlawful behavior."

Always seeking to cast WLBT in a new light, its lawyers pointed to editorials that WLBT had aired more recently. In 1966 it editorialized about what it called the "irresponsible attack" on James Meredith's life as he conducted his "march against fear." In 1967 station manager Bob McRaney Jr. had editorialized against the "revolting incident" when a bomb killed Natchez NAACP official Wharlest Jackson. There had also been an editorial for Jacksonians to be calm after a civil rights worker was killed in rioting at Jackson State in 1967.

The Office of Communication's petition to deny WLBT's license had also charged that courtesy titles were used on second reference only for whites, not for blacks, a charge WLBT denied. And look what happened on occasion when those titles were used, the station said: irate viewers objected. Said one anonymous letter writer: "While listening to your sportscast this afternoon, I was appalled at your reference to Willie Mays' wife as Mrs. Not once but twice. Surely you are aware that true Southerners never address a Negro as Mr., Mrs., or Miss. The fact that she is the wife of a famous baseball personality holds no more significance than the wife of a field hand does where this is concerned."

WLBT was changing, its lawyers insisted. Station personnel had met with black leaders such as Charles Evers and the Reverend R. L. T. Smith, who made various suggestions about programming, all of which were adopted. Since blacks had started appearing on WLBT, the lawyers said, "the question then becomes whether they appeared often enough. There was testimony that while Negroes had been asked to appear on WLBT, very few ever would appear." One of the church's witnesses said that as soon as a white religious program came on the air, "most Negroes would turn the set off." To satisfy such attitudes, "only an all-Negro station would be sufficient. But that is not the standard WLBT must meet. If it is, then every station in the United States must have its license revoked."

WLBT could never do enough to satisfy either side on the emotional issue that divided its community. WLBT's challengers "apparently misconceive the role of a television station—as they misconceived the role of television news," its lawyers said. "Television news is not meant to 'create' a movement. Nor is television to be used as an instrument to advocate a particular social philosophy, or political position, to the exclusion of others. It is only to report events and provide the means for discussion of issues as they happen—fairly and accurately." WLBT believed that it had done this.[3]

The FCC's Broadcast Bureau in general agreed with WLBT's positions about the hearing examiner's potential ruling. For example, the FCC lawyers accepted WLBT's explanation that it had substituted a program for the interview with Thurgood Marshall to avoid giving the Citizens' Council a half hour of response time and that no "Sorry, Cable Trouble" sign was shown.

The Broadcast Bureau's proposed findings, signed by Thomas B. Fitzpatrick, chief of its hearing division, and the two FCC staff members who had been in Jackson, William A. Kehoe Jr. and Leo I. George, questioned the objectivity of the challengers' monitoring study on which much of their case was based. The church had submitted no analysis of WLBT's programming that would sustain the charge that it had not afforded reasonable opportunity for the discussion of conflicting views, the FCC lawyers said. They also did not think WLBT had behaved inappropriately faced with the Reverend R. L. T. Smith's request for airtime well before the election.

The FCC attorneys acknowledged that even though WLBT's editorials about James Meredith were couched in the language of states' rights, they "espoused a view against racial integration." Nonetheless, the FCC lawyers said that when asked for information about its editorial position, WLBT honored all requests and never tried to hide any information. Thus they concluded that the station did not deliberately misrepresent to the commission or to the public its policies with respect to the issue of racial discrimination.

As for a complaint that one of the announcers referred to members of the black community as "niggers" or "negras," the FCC lawyers said that when that matter was brought to the announcer's attention, he indicated that he had difficulty pronouncing the word "Negro" and meant no harm. "The record will not support any contention that the station had a policy of referring to members of the Negro community in a disparaging manner," the Broadcast Bureau said.

The FCC attorneys concluded that WLBT's license should be renewed. In their eyes, the station was serving the needs of its entire service area.[4]

The challengers were not hopeful about the hearing examiner's decision because of what Earle Moore called Kyle's "snappy" way of dealing with the church's lawyers and their witnesses.[5] The lack of optimism was well founded. On October 13, 1967, Kyle ruled that the challengers had not proved their case and that WLBT's license should be renewed. He considered the church group's monitoring study of little value and its witnesses generally not credible.

Point by point, Kyle rejected the challengers' arguments:

- On the Reverend R. L. T. Smith's attempts to buy time on WLBT, Kyle found that Smith was accorded fair and equitable treatment by Fred Beard and station WLBT.
- On the Reverend Edwin King's charge that Beard had said he had received an award from the Citizens' Council for pulling the Thurgood Marshall interview off the air (which Beard denied), Kyle compared the demeanor of both witnesses and preferred that of Fred Beard.
- On whether WLBT interrupted programs involving black people or issues of concern to them by claiming cable trouble, Kyle ruled "a myth" the allegation that the station arbitrarily regularly utilized a "Sorry, Cable Trouble" sign.
- On WLBT's editorials on the Meredith controversy, Kyle echoed WLBT's lawyers: "These editorials did not call for open defiance of the U.S. Government—these editorials did not call for disobedience to law and order—these editorials did not constitute a call to arms—these editorials did not urge people to go to Oxford, Miss., to oppose Federal forces, and these editorials did not advocate violence or unlawful behavior." The hearing examiner did acknowledge that the editorials had praised Governor Ross Barnett and other state officials for the stand they had taken to prevent school integration.

Kyle concluded that the station had allowed airtime to responsible citizens and organizations without hesitation over a period of years.

"It must be pointed out here that there has been obviously personal animosity directed toward Fred Beard, former general manager of the station," he added.

Thus, on the first issue before the FCC hearing, whether the station afforded reasonable opportunity for discussion of conflicting views on important public issues, Kyle ruled that it had. On the second issue, whether the station made its facilities available for use by significant groups in the area, he concluded that it had. On the third issue, whether WLBT had acted in good faith in terms of presenting programs dealing with racial discrimination and whether it misrepresented itself with respect to such programming, Kyle said there was no evidence of misrepresentation.

Kyle then outlined his strong opinion on who had the burden of proof in this case, revealing an attitude with which the federal court of appeals would later take issue. The hearing had allowed the challengers ample opportunity to sustain their serious allegations against WLBT, Kyle wrote. "They have woefully failed to do so." The challengers seemed to believe that it was up to Lamar to disprove their allegations, Kyle said, adding that most of their witnesses' testimony was based on hearsay, exactly the point that the station attorneys had stressed. Kyle pointed to the fact that only six people from Jackson and its immediate area and two others from within the service area, which consisted of more than 850,000 people, appeared at the hearing to complain about the station, while a large number of "substantial citizens" from Jackson and Greenville testified on behalf of the station. Kyle either dismissed the idea that potential viewers/eyewitnesses might fear retribution if they testified or did not consider the concept at all. In view of his findings, he concluded that renewing WLBT's license "would serve the public interest, convenience and necessity."[6]

Kyle's decision cheered WLBT and its attorneys. Although expected, it was a blow to the challengers. It gave WLBT a major weapon as the case moved before the full FCC. The church stood its ground, though, because it thought it had to—or see citizen involvement die. Few people would intervene in FCC matters if they spent the time and money to become involved only to be reversed by an examiner who, the church believed, was disregarding the appeals court and even the FCC's directives in the case. "Examiner Kyle is evidently very hostile to public participation in licensing proceedings and takes the view that any digest or analysis of programming is necessarily subjective and unreliable if it comes from a public participant," Earle K. Moore wrote to Everett Parker.[7]

The next step was oral argument on the case, which the FCC heard on June 4, 1968, at its Washington headquarters. Present that day were Commissioners Rosel H. Hyde, Nicholas Johnson, Lee Loevinger, Robert E. Lee, Robert T. Bartley, Kenneth Cox, and James Wadsworth.

E. William Henry, a dissenter in the first WLBT renewal, was gone from the commission by this time. The Johnson White House had announced the appointment of the newest FCC member, Nicholas Johnson, and the elevation of Rosel Hyde to be FCC chairman on the same day in June 1966. Any similarity between the two men ends there. In naming Hyde, President Johnson was tapping a career FCC man. Hyde held a variety of legal positions, including general counsel, before President Truman named him a commissioner in 1946. Hyde had served as commission chairman in 1953 and 1954 and had been acting chairman after Henry resigned in May 1966. A Republican and a Mormon born in Idaho in 1900, Hyde first worked for the federal government in 1924 on the staff of the Civil Service Commission. He joined the Federal Radio Commission in 1928 after obtaining his law degree at George Washington University.[8] *Broadcasting* magazine commented that the Hyde appointment "formally brought to an end the New Frontier era at the FCC—an era that had been marked by controversy and studded with proposals that would affect the foundations of the broadcasting industry." It described Hyde as "one who feels broadcasting will improve if the governmental climate is favorable. His criticism of broadcasters in the programming area has been limited to what he regards as their failure to fight back against government interference."[9] *Variety* reported that Hyde was "far from the liberal crusader image of E. William Henry or Newton Minow."[10]

Nicholas Johnson was another story. At thirty-one the youngest person ever named to the commission, he had served for two years as the head of the Federal Maritime Administration. Shipping interests were reportedly so annoyed at his decisions that they asked the president to move him out of that job. That industry was still loading and unloading ships the way the Phoenicians did, Johnson told Cox soon after he joined the commission. Engendering the kind of ill-feeling he received from shippers, said *Broadcasting*, "was the price he paid for doing the kind of job he was hired to do: develop ideas for infusing new life into the barnacle-encrusted merchant marine and make it more competitive in world commerce."[11] Johnson would take the same iconoclastic approach at the FCC. A native of Iowa, where his father was a university professor, Johnson was a Phi Beta Kappa graduate of the University of Texas and an honors graduate of that university's law school. He clerked for Hugo Black at the Supreme Court and taught law at the University of California before joining the prestigious Washington law firm of Covington & Burling.[12] "Looking at him," said *Broadcasting*, "one wouldn't think a harsh word could be said" about him.[13]

By the time Johnson left the commission, *Broadcasting* had changed its perspective, predicting that there would be "dancing in the streets" over his departure.[14] During his seven years on the FCC, Johnson became "enemy No. 1 to the broadcast industry," said television writer

Les Brown, who described him as "a noisy reformer who campaigned for virtually everything the industry feared: counter-commercials, license challenges by citizens at renewal time, the break-up of media monopolies, an informed and activist FCC and access to the airwaves for minorities, political dissenters and representatives of the counter-culture."[15] In a world of buttoned-down lawyers, Johnson wore his hair long and rode his bicycle to work. Brash and flamboyant, Johnson made sure the press knew about his dissents—and they were frequent.

I was covering the FCC during Johnson's last years on the commission, and I well remember late-afternoon calls from him when he thought the FCC was trying to sneak by with an unpopular decision—a long-distance telephone rate hike increase, for example—just as a holiday weekend was starting. His colleague Kenneth Cox said his wife used to ask him, "How come your dissents aren't printed on the front page of the *Washington Post*?" and he would reply, "Because they aren't written for that purpose." Cox called Johnson "a great word-smith" but expressed disappointment that he closed himself off from broadcasters.[16] Johnson, a hard-working commissioner, had a loyal following among liberal organizations and a string of able assistants.

At the oral argument, Earle K. Moore led off for the Office of Communication. Ann Aldrich appeared with him. Paul A. Porter and Reed Miller represented WLBT, and William A. Kehoe Jr. represented the FCC's Broadcast Bureau. Now the attorneys were speaking directly to the commissioners who would make the decision, not to an intermediary like the examiner, so in the limited time allotted them, they made their key points.

Once again, Moore argued that the hearing in Jackson had established that WLBT's programming was directed almost exclusively to whites throughout the renewal period. He particularly pointed to the lack of any black children on WLBT's daily kindergarten program. "It should not be necessary to point out that the decision of the Supreme Court in *Brown v. the Board of Education* about integration of school children was announced in May 1954, which was several years before the beginning of this renewal period." That decision pointed to the harm segregation caused black children, Moore said, adding that it was incongruous that a federal licensee in presenting children on the air should not only ignore the Supreme Court's school desegregation decision "but shouldn't even comply with the rule of Plessy against Ferguson in 1896, which required 'separate but equal' facilities."

The hearing examiner would not let him go into the character of the Freedom Bookstore located at WLBT, Moore said, because he thought it was irrelevant. "But we think that the making available of station facilities to an organization which promoted anti–civil rights views, promoted segregation, and the repeated making of promotional announcements for this organization was a very clear violation of the Fairness Doctrine."

After outlining the challengers' arguments about the lack of balanced coverage of the controversial issue of segregation, Moore said, "This is a case which should outrage the conscience." If the FCC's standards were to have meaning, the commission must punish a station that defied them. "WLBT's behavior was not careless or inept. WLBT deliberately disregarded the needs of half its service area. WLBT deliberately insulted half its listeners. WLBT deliberately used its license to promote segregation and racial hostility. Now it should account for its stewardship."[17]

Next, Ann Aldrich addressed the commission about WLBT's candor and honesty in responding to FCC queries about its programs. The station consistently said it did not afford time for programming that involved racial integration, while also running what Aldrich described as "inflammatory" editorials about Meredith's entry into the University of Mississippi. Aldrich underscored this point to the commission because she knew from working there that it had not appreciated misrepresentation in the past.[18]

When the time set aside for the challengers' presentation ended, Paul Porter wasted no time before going on the attack. Although he would have preferred simply to move for the adoption of the examiner's decision, he said, he found it difficult to suppress "a justifiable indignation in dealing with the kind of reckless and unsubstantiated allegations which prompted the court to require this commission to conduct this hearing." Porter, whose words carried extra weight because he was a former FCC chairman, charged that the challengers were guilty of abusing both court and commission processes. However laudable their intent, "the negligence and carelessness with which these intervenors sought to merchandise unsubstantiated rumor and to market unsupported scuttlebutt and their failure when put to proof is tantamount, in my view, to a fraud on this commission and a fraud on the court."

Noting the record of 1,500 pages, 200 exhibits, and twelve days of hearings with forty-seven witnesses, Porter concluded that even during the tension-ridden period of severe racial crisis in Mississippi, WLBT had an acceptable record of performance. However, the challengers apparently expected WLBT to become "a crusader for instant social change and to assume an extremely advanced position in the community and civil rights causes."

At that point, Commissioner Kenneth Cox interrupted Porter. "Do you regard the editorials in September of 1962 as acceptable?"

"I disagree with the editorials but I defend their right to say it. I believe they are advocating state sovereignty . . ."

Cox: "They were advocating resistance to the federal policy."

Porter: "They were not, Commissioner Cox."

As for the allegation that WLBT cut Thurgood Marshall's appearance and substituted a "Sorry, Cable Trouble" sign, Porter emphasized that the hearing examiner had called this a myth. "I will refrain from using a more vivid description. However, I must observe that one would expect an intervenor, particularly a church, to exercise more circumspection."

Finally, Porter discussed "the so-called monitoring study, which gave an aura of false responsibility to some of these allegations." It turned out to be "an irresponsible farce," Porter said, adding that the hearing examiner characterized it as worthless. Down the road the appeals court would not agree.

Near the end of his presentation, Porter said that the record in the case completely supported the conclusion that WLBT should have its license renewed. The results of the hearing had also showed that the FCC had been right to argue that its own procedures were adequate to deal with even the most serious allegations, Porter stated. He contended that the challengers made frivolous charges, lacked good judgment, and misled the commission.

Porter regretted that the FCC lacked the power to assess costs to penalize the Office of Communication. However, when it adopted the examiner's recommendation, as he thought it must, he hoped it would serve notice on the United Church of Christ and others to act responsibly. The commission should not tolerate "this kind of abuse of its processes," Porter said. "Criticism, dissent, pressure, yes, these are all vital values and protected values in our system. But they must not be used to the detriment of others by those who have such a regard for the truth that they seem to use it sparingly."[19]

Everett Parker was not impressed by Porter's presentation. The next day he wrote Earle Moore to congratulate him on his handling of the argument. "Your statement was far superior to Mr. Porter's bombastic speech."[20]

During the question period, Commissioner Johnson asked Porter whether in a city that was essentially half black, a station had a special obligation to serve as a forum for discussion of their needs.

"I don't believe they have to operate on a quota system, forty-seven per cent of this," Porter responded.

"I am asking whether a community that is one half Negro and a station in that community assumes a burden that is perhaps greater than a city where the Negro population is less than five per cent?" Johnson said.

"No, I don't think I would necessarily make that concession. I think a well programmed station can have an appeal to all ethnic groups," Porter replied. If an effort was made to cater to one group instead of another, he added, "a disservice may be done both groups. I think it may tend to create wider separation rather than needed reconciliation."

Johnson asked Porter whether he felt WLBT had fulfilled its obligation to go into the community and to find out its needs and to serve those needs, to which Porter replied: "Commissioner Johnson, I am not claiming that this station was a paragon of perfection during the 61–64 period. What I am claiming is that it did in the environment of its own community do a sensible, responsible job."

Johnson: "In the environment of its own white community?"

Porter: "In the environment of the entire community."

Johnson: "I gather there are some citizens of the community who would not share your judgment?"

Porter: "I think so, but I think the majority would. They could not produce any witnesses except a few."

Then Johnson spoke to the issues of a challenger's responsibility and the balance of power in public dealings with broadcasters and the FCC, basic issues in this case: "What do you think a member of the public who is dissatisfied with the programming of his local station ought to do beyond what these parties have done in bringing the case to the Commission and being turned down by the Commission and going to the U.S. Court of Appeals, going through a hearing, going

Fred Beard, manager of WLBT from 1953 to 1965, editorialized against the entry of James Meredith into the University of Mississippi. (Courtesy of WLBT files)

Medgar Evers, executive secretary for the Mississippi NAACP, frequently sought airtime on WLBT to respond to its broadcasts on civil rights issues. (Courtesy of AP/Wide World Photos)

WLBT, located near Pearl River south of downtown Jackson, had the strongest television signal in the state and was the market leader. (Courtesy of the Mississippi Department of Archives and History)

Richard Sanders, WLBT news director from 1954 to 1965, interviewed victorious gubernatorial candidate J. P. Coleman on primary election night in 1955. (Courtesy of Richard Sanders)

The Reverend Everett Parker, director of the Office of Communication of the United Church of Christ, organized the challenge of WLBT's license. (Courtesy of Everett Parker)

Gordon and Martha Henderson, shown in 1966 with their three children, helped the Reverend Everett Parker monitor WLBT in 1964. (Courtesy of Gordon and Martha Henderson)

The Reverend R. L. T. Smith, who had sought airtime on WLBT as part of his campaign for Congress, helped challenge WLBT's license. (Courtesy of the Mississippi Department of Archives and History)

Aaron Henry, a Clarksdale pharmacist and state civil rights leader, challenged WLBT's license and later became the station's chairman of the board. (Courtesy of Mississippi Department of Archives and History)

Earle K. Moore represented the Office of Communication in the WLBT license challenge and was general counsel for Communications Improvement, Inc., which ran the station in the 1970s. (Courtesy of Patricia M. Patterson)

E. William Henry, chairman of the Federal Communications Commission from 1963 to 1966, dissented from the decision to renew WLBT's license. (Courtesy of E. William Henry)

Warren Burger, as a federal appeals court judge, wrote decision in the WLBT case that established the public's standing to participate in FCC matters and later opened the way for a new station operator. (Courtesy of AP/Wide World Photos)

Randall Pinkston, CBS news correspondent, began his television career at WLBT in 1969 when the station started reaching out to Jackson's black community as a result of the license challenge. (Courtesy of Randall Pinkston)

Kenneth L. Dean was president of Communications Improvement, Inc., and active in WLBT's operations in the 1970s. (Courtesy of Kenneth L. Dean)

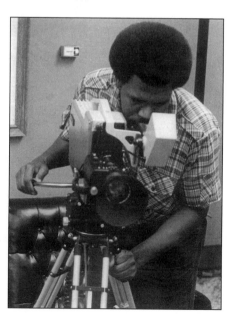

Tom Alexander was a cameraman and producer for WLBT while it was run by Communications Improvement, Inc. (Courtesy of Tom Alexander)

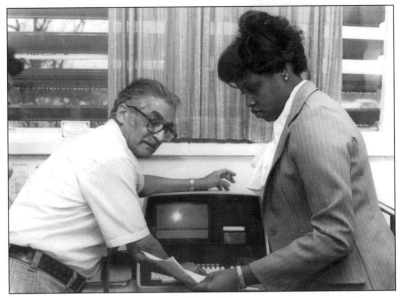

Woody Asaf, longtime staff member, and Mary Ann Lindsey, program director, confer at WLBT. (Courtesy of the WLBT files)

Walter Saddler, WLBT anchorman, poses with network newscaster John Chancellor during his visit to WLBT. (Courtesy of the WLBT files)

Michael Rubenstein (left), sports director, talks with William Dilday, named the first black station manager by Communications Improvement, Inc., in 1972. (Courtesy of the WLBT files)

Walter Hall (left), with Lady Bird and President Lyndon Johnson, financed the legal work that kept alive the fight for the permanent license at WLBT and was subsequently a board member. (Courtesy of the Estate of Walter G. Hall)

through oral argument, doing the monitoring study they did, getting the witnesses they did? You are a most distinguished lawyer and former chairman of the Commission and broadcasters have access to this kind of talent and the services of your firm. What do you think the public ought to do beyond what they have done here? How could they have handled this case better?"

Porter responded that it was the commission's responsibility to evaluate the claims about stations and to reach conclusions. Even though Judge Burger might be trying to limit that authority, the commission still should insist that public participation be conducted responsibly, he added.

Johnson: "This is what I am asking, because you are essentially rearguing the case which has now been decided and so the standing of these parties is now acknowledged. What could they have done that would have in your judgment been more responsible and more thorough?"

Porter: "They would have been more responsible proving their case. They should not have relied upon remote hearsay saying sorry, cable trouble. That is a myth that will haunt this station for the rest of its electronic life."[21]

William Kehoe of the FCC's Broadcast Bureau then answered questions from the commission, including whether Fred Beard had said that WLBT labeled network news as biased or northern Yankee news. He said WLBT did that for two weeks during the *Today* show in the midst of the Meredith controversy after receiving complaints from people that they couldn't differentiate the local news broadcasters and NBC newscasters. While he did not excuse the practice, he implied that this confusion adequately explained it.

Commissioner Cox asked Kehoe about the examiner's statement that the record was "replete with efforts made on the part of management, especially in recent years, to encourage groups, particularly

Negroes in the community, to participate" in programs. "Would you say the record is replete with evidence of such efforts prior to 1964?"

"No, sir," Kehoe responded, "I could not say that."

Did he think the station proved that it had fairly served the black community in Jackson, Cox asked Kehoe, and that it worked overall in the public interest?

"Yes, sir, that is the position we took in our proposed findings."[22]

Nicholas Johnson asked Kehoe what he had meant by a comment that the case ought to be considered in light of conditions in Mississippi from 1961 to 1964.

"In Mississippi you didn't have integrated programs, you didn't have integrated churches, you didn't have integrated schools in 1961. But when the public schools were integrated in Mississippi they had riots. . . . I think when you consider having integrated programs on a television station where you don't have the protection of marshals and troops, if necessary, that you have a serious question." Only when a Catholic school in Vicksburg was integrated was there an integrated *Teen Tempo* program, he added.

"Is it your position that the standards of this Commission and of licensees ought to be that it is the licensee's responsibility to reflect the morals of the majority establishment in his community, whatever they may be?" Johnson asked Kehoe. Suppose a state had a large American Indian population. If there were feelings against American Indians or if other communities had negative feelings about Jews or other minority groups, did Kehoe think a station would be warranted in excluding those people because it would cause disruption among the white establishment?

Kehoe: "I will dodge that question by not giving my personal view, but the commission has said many times when it comes to the selection of programming in the community, the responsible good faith judgment of the licensee must be given a good deal of weight."

Johnson agreed that the FCC should rely on good judgment. However, he said, that did not address whether a broadcaster could justify essentially excluding almost half the viewing audience on grounds that its interests would be offensive to the white establishment. He believed that this question was at the heart of the case.[23]

Less than four weeks after the oral arguments, the commission renewed the WLBT license on a 5–2 vote. The majority agreed with the examiner that the challengers had failed to substantiate virtually all of their allegations on which the hearing was based. The *New York Times* and the *Washington Post* teed off on the FCC. The commission "usually goes through the motions at license-renewal time, continuing franchises with little regard for station performance in the public interest," editorialized the *New York Times*. It did so again, "shockingly," in renewing WLBT's license, the editorial added.[24]

The FCC majority said that while it could not conclude that the licensee's history of Fairness Doctrine compliance had been exemplary, it agreed with the examiner that the challengers had failed to prove the many serious incidents they alleged. For example, WLBT's program in 1957 on the Little Rock crisis might have triggered the Fairness Doctrine had it been partisan, but the record was devoid of any evidence on the content of the program "other than the unsubstantiated allegation that it discussed the maintenance of segregation." Given the positions that the program's participants held favoring segregation, it should have been obvious to the FCC that the 1957 program on the crisis did, in fact, discuss maintaining separation of the races. Evidently, it was not.

As for whether the station afforded reasonable opportunity for significant groups in the community to use its facilities, the FCC dismissed the evidence in this area—the challengers' monitoring study. Disregarding this element of the challengers' case would later be a key factor in the appeals court decision. The study had "little probative value," the majority said.

The FCC was persuaded, however, that in the 1961–1964 period "Negro participation per se in WLBT's locally originated programming was limited." But while the absence of blacks in programming might indicate lack of service to the black community, "it is by no means determinative of it," the FCC majority wrote, making an odd distinction. One would be hard-pressed, however, to interpret the absence of black Mississippians, a major section of the community, from a station's news, religious, and cultural programming in any light other than as a lack of broadcast service to that community.

The commission noted that WLBT had improved markedly in terms of black participation in locally originated programming. "We caution, however, against any conclusion that WLBT's performance during the period in question was spotless or a model of perfection to be emulated by other stations." Nonetheless, the majority said, the challengers had failed to prove their charges. The commission added, however, that it sincerely appreciated the strenuous efforts by the United Church of Christ and the other challengers to learn the nature of WLBT programming and to bring it to the FCC's attention. "They have performed a valuable public service, and they can be sure that the recent marked improvement in WLBT's local programming which this record discloses is due in no small part to their efforts."[25]

Once again, Kenneth Cox disagreed with his fellow commissioners, joined this time by Nicholas Johnson. In a dissent twice as long as the majority opinion and bristling with indignation, Cox and Johnson wrote that the FCC had replaced its former show of concern for the public interest with "all-out indifference." After in effect putting WLBT on probation with a one-year license renewal in 1965, the FCC in 1968 "looks over the same record and declares it clean enough to justify a routine, rubber-stamped, three-year renewal."

The appeals court had cautioned that a station had to run on its record, but the FCC was shifting its standards away from the relevant period of that record, 1961 to 1964. Cox and Johnson pointed to three other cases between 1960 and 1963 in which stations had not been permitted to profit from upgrading their practices after a hearing had been set. "Of course, administrative precedent can be ignored when its teachings appear inconvenient." The Communications Act would be meaningless if broadcasters thought they could shower the FCC with promises "to sin no more" once their licenses had been designated for a hearing, the dissenters said.

The Cox-Johnson dissent incorporated points that would undergird the final appeals court decision, one seemingly inevitable because of the way the FCC majority had misread the sense of the first ruling by Burger and his colleagues. For example, Cox and Johnson argued, the commission made it virtually impossible for the challengers to succeed against WLBT when it put the burden of proof for the two most important issues on them, not on the station. Using this standard, broadcasters, who controlled virtually all relevant information about past programming practices, such as logs, tapes, and scripts, were safe from challenge. "This is an unfair burden for the commission to impose on members of the public who are sufficiently concerned about a license's performance to take the time, trouble, and expense to engage in litigation before this agency."

Cox and Johnson also questioned the majority's reasoning when it found, for instance, that WLBT had not violated the Fairness Doctrine in refusing reply time to its 1957 program on the Little Rock crisis. The commission had said that there was no evidence that the program, which featured elected public officials, discussed the maintenance of segregation and was therefore partisan. "Do public officials not hold partisan views? And whether they do or not, are programs on which they appear presumptively not subject to the fairness doctrine?" Furthermore, the commission had said the challengers had presented no evidence to substantiate their charge that the program

participants discussed segregation. "Testimony is evidence," argued
Cox and Johnson, and the challengers had testified that three officials
discussed maintaining segregation in favorable terms.

The commission majority had ruled that the only instance in which
WLBT had violated the Fairness Doctrine was during the Meredith
controversy when it carried repeated spot announcements by the
Jackson Citizens' Council that Communists were behind the civil
rights movement. One mistake, it said, should not result in denial of
a station's license. Carrying this unanswered "saturation campaign of
anti–civil rights material" was not simply a good faith error in judgment, Cox and Johnson wrote, and furthermore it was not true that
this campaign was the only fairness violation in the record. In this and
other instances, WLBT's attitude represented active rebellion against
requirements that it present contrasting views on controversial issues
of public importance. "It is unlikely that a more flagrant deliberate
and serious offender against the fairness doctrine will ever appear
before us."

As for the majority's dismissal of the challengers' monitoring
report, Cox and Johnson said that the commission had in the past
accepted studies with categories different from its own. How long,
they asked, would the commission have a group monitor a station to
be considered valid? A year? Three years? That would be too difficult
and too expensive, and so no such efforts would be undertaken. The
dissenters argued that the one-week monitoring study was every bit
as fair as the composite week of programming that the FCC used to
evaluate station performance.

As for the allegation that WLBT flashed a "Sorry, Cable Trouble"
sign when it did not run an interview with Thurgood Marshall in
1955, Cox and Johnson scored the commission for simply taking Fred
Beard's word that he had been misquoted in a local news article.
Even Beard's version was damaging enough in that he acknowledged

cutting off the program. He "admits he took this step in order to prevent the people of Jackson from seeing a Negro—this man who had risen to the position of distinction and respect even then held by Mr. Thurgood Marshall."

The majority said that there had been improvements at WLBT since its license was challenged. "One may or may not be impressed by this new spirit of brotherhood in Jackson. But it has only occurred since WLBT's Washington counsel advised its principal owners, the Murchison brothers of Texas, that their license to operate this several million-dollar television station was in serious jeopardy. It is indefensible for the commission to consider such evidence of decisive significance."

It is undeniable, the dissenters maintained, "that bigotry was a watchword at WLBT between 1961 and 1964, and it is difficult to doubt, prior to 1961. Whether it is now still the case is, to say the least, unclear from the record. That WLBT's recent show of contrition should not be allowed to counter WLBT's prior open and unmitigated scorn and indifference to the half of its viewers who happen to be black seem to us beyond argument."

Remembering Ann Aldrich's oral argument, Johnson and Cox spoke, too, of WLBT's misrepresentations. The station said it had a policy not to present local programs dealing with segregation when in fact it did present such programs and that it tried to notify opposing groups on controversial issues when in fact it did not. It used to be that the FCC took stern action where misrepresentation was concerned, they added, quoting the saying that "it makes no difference what you do, just make sure you tell the Commission the truth about it if you're caught." Now it appeared to the dissenters that even that modest standard had been eroded.

Cox and Johnson then summed up the elements of the challenge that make it worth studying even today: "This case has everything.

A racist television station in Mississippi. An offended citizenry that actually takes the expensive and frustrating course of involving itself in the license renewal process. A church as a party. Negroes protesting the programming abuse received by that nearly 50 per cent of the people in the station's viewing area who are black. A landmark, first-impression decision by the U.S. court of appeals awarding 'standing' to such parties. The station's misrepresentation to the Commission over the years. The Commission's contortions to keep the public out entirely, then to place upon them an impossible burden of proof, then to reverse long-held precedents and ignore the clear suggestions of the court as to the standards to be applied."

Clearly, in the dissenters' view, the commission was not going to ride the wave of participatory democracy sweeping the country. "Everyone, from States' Righters to New Leftists, from the highest echelons of the establishment to the storefronts of the ghetto, has embraced the ideal of extending democracy in all levels of government—everyone, that is, except for this FCC majority."

The commission, Cox and Johnson believed, had gone to great lengths to protect a licensee with a very bad record. The majority had ignored the court of appeals' directions. It rejected valid evidence. It sanctioned obstruction that could only discourage citizens from exercising their rights. "Indeed, it would appear that the only way in which members of the public can prevent renewal of an unworthy station's license is to steal the document from the wall of the station's studio in the dead of night, or hope that the courts will do more than merely review and remand cases to the FCC with instructions that may be ignored."[26]

The commission majority was stung by the dissent. Commissioners Hyde, Bartley, Lee, and Wadsworth took the unusual step of issuing further comments. In his one-page statement, Bartley said that the dissent was full of "vituperations and self-serving characterizations."

The allegations brought against WLBT, "if true, might well have been grounds for denying the renewal. However, the allegations were not substantiated, were not considered true, and were *not*, therefore, grounds for denying the renewal as requested by the intervenors."[27] Commissioners Hyde, Lee, and Wadsworth said that "to deny renewal of this license on the basis of this dissent—stripped of its inaccuracies, errors and misinterpretations—would indeed have been a gross miscarriage of justice and an abuse of agency discretion."[28]

The press howled. The *Washington Post*, under a headline "A Farce at the FCC," editorialized on July 9, 1968, that the commission had done itself, the television industry, and the viewing public "an immense disservice" in renewing WLBT's license. "By a use of legalisms almost beyond description a majority of the FCC decided that WLBT never violated the fairness doctrine except in connection with James Meredith's efforts to enroll at the University of Mississippi. Any station, the majority said, must be forgiven one slip. The FCC could reach this result, however, only by requiring those who complained about WLBT to document every complaint they made while accepting as true, with or without documentation, almost everything WLBT said."[29] Robert Lewis Shayon wrote in the *Saturday Review* that the majority decision in the WLBT case was "a model of casuistry." The FCC had cautioned against concluding that the station's history was exemplary yet had argued that the church had failed to prove serious misconduct, he added in a tone of incredulity. "As for the Johnson-Cox dissent," Shayon continued, "it ought to be assigned reading for every high school social studies class in the nation as a visceral illumination of just who owns the country's airwaves."[30]

Within a week after the FCC decision, the United Church of Christ pledged to appeal, saying the result was not unexpected. When the Office of Communication undertook the case, it said, it did not seek the license for itself. "We sought to establish the basic moral principle that black men and women, who own the air frequencies along with white men and women, are entitled to a service equivalent to that afforded white citizens. These have been four long and wearying years for the Office of Communication of the United Church of Christ and we do not look forward to continued litigation. But there is no choice left open to us in conscience." It would pursue its appeal to the U.S. Court of Appeals.[31]

The same court panel that had heard the first appeal on the FCC's decision about WLBT heard the second on February 18, 1969: Warren Burger, Carl McGowan, and Edward Tamm. The courtroom was packed—every communications lawyer in Washington must have been there, Earle K. Moore recalled. As the court started to hear the oral arguments, it was clear to Moore it was "very, very hostile to the Broadcast Bureau" of the FCC. The court was also aggravated by the way the hearing examiner had allocated the burden of proof. "I had sort of trapped the hearing examiner into giving his views on the burden of proof which were diametrically opposed to the court," Moore said. "I mean, there was no way they could get around that."[32]

The three-judge court focused on the issue of burden of proof, according to a report in *Broadcasting*. In his argument, Moore repeated the challengers' contention that WLBT's record on serving the needs of the black population in its service area and on meeting Fairness Doctrine obligations on civil rights matters did not justify renewing its license. Lawyers for WLBT and for the FCC argued that the Jackson hearing had provided a reasonable basis for the commission's decision. Stuart Feldstein, representing the FCC, agreed with Moore that the commission did have the policy of requiring stations to deal with controversial issues, but he added that it gave them discretion over their programming.[33]

Moore later expressed surprise that the Broadcast Bureau attorneys had been, in his view, so clearly on the side of WLBT. He had argued before the New York State public service commission, where he felt the lawyers and the staff had a different approach. They knew that the public did not always have the same access to information and experts that regulated companies had, so it was their job to try to take apart the case of the licensee. But at the FCC, Moore found it quite the other way around. "They sit and decide who they think should win and then throw their weight on that side. In the case of someone like ourselves, I think there was a deep resentment that we were intruding into their function and who were we telling them what to do?"[34]

As the argument unfolded at the appeals court, Moore said he had the feeling "that the fix was in, my way for a change. The case was argued and the bench was extremely favorable to me, and they crawled all over the FCC and they gave Paul Porter an even worse time. He was in a horrible mood. It was pretty clear at the end of that argument that we had won." But Moore added that he practically got on his knees in front of the court and asked that the case not be sent back to the FCC again.[35]

On May 21, 1969, Warren Burger moved from the comparative obscurity of a seat on a federal appeals court to President Richard M. Nixon's nominee as the next chief justice of the United States. He would succeed Earl Warren, who had served since 1953 and was retiring. On June 9 the Senate overwhelmingly confirmed Burger after a Judiciary Committee hearing that reportedly lasted only an hour and forty minutes.

But before Burger headed up the hill from the federal court building to his Supreme Court post, he had one last appellate opinion to write—one that would stun the FCC and the television stations it regulated. Eventually, it would also lead to Lamar Life Broadcasting losing its license for WLBT. Writing for the court, Burger scored the FCC for its renewal and its treatment of the public challengers. He and his fellow judges ordered the case sent back to the commission, but not for more renewal deliberations. Other groups would now be allowed to compete for the license.

"The court did something very, very unusual," Moore commented. "They said that they were convinced that the station had the burden of proof and had failed to prove that it was entitled to renewal of its license. Since the case had gone on so long, they were going to send the case back to the commission with instructions to hold a comparative hearing to pick a new licensee. They would allow Lamar Life to compete but without the presumption of favor that an existing licensee would be entitled to." He added that most people interpreted that to mean Lamar could compete, "but there was no way they could win."[36]

The court was emphatic in its opinion, saying that the station had yet to demonstrate that it was in the public interest for its license to be renewed. The FCC had put WLBT on probation for one year, which meant the station was in a less favorable posture entering the Jackson hearing than would have been the case otherwise, the court said. "This is important, but its significance seems to have eluded the hearing examiner and the commission as well." The examiner seemed to have regarded the challengers as "plaintiffs" and the station as "defendant," the court added, with burdens of proof allocated accordingly. This approach, though possibly fostered by the commission's own action, "was a grave misreading of our holding on this question. We did not intend that intervenors representing a public interest be treated as interlopers." The commission's duties did not end by allowing the challengers to intervene in the case, Burger wrote. "Its duties began at that stage."

"A curious neutrality-in-favor-of-the-licensee seems to have guided the examiner in his conduct of the evidentiary hearing," Burger stated. For example, the examiner completely discounted the challengers' monitoring study, as the challengers and the FCC dissenters had emphasized. Yet, the court said, the commission had often complained, no doubt justifiably so, "that it cannot monitor licensees in any meaningful way; here a seven-day monitoring, made at no public expense, was presented by a public interest intervenor and was dismissed as 'worthless' by the commission."

The court may have revealed one motivation for ruling as strongly as it did with these lines: "The infinite potential of broadcasting to influence American life renders somewhat irrelevant the semantics of whether broadcasting is or is not to be described as a public utility. By whatever name or classification, broadcasters are temporary permittees—fiduciaries—of a great public resource and they must meet the highest standards which are embraced in the public interest concept. The Fairness Doctrine [which had just been upheld by the Supreme Court] plays a very large role in assuring that the public resource granted to licensees at no cost will be used in the public interest." The hearing examiner had dismissed many factors that he should not have dismissed. "The pervasive impatience—if not hostility—of the examiner [toward the public intervenors] is a constant factor which made fair and impartial consideration impossible." The members of the public who had challenged the license deserved a more hospitable reception. A potential FCC ally was regarded as an opponent, the court said.

The FCC in effect placed on the challengers the entire burden of showing that the station was not qualified to be granted a license renewal, the court observed, adding, "The examiner and the commission exhibited at best a reluctant tolerance of this court's mandate and at worst a profound hostility to the participation of the public intervenors and their efforts." Furthermore, the record left the court with deep concerns over the entire handling of the case at the FCC. "The impatience with the public intervenors, the hostility toward their efforts to satisfy a surprisingly strict standard of proof, plain errors in rulings and findings lead us, albeit reluctantly, to the conclusion that it will serve no useful purpose to ask the commission to reconsider the examiner's actions and its own decision and order under a correct allocation of the burden of proof. The administrative conduct reflected in this record is beyond repair."

For the first time, a federal court was overruling the FCC on a renewal case and in effect terminating a broadcasting license. The court held that the commission's decision to renew the license a second time had not been supported by substantial evidence. Even as the court ordered the FCC to invite new applications, however, it did not disqualify Lamar Life from that proceeding, saying that "the conduct of the hearing was not primarily the licensee's responsibility."[37]

The case was a bombshell for broadcasters. "And particularly, of course, at the southern stations," said Moore. "It was interpreted as meaning that 'we better get our acts together on the racial issue.' "[38] In addition to being the first time a court had ever taken away a license, this case also marked the first time that a television station had lost its license over programming issues.[39]

The *New York Times* editorial page heralded the decision, calling it "of major significance not only for broadcasting but for other federally regulated businesses." The first court of appeals decision, which had granted standing to the public whenever its interest was at stake, already had encouraged conservationists to take action in matters before the Federal Power Commission, the editorial pointed out. This second decision meant "that TV and radio stations holding franchises of the public air do not have, in the cynical phrase, 'a license to print money.' " They hold temporarily a great public resource and must meet the highest standards, the newspaper said, concluding: "Broadly, this decision will help educate the Federal regulatory agencies and the courts as to the inherent rights of public challenges against licensed private interests."[40]

For its part, *Broadcasting* reported that the Burger opinion was "probably unprecedented in the tone of its condemnation of the commission and extraordinary in taking the resolution of the WLBT case out of the hands of the so-called 'expert agency.' " Communications attorneys saw the decision as encouraging community groups to file protests against license renewal applications. Such challenges were already a fact of life.[41]

WLBT's attorneys were stunned. They had argued that "okay, we were a bad citizen for a while, but we came in and cleaned it up and fixed it and we're now very good citizens. In fact, exemplary citizens, and that ought to have some weight," Harry Huge said.[42] Huge was convinced that there was nothing in the record casting doubt on the present status of the station because it had worked so hard to correct its problems. When he was younger, Huge said, he had speculated that Burger was "getting his civil rights ticket punched" with his decision or that Burger had thought FCC proceedings were stacked in favor of broadcasters.[43]

Former WLBT news director Richard Sanders followed the case to its conclusion and years later reflected on its outcome. He did not think the challenge was fair or the court's decision correct, even though his thinking about the issues the black community was raising had changed while he was in Mississippi. The turning point, he said, had come when the head of a small black college in Mississippi had posed the question about how could he teach civics when his students "ask me if I can vote and I have to say I can't." So when Myrlie Evers was mentioned in accounts of the trial of Byron de la Beckwith, accused of murdering her late husband, Sanders had thrown out his previous reservations and identified her as "Mrs. Evers" on second reference.

With all the pressures, Sanders said, "I probably got out just in time. . . . When we got away from it, you wondered how did you live with that" and have a normal home life. The fact that he wasn't fired for his coverage should have meant something, Sanders believed. Furthermore, by 1969 Fred Beard was gone. "They had made a complete change. They were doing what was right. It really was unfair to Lamar Life. We got into all that trouble—when we were the only station giving blacks even any coverage. The competition never covered any of those things."[44]

After the appeals court decision, the challengers and the FCC faced new questions. Who would run the station permanently, and who would run it over the short haul? Would the United Church of Christ's Office of Communication play any role? For the moment, Lamar Life would remain in charge. That would soon change. For the long term, another player had already entered the arena, and others soon would. On March 12, 1969, as the court of appeals was mulling its decision, a group calling itself the Civic Communications Corporation asked to intervene in the case and filed an application for the station. One of Civic's key participants was Aaron Henry, who had joined with the Office of Communication in its complaints against WLBT. Other Mississippians in the group were Charles Evers, Patricia Derian, Hodding Carter III, and Charles Young, a cosmetics manufacturer and NAACP activist from Meridian, Mississippi. The presence of this group with its clear roots in the civil rights movement—especially Aaron Henry's participation—would draw others into the fight for the permanent license. No one could have predicted then that it would take another ten years before the FCC could finally designate a permanent licensee for WLBT.

6. EXIT LAMAR LIFE, ENTER WILLIAM DILDAY

One Sunday morning early in 1973, five young black men and women arrived at the First Baptist Church in downtown Jackson to attend worship services. Church deacons turned the young people away at the door—only whites attended First Baptist. Unbeknownst to the deacons, a camera crew from WLBT, acting on a tip, was hiding in nearby shrubbery, and the station aired the confrontation on its 6 P.M. news that evening.[1] This aggressive coverage of an issue involving race marked a major transformation at WLBT following its hiring of the nation's first black station manager. It also marked change for Jackson's television viewers as well, the kind of change that had been the reason for challenging the station's license in the first place.

After the federal appeals court decision in 1969, the Federal Communications Commission invited new applications for the license. The commission said that it would select someone to run the station until it chose a permanent operator, raising the possibility that a group not seeking the license might become the interim management. That's what happened, and that's when the pace of change accelerated. The interim management ran WLBT for almost a decade, giving it time to respond to the interests of black as well as white viewers and to change the station's coverage to reflect those interests. The interim management also increased minority hiring at WLBT.

This nonprofit group, Communications Improvement, Inc. (CII), was incorporated in February 1970. In its application to be interim operator, CII pledged not only to improve minority coverage and employment but also to give half its net profits to help develop educational television in Mississippi. The group said that it would also try to develop communications training at a predominantly black college.

Lamar Life had lost its license at WLBT in part because of charges that it failed to learn—or "ascertain," in FCC jargon—what a significant portion of its community wanted in local programming. For its application, CII consulted with area leaders on state problems, asked college students by questionnaire to help them identify such problems, and polled community members randomly. It surveyed blacks and whites—civil rights leaders, poverty group officials, educators, doctors, ministers, government figures, businesspeople, even a member of the Ku Klux Klan. Many mentioned race relations as a problem; others viewed the quality of education, unresponsive government, and lack of sufficient low-income housing and economic opportunity for poor people as important issues. Many urged more documentary programming on public affairs. As a result, CII proposed to use more than 13 percent of its schedule for news and public affairs and said that blacks would participate in programs about all community problems, not just those of special concern to the black community.

In its application, CII said that broadcasters could make only limited contributions to solving complex social and political issues, but they could provide service by calling public attention to those concerns. The group said it was well aware that exposing serious problems "will be disturbing and disquieting to many of its viewers and may produce some adverse audience reaction." But it didn't intend to present "bland non-controversial, reassuring interviews and discussions, but rather to seek out critical opinion and to reflect controversy."[2]

On September 8, 1970, the FCC selected CII to run the station until it chose among the five competing applicants for the permanent license. "We thought we'd be in for 18 months but it took nine years," said Dr. Aaron Shirley, a black pediatrician who was on the CII board.[3] Whether a short-time or longtime operator, CII was determined to make its mark.

The key person within CII was Kenneth Dean, the former executive director of the Mississippi Council on Human Relations and a Baptist minister. He took an active role in setting station policy and helped establish an integrated board of directors to oversee the station in an era where such boards were rare nationally, let alone in Mississippi. Mississippi, one must recall, was still resisting legislative redistricting to give fairer representation to African Americans statewide as well as in city and county government. Most white Mississippians sent their children to private, segregated academies rather than to the public schools. Whites still retaliated against blacks seeking political advancement, sometimes sweeping innocent people into the violence. During a successful voter registration drive in the small town of Drew in Sunflower County, for example, several whites killed Joetha Collier, an award-winning black student who had just graduated from high school the night before her death. This, then, was the Mississippi in which the interracial CII board took over the state's leading television franchise.

CII needed money to start its operations, including paying Lamar for renting its equipment. The organization went to the Mission Enterprise Loan and Investment Committee of the United Methodist Church, which gave CII a $300,000 line of credit. The committee lent a total of $200,000 of that to CII, which paid back the loan in

March 1974. It would have been difficult to attain the success that CII had achieved without the church's loan and support, Dean told the Methodists when he made the final payment.[4]

The first CII board of directors included Dr. Shirley, who had been active in civil rights work and who headed a local comprehensive health center; Earle F. Jones, a white man whose management firm ran several Holiday Inns; white insurance executive Jack Shuford; white Millsaps College religion professor Lee Reiff; Thelma Sanders, a black woman who ran an apparel store and was active in local civic and professional groups; George Owens, president of predominantly black Tougaloo College; and several other Mississippians. The Reverend Everett Parker, although not part of CII, was instrumental in helping shape its public service vision and also aided in recruiting some national members for the board. These included Edward Barrett, the former dean of Columbia University's Graduate School of Journalism, and James Day, president of National Educational Television; both were white. CII's attorney was Earle K. Moore, who had represented the United Church of Christ in challenging WLBT and later was the attorney Action for Children's Television. He also served on the board of directors.[5] But it was Ken Dean who had the most day-to-day impact on the station's operations.

For example, in a lengthy memo that he wrote to the board of directors on July 28, 1971, Dean listed more than a dozen concerns that he had about station practices, ranging from fiscal operations to failure to schedule black programs or use black staff in prime time. Dean noted that much of the black presence on WLBT at that point was "in the form of preaching, singing, or some other form of religious expression. It is as if blacks can sing, preach and play baseball but do little else." Dean was also concerned with the tendency he said he detected in station manager Bob McRaney Jr. to "play down the bi-racial composition of the board, our commitment to civil rights and race relations, and the fact that a number of board members have been and still are active in civil rights and federally-sponsored projects."[6] Dean was already wondering "how much the present management can change from a Lamar to a CII operation," a feeling that would only grow in the months to come.

Dean was born in Rogersville, Tennessee, and moved to Marysville when he was six. His family had been active in the local Southern Baptist Church, and Dean said that made him sensitive to the suffering of others. When he was ten years old in 1945, he recalled watching newsreels at the Saturday morning movies about the Holocaust. Seeing pictures of the bodies of Jews stacked up like cordwood made him think that all people should be treated in more humane ways. "That of course prepared the background in my mind for later considerations of race."

He received his bachelor's degree in philosophy from Carson-Newman College, a Baptist school in Jefferson City, Tennessee, and then graduated from Colgate-Rochester Divinity School in Rochester, New York, in 1965. In Rochester, he became involved with protests against housing discrimination. Leslie Dunbar and Will Campbell of the Southern Regional Council heard of his involvement in civil rights and asked him if he would be interviewed for a job as head of the Mississippi Council on Human Relations. Like Harry Huge, he had never really heard much good about Mississippi, but he went to Jackson in 1965 and stayed until 1970. He returned to Colgate-Rochester Divinity School and taught there while earning a second degree, moving back to Mississippi during CII's operation of WLBT.

The Council on Human Relations worked on issues involving public accommodations, police brutality, voter registration, and school integration. "Black people were being demeaned and dehumanized," Dean said, "and whatever you need to do in society, you need to do to correct that."

While he was with the council, Dean was asked to testify at the FCC hearing about how WLBT had treated the Council on Human Relations, "which was very good," Dean said. "I was on that station regularly. So I said sure, I'd say how they treated me. Actually, in the hearing process there, I testified in favor of WLBT under Bob McRaney and didn't really think much about it."

Looking back more than thirty years later, Dean said of the hearing: "My assessment would be that the attitude of the hearing examiner, the attitude of Lamar Life, and the attitude of management of WLBT at that time was 'this is no big thing, we don't really have to give serious consideration to it.'" They believed that FCC decisions would continue to turn not on law but on politics, so they didn't give serious thought to the fact that they might lose.[7] McRaney himself said later that, until the interim management took over, he, too, did not think Lamar would forfeit its license.[8] Broadcasters in that era may have had a good reading of the attitudes of the FCC, but it proved harder for them to get a fix on the court until the hammer came down.

CII took over at WLBT in June 1971. The staff was understandably uneasy, asking who these new people were and what they would want. Staff members wondered if they would keep their jobs. J. Hewitt Griffin, longtime program director at WLBT, remembered the meeting that key CII board members held with station employees. "I know all of you have reservations, that you're worried about your jobs," Ken Dean told them. "You're not going to lose your jobs, we're not going to fire anyone. But by attrition we're going to get this station up to where the percentage of black employees is equal to the black population in the state."

After the meeting, Griffin recalled, "I started to get a steady stream of people in my office. People were saying, 'I won't work with niggers.'" "Well, you'd better get out of here," Griffin told them, "because those people are coming. I don't want you to go, but

I don't want you to stay if you're going to fight it. I lost a lot of folks. We lost a lot of viewers in the beginning—they thought we were going to turn into an all-black station, and they weren't ready for that in 1971."

Hewitt Griffin's career offered a profile of how WLBT and its staff evolved. Griffin considered himself a typical white Mississippian in terms of upbringing and attitudes—he went along with WLBT's outlook under Fred Beard. But he emerged as a mentor to black employees like Randall Pinkston and Mary Ann Lindsey, who later became the WLBT program director. Despite some rocky encounters, he also became good friends with the first black station manager, who was hired about a year into CII's operation of Channel 3. Griffin talked to me about his experiences less than two months before he died of a heart attack in August 1999.

Griffin, who had moved to Jackson in 1936 when he was eight years old, wanted to be a writer. He had worked for the *Shreveport Times* and had a job waiting for him at the *Memphis Commercial Appeal* when WLBT executives approached him about coming to the TV station. "I said I didn't know much about television," then in its adolescence. "I watched *Bonanza* every once in a while and that was it." Hired in May 1961, Griffin said he would try the job for ninety days. Those ninety days turned into more than thirty years. He worked for Fred Beard, then Bob McRaney, then William Dilday.

Of Beard, he said, he was "a fine man, had a fine family. But he saw Communists under every bed, and he fought integration. He was a fine broadcaster, a great businessman." But, yes, when a black man might be on television, technical difficulties did seem to occur. "It didn't happen all the time or we'd have been doing it every day," Griffin said. He excluded news director Richard Sanders, whom he described as a liberal, from the indictment he was about to make, then said that people at the station "were not racists but were willing to let it happen. I had to write promos for the Freedom Bookstore and I did it." Remembering the station under Beard, Griffin said of his own performance, "We were raised that way. Compassion was different than activism. I wasn't any shining hero. I went along with it. I saw the injustice of it but I didn't do any fighting."

Once Beard was fired, Griffin said, "we promised the world." Reed Miller and Harry Huge, Arnold & Porter attorneys, made the station change many things. News stories, for example, had to include courtesy titles for black people. Griffin took news copy that he had written to Alon Bee, the morning announcer, who said, "I'm not going to do that here. I ain't going to get my house blown up." Someone else went on the air that morning. The lawyers told the station to integrate the teenage dance program. "We didn't know how," Griffin recalled.

Bob McRaney and Hewitt Griffin got to be close friends, the latter said, and Griffin understood that McRaney, whom he described as "an ambitious guy," liked his red convertible, big house, and country club membership, "which finally got him fired."[9] Given McRaney's ambition and that of Ken Dean, who later ran unsuccessfully for Congress, it was inevitable that they would clash. If it hadn't been the country club membership, it would have been something else. Dean kept stirring the WLBT pot and pushed McRaney to hire more minorities. When CII took over, there were thirteen black employees, or 15.5 percent. Not long before he left the station, McRaney reported to the board that WLBT then had eighteen black employees.[10]

As much as possible, CII wanted to keep the staff that it inherited from Lamar Life to show that a staff of mostly white southerners could, with different leadership, go in a different direction. At the same time, it also wanted a more biracial staff, Dean said, and so the board soon adopted a policy not to hire any more white employees until the black staff reached equity with blacks in the local population.[11]

In addition to the basic equity issue, smart newsroom managers know that one of the key reasons for diversity in the media is that people with different backgrounds see different stories—an element that certainly would have been true in Jackson in the early 1970s. Adding women to newspaper and broadcast staffs over the years has altered the definition of news as more stories about children, credit discrimination, or women's health started making the front pages or the evening newscasts. Likewise, having more black staff members helps a newspaper or station increase its range of stories. As communications sociologist Michael Schudson has written, "Who writes the story matters. When minorities and women and people who have known poverty and misfortune first-hand are authors of news as well as its readers, the social world represented in the news expands and changes."[12]

At WLBT, the CII board recognized that at times it might have to make exceptions to its hiring policy because, in a technical field like television, the station might have to fill a particular job in which blacks had little experience. The board's executive committee decided that it would have to rule on any of those exceptions.

"Bob McRaney came to me and said, look, we've got a camera position that's come open and we can't find any blacks," Dean recalled. "He said I've got a good candidate here who's white. I've got to hire this white candidate. We can't continue without this position being filled. It's running into overtime."

"And I said, well, Bob, what are you going to do with our policy?" He said he would hire a black trainee. Then another position opened up. Same thing. Black trainee, white full-time employee. Finally, the job of receptionist came open. "McRaney came to me and said there's no way we can put a black face at the front door. We're going to have to hire a white woman to be out there. This affects sales. It affects everybody who comes in here. Well, we had a number of applicants for that job, some of them white, some of them black. The executive committee said, you tell Bob McRaney he's going to put a black in that position. He's not going to tell us that he can't find a black that can come in here and answer our telephone and greet people. So we did that."

After McRaney had hired several black trainees, Dean recalled saying to him, "Bob, we're going to end up with a station that's got eighty-four white employees and eighty-four black trainees." The board had been supportive of McRaney but was beginning to get restive, Dean and several other members said. The issue that precipitated McRaney's departure did not involve hiring practices, however, but rather his membership at a Jackson country club, which Dean said discriminated against both blacks and Jews at that time.

McRaney wanted to maintain the membership in order to do business in the community. CII was paying for the membership, and Dean told McRaney that the country club's discrimination violated board policy. "This was flagrant to us," Dean said, "flagrant for three reasons: the issue of segregation of blacks, the issue of Jews, thirdly, whose money it was," that is, that the integrated CII board was paying for a membership in a discriminatory club. Earle Jones suggested that Dean discuss with McRaney giving him a salary increase equal to the amount he would have to pay to get a personal membership in the country club if he thought he was going to have to do business there. Dean said that McRaney told him that wouldn't deal with his monthly costs at the club, so Dean returned to the board, which decided what it thought would cover membership and monthly costs. "I took it back and told Bob what we wanted to do. And he refused." When Dean reported to Jones, Dr. Shirley, and the board's lawyer, they said, "We don't like this but, Ken, you've got to go fire Bob for this reason." Dean said he saw McRaney at about noon on April 13, 1972, and told him to give him his keys, that they were relieving him of his duties.[13]

In a statement issued after the firing, CII said that it had high regard for McRaney as a professional broadcaster and as a person but that the board felt that it needed a new manager.[14] The day after McRaney left, the station received a dozen calls protesting his dismissal. Several callers asserted that "blacks have taken over the station completely now."[15]

Clearly, this incident marked a turning point both for the station and for McRaney, who still found it painful to discuss his experiences under CII almost thirty years later. When the interim group had been appointed, he said, "I told them I would serve them, be responsive to them, and give them my best professional judgment on what to do and what ramifications were there. And everything they proposed doing, I was prepared to implement but I also told them what the consequences were."

For instance, WLBT had carried a Presbyterian church service every Sunday morning. It paid for the time. "They wanted me to cancel that and put on a black church and move [that time slot] around among black churches every Sunday morning. I said fine. We can do this. Here's what it's going to cost. It's going to cost X number of dollars to buy a mobile unit, which we do not have. . . . Hire a crew to go to each church to set it up, light it, mike it, do the technical for each week. These are the out-of-pocket dollars for each week. Who's going to pay for those? . . . I gave them a list of the members of the board of aldermen or whatever they were called—the deacons of the Presbyterian church—biggest advertisers we had. I said we're likely to lose Coca-Cola, likely to lose whatever the beer distributor was, all of the above. They said, okay don't do it." Ultimately, however, WLBT did replace the telecasts from the First Presbyterian Church with a rotation among various denominations.

McRaney viewed his firing as a product of the board's mind-set. "They learned enough to run a TV station. Didn't need me. They also wanted to hire the first black general manager in the history of the business in the world, in the country. I have no respect for Ken Dean, is what I'm leading up to. When they hired Bill Dilday, he was a personnel manager. This is when it gets emotional. This is when my life is affected."[16]

McRaney moved out of the state then, going first to Richmond, Virginia, then to New Orleans. Before he was fired, McRaney said years later, he had a commitment to Mississippi, wanting to stay there rather than move to a bigger market as some of his friends had done. He had also contemplated getting into public service, perhaps running for office. After living out of state for several years, McRaney remarked, "I finally got tired of jumping through corporate hoops and went back to Mississippi" as a better place to raise children. He was running AM and FM radio stations in West Point, Mississippi, when we spoke.[17]

Earle Jones, who was on the station's executive committee the entire time that CII ran WLBT, was a Californian who had attended Harvard Business School and moved to Mississippi in 1956. Jones said the issue that led to McRaney's dismissal was his stonewalling on hiring blacks. Jones prefaced his remarks by saying that McRaney was "a good diplomat, smooth salesperson, very likeable." But the station had a policy to hire blacks when there were openings. "Time after time we would hear from Bob that there weren't qualified people so he'd ask for an exception to hire somebody white. Finally, the board gave up. It was never going to be easy until we got somebody else." The country club membership may have been the issue that precipitated the dismissal, but the disagreement over hiring practices was the underlying cause, Jones said.[18]

McRaney had his adherents on the staff, however. John Milton Wesley, a young black man hired at the station not long before McRaney left, recalled that McRaney had been helpful and had encouraged him to apply for a summer training program at Columbia

School of Journalism. "It was Bob McRaney who came to me and said only one other person in the state has gotten this fellowship. He walked me through it." The day McRaney was fired, he had given Wesley a check and told him to take his application to the post office. When Wesley returned to the station, McRaney was gone and his belongings in boxes.

"It was sad for me but I understood what was going on. We literally loved Bob McRaney," Wesley recalled. "He really fought for employees. We thought that in terms of implementing changes," he would have been the best. "He was treated so unfair." He had had to appease first Lamar Life, then CII, Wesley said. "They could have given McRaney a chance to emerge as an example for other whites who were in communication and other whites who were in business. They could have allowed McRaney to be a drum major for justice. He could have shown that with his understanding and leadership," blacks and whites could work together.[19]

With McRaney gone, the board did indeed hire a black general manager. "We believed that in order for our policy on hiring to be authoritative that we too had to follow it," Ken Dean said. "So if we had a general manager's position open, we had to hire a black." But no blacks had held jobs like that. Some of the board members believed they would be going too far, too fast. Some also thought that it would set back race relations for the station to have fired a popular white general manager to replace him with someone black.[20]

William Dilday, a graduate of the Boston University School of Business, was then personnel manager at WHDH in Boston. He had previously worked for IBM in Boston and for a Roxbury, Massachusetts, metal fabrication firm as personnel administrator and public relations director. He heard about the WLBT job from a field representative for the United Church of Christ in Boston, who told Dilday that he had good news and bad news. The good news was that he knew of an opening in which Dilday could be the country's first black general manager of a TV station. Dilday recalled saying, "That's fine. What's the bad news?" The job was in Jackson. He had no interest in going there.[21]

Ken Dean asked Dilday to visit him in Rochester so that they could talk about the job. "I had reservations as to whether somebody in personnel could move from that position to general manager because, quite frankly, personnel and community relations were the two showcase areas in which the industry was putting blacks, and I knew this." When he met Dilday, Dean was impressed. He found Dilday friendly, obstinate, and with a healthy ego. "I thought it's a damn shame he doesn't have more hard-core business experience." Looking through Dilday's résumé, Dean saw that he had been through the IBM management training program. That convinced him Dilday would be a good risk, even though Dean thought his attitude a bit cavalier.

Dilday's attitude could be devastating for him in Mississippi, Dean thought. "He could not go there from Boston and project that image." He decided to wait to see if Dilday would contact him. Hewitt Griffin was sitting in as general manager, and the station seemed in good hands at the moment. Sometime later, Dilday called Dean to find out why he hadn't gotten back to him. Dean asked why Dilday hadn't contacted *him*, adding that he thought he hadn't been much interested in the job. Dilday replied that he was very interested. He went to Mississippi to meet with the board, and he was hired.[22]

"The farthest south I had been was Washington, D.C., and my wife had been to Tarrytown, New York. We were provincial northeasterners," Dilday said. His father hadn't wanted him to go to Jackson. "He said I had never lived in the South. He was from North Carolina and he said he didn't think I'd survive because I had a way of speaking my mind. He really did not want me to go."[23]

But go Dilday did. He went to Jackson in May, and his wife and two daughters followed in September. When Dilday's appointment was announced, the station had eighteen phone calls. Most were considered violent, according to the telephone logs, with callers saying they would never watch the station again. (As an aside, the station received more critical phone calls when Randall Pinkston left WLBT several years later than it had when either McRaney was fired or Dilday hired.)²⁴ Despite this phoned-in hostility, though, Dilday received a warm welcome from the black community. "I had more invitations from black families than I could handle. They were great. I didn't realize until I had been here about five or six years that I actually had gotten a very cold reception from the white community. I was used to seeing people at business and then going home. I guess they were upset that Bob McRaney, who had been very popular, had been fired. I didn't realize, coming from the Northeast, that it wasn't as cordial as it could have been."

Dilday had only been at WLBT a short time when he had the opportunity to speak his mind—on the air. Governor William Waller vetoed a federal grant for a community health center for the poor in Mound Bayou, a historic Mississippi Delta town that had always been run by black people. Later the same year Waller vetoed another grant for the health program in Jackson and Hinds County. Dilday editorialized against the vetoes, pointing out that through them the state was refusing $7.6 million in federal money, "money that could help us solve our acute health problems, help stimulate our economy, money that our state sorely needs." WLBT believed, the editorial said, that this issue should not become a political football. "One thing is certain—when politics become paramount, it is the people who suffer."²⁵ The switchboard lit up. "My being there and being black hadn't really registered with people. General managers aren't seen much. But when I went on the air, it was, 'Whoa, here's this black guy telling us how to spend our money.' Even though they knew it [that he was there], this made them really *know* it."²⁶

The new station manager made his mark in news coverage as well. That December the Channel 3 news team confronted a dilemma about whether to cover a demonstration being held by J. B. Stoner and members of his white racist National States Rights Party at the state capitol. Stoner's group was countering a memorial service being held for slain civil rights leader Vernon Dahmer, killed by Ku Klux Klansmen in 1966. Jewish leaders in the community and the FBI asked local media not to cover the counterdemonstration. Everyone but WLBT acceded to that request. Dilday sent a black reporter to the demonstration, which included Stoner waving a sign saying "Bilbo Was White and Right," referring to the former Mississippi politician who wanted to ship blacks back to Africa. "We got a lot of flak" for covering the demonstration, Dilday said at the time, "but if it happened tomorrow, I'd do it again." WLBT aired film showing Stoner's speech in which he said that "Hitler was too conservative, that he didn't kill enough Jews. . . . I think putting him on like that, we did so much to refute any credibility he might have had." But many in Jackson disagreed. Once again the switchboard lights blazed.²⁷

Dilday increased public affairs programming and emphasized problems of minorities and the poor. And he began the integrated children's program that the CII board so badly wanted. Before he left the station, McRaney had told the board that he was having difficulty finding someone to direct the program and asked the board to suspend the policy of hiring only blacks to give him more flexibility.²⁸ In July 1972 Dilday hired Dorothy Gibbs, a young black woman from Greenwood who had a bachelor's degree from Jackson State University and a master's degree in early childhood education. Her assignment was to produce and teach on an educational program for preschool children, black and white. *Our Playmates* debuted in October 1972. A half-hour program, it ran five times a week with a different group of children appearing each week. The children played games, sang songs, did exercises, participated in art activities, and learned how to relate to one another, much as they would do in a Head Start or kindergarten class. Said Dr. Shirley: "So some white mommas had an opportunity to see a talented black person locally. . . . They had white kids and black kids on together. That kind of thing set the stage for dialog between the races that never had occurred before."[29]

Of critical importance to the CII board, Dilday increased minority employment at WLBT from 15 percent to 35 percent (it eventually reached 40 percent) within the first year he was general manager. He faced some hostility from white employees, and, as he told reporter Phil Gailey, "There are still a few people around here fighting the civil war, but a lot of them have resigned or been fired—not for prejudice— but for incompetence." Dilday planned to promote Tom Alexander, a young black man, to assistant production manager when word reached him that if he did so, the production department would walk out en masse. He called a department meeting and announced the promotion. "In a few minutes, three resignations were turned in. The funny thing is that two of those men who resigned worked a different shift and wouldn't even have been around Tom. That's a good case of racism over common sense."[30]

When Dilday became general manager, "there were two different stations, a black station and a white station. The two camps never came together. I tried to instill a sense of unity among them. I came in and became sort of a hard ass and that made them bond together to show me" what they could do. "I knew when I started that after a few months, the blacks would be disappointed and the whites would say he's not as bad as we thought he would be."

The CII board members had wanted not only black employment figures improved and better integrated programs but also that the station continue to show a profit. It did. Although the station lost several advertisers when Dilday took over, all but one came back because the station consistently had the number one ratings in the city. "Whatever social engineering we did," Dilday said, "it wasn't at the expense of ratings or revenues."[31]

Before Dilday came to the station, WLBT's black employees had sought a share in decision making for everyone at the station, not just its administrators. Their request for greater involvement was not uncommon in the media of that era. They formed the Minority Group Employees and sent a memo to McRaney and Griffin on February 21, 1972, suggesting that minority group representatives actively participate in all executive committee meetings. The minority staff urged WLBT to seek a full-time black salesman and make it clear to advertisers that black as well as white talent would be used in commercials. WLBT should also seek blacks for jobs in engineering, accounting, and programming administration and should not discriminate in pay. Fourteen black employees signed the memo, including Tom Alexander, a director; Mary Ann Lindsey, then a film editor; newsmen Willie Pinkston and John Wesley; and several maintenance workers.[32]

"We knew we were very much a minority here, we knew that we could be targeted," said Lindsey, at whose home the group often met. "We made very sure to clock in at 8 A.M. We didn't want what we were doing to affect our job performance." Lindsey said that many of the white managers, including McRaney, were nice to her even as she was learning to edit film. "I loved every bit of it. I could edit anything. But I also knew that I always had to be better than that white person standing over there." Hewitt Griffin was always especially supportive. "He was a person who cared about people. I could go to Hewitt with any problem I had."

The minority employees formed their caucus because they wanted better working conditions, equal treatment, and raises. "We wanted the things that other people got. There was so much racial tension then. Your work atmosphere can either contribute to that or make it better," Lindsey said, remembering that some people spoke in blatantly racist terms—" 'that nigger this' or 'that nigger that.' " Yet "if we had said 'that honky,' we would have been immediately thrown out. The black caucus was a means of survival."[33]

In addition to raising their grievances internally, the black employees complained to the FCC on June 14, 1972, that despite the board's resolution that only blacks should be hired without express approval of CII's officers, five whites had been hired for the news, engineering, audio, art, and sales departments. "Although CII has hired a black manager (William Dilday), this action should in no way negate the board's efforts and determination to implement" its resolution.[34]

Dilday himself was not exempt from criticism from the black employees' group. He wanted to meet individually with its members. The minority employees said it was all or no one.[35] The day after the group insisted on collective talks, Dilday expressed his frustration with the group. "I thought most black people had moved to a degree of sophistication which would allow them to trust the integrity and ability of any brother or sister THEY had selected to represent them. If among your whole group, you do not have two people you feel are intelligent and articulate enough to effectively express your feelings and concerns, then you have far greater problems than you realize."[36]

Addressing the employees' complaint about his hires for the sales department, Dilday stated that any openings there would be filled by a black. But he indicated his awareness of local practices when he said he was not as optimistic about changing the minimal use of black talent in local commercials. It was exceptionally difficult for the station or a salesperson to tell advertisers what they must do in their advertisements. "This is an area where community pressure on advertisers, particularly those doing a large amount of business in the black community, would be an invaluable aid." By the time Dilday was making his first annual report to the board in May 1973, he added that WLBT had 38 percent minority employment. "In terms of pay, all my employees would probably state I am completely fair and unbiased in underpaying them."[37]

Dilday had the support of his board. He was a good businessman, Ken Dean said. "That's who we hired him to be. He always stayed focused. He was there to make a record as a good broadcaster in a commercial station. He didn't consider himself a part of the nonprofit orientation of CII. Rather, he saw his role as that of maximizing profits for WLBT. He always drove a hard bargain. He never did take off his lenses as a businessman. He was criticized and CII was criticized because he didn't become an activist type in the community. . . . He implemented CII policy, which was in itself a social agenda." Dean thought that as the first black general manager of a commercial TV station, Dilday was highly successful. Even the chief engineer, who was known as being philosophically committed to racism and was at first critical about Dilday, came to respect him as a good businessman and a good general manager, Dean said. Dilday had the opportunity to appoint several sales directors, Dean said, and he picked white men. Dean saw him work with those white sales managers "in very friendly, collegial ways that you don't always see between business partners. Their language was very much the language of buddies."[38]

It took time, however, for Dilday and Hewitt Griffin to come to good terms, reflecting again deep-seated attitudes on both sides. "Dilday thought he was going to be met by the guys with white sheets," said Griffin of the new general manager's attitude when he arrived at the station. "He was arrogant, unqualified, authoritative. I had been managing the station after McRaney was fired. We clashed from the very beginning." According to Griffin, Dilday was determined that he was going to make the decisions, and "he didn't know anything about TV at the time." Griffin quit, ostensibly to write a novel, he said, but he completed only ten pages in six months. "All

I was doing was drinking," said Griffin, who later became a local spokesperson for Alcoholics Anonymous.

Eventually, Ken Dean asked Griffin to meet him for lunch and tried to talk him into coming back. "I said, 'I can't work for Dilday.' The next morning Dilday called. I noticed a change in how he talked to me. He asked me to come down and meet with him at 1:30. I spent three hours in his office. Bill owned up to the fact that we had started out wrong." That afternoon, Griffin said, the two men were "just gut-level honest with each other. We both owned up to mistakes we had made. We never had another cross word. We went all over the country together. He became one of the best friends I ever had."[39]

Dilday was the "right package at the right time," said John Wesley. "He was the right general manager if excellence was what we were going to hang our hat on. He had an ability to make you want to do your best. He didn't do it the way McRaney did. McRaney did it through devotion, loyalty and all that. Dilday was much stricter, more a taskmaster."[40]

The program that brought the most national recognition to WLBT—*Probe*—went on the air in the fall of 1974. Because the station still considered itself weak in public affairs programming, Dilday and Griffin wanted a program that would go beyond the headlines. Dennis Smith served as the original producer for *Probe*. Two years later, on October 20, 1976, *Probe* reported on conflicts of interest involving State Senator Bill Burgin, influential chairman of the state senate appropriations committee and a member of the state college board. Burgin, a fiscal conservative, had saved the state millions of dollars but at the same time had reaped huge legal fees by representing clients before state agencies in his capacity as an attorney, WLBT reported. Burgin's positions gave him clout over state agencies' budgets, so those agencies were receptive to his requests for his clients. His law partner also received a contract to construct a dormitory.

"I said to the staff to take a good hard look at this man," Dilday recalled. "Anybody who has that many conflicts must have stepped over the line somewhere. This man hated us." The program showed a series of conflicts, and the federal government investigated Burgin. He resigned.[41]

That thirty-minute *Probe* won a George Foster Peabody Award for meritorious public service, broadcasting's equivalent of the Pulitzer Prize. It was one of twenty-four programs nationwide to win the award that year, along with ABC's coverage of the 1976 Olympics and a segment of CBS's *60 Minutes*. WLBT was one of only three commercial stations in the country to receive the award that year and the first commercial station in Mississippi ever to achieve such an accolade. The National Peabody Advisory Board called the WLBT broadcast "an example of greatly needed documentary reporting in an area seemingly untouched in the recent past."[42]

CII made changes in the broadcast industry in Jackson and the South, Dilday believed. "I wanted to promote our news very heavily, and that meant that the other station finally got time to promote its news as well." He also put the first black male and white female anchor team on the air in the South, Walter Saddler and Marsha Halford. He wanted the historically black colleges to receive the same sports coverage as the historically white colleges. "We covered Jackson State, and that started to build up our viewership." Some people complained that the black schools were getting too much coverage. "I suppose if you've been getting it all and then it is reduced, you think the other fellow is getting too much," Dilday added.

"We had some very bright young people on our staff and we just turned them loose," Dilday said. "We told them get your facts right. If you do that, we'll put it on the air."[43]

Walter Saddler was one of the young people who helped change the coverage at WLBT. A native of Madison County northeast of Jackson, Saddler had majored in business administration at St. John's

University in Jamaica, New York, graduating in 1970. He worked at an all-news radio station, WINS, in New York while he was in college and shortly afterward. He returned to Mississippi because he didn't want to spend his life in New York and got a job at WLBT. He anchored the early morning newscast at 6:45 A.M. and thought he was awful. He was in his early twenties and had "a severe case of nerves and anxiety. I didn't come with a whole lot of personal experience in the TV arena. I made up my mind that it was something I liked and I would learn how to do it."

Saddler had to deal with some obstacles. One engineer, for example, "would leave me with an unexpected minute and a half [of airtime] just as my newscast was to start" by failing to play the public service announcements usually used when there were no commercials. "I wasn't too stable anyway when I started. This would happen two out of three mornings." He was hesitant to report it but finally did tell the news director and the harassment stopped.

After anchoring the news, Saddler spent the middle of the day reporting, which he considered his strong suit. He tangled often with the mayor because WLBT focused on the lack of any black department heads then in Jackson city government. "There were still pockets of segregation in many places, especially in the rural areas, but even some in the city. We looked at those. We looked at allegations of police brutality."

For the first time, no areas were sacrosanct. "Our job was to question, question, question and to push and probe and not accept political answers. If they weren't going to give us answers, then we'd put that on the air. We got reaction from both the white and black communities. There were a lot of people in town who knew things were wrong and wanted to see them corrected."

Still, he received hate calls. "I always got hostile reaction. I always got hate calls. Some at home, some when I was covering stories." Twice he was really frightened. "I was in one of the smaller towns . . .

and we weren't allowed in the courthouse even though it was a public place. We were really threatened. There was this big deputy standing there on the step with guns and there I was, one little guy with
a microphone saying that it was a public building and we had a right
to go in. [Citing] the law didn't play well in small towns in those
days." The other time he was with the Reverend Emmett Burns, an
NAACP leader, surveying stores in Carthage outside of Jackson to
see how many blacks were employed. Although blacks were expected
to shop there, the stores hired no black cashiers, indeed few black
employees at all. Burns and Saddler drew many hostile comments.

Once Saddler and photographer Tom Alexander, also from
Madison County, went to Canton to check whether votes there were
being fairly counted. A number of black candidates were running,
and some might have a chance of winning. "There was always an air
of secrecy in Canton elections," Saddler said. "Our effort was to get in
for the first time and see what was going on and if it was being done
fairly," but the head of the election commission tried to have them
thrown out. The commissioners believed they weren't required to give
a public accounting, and the commission head called the chairman of
the board at the station, who backed the reporters.

"The other station wasn't as aggressive in covering the news. Those
were tension-filled days. That was the kind of story nobody else
would have covered. . . . We didn't ask anybody. We just grabbed the
equipment and went. Nobody else was there." Saddler thought that
black candidates were often cheated during the vote-counting
process, especially in Canton. Because the election commissioner
would not let the pair from WLBT inside the building, Alexander
focused his camera on an upstairs room lit by a bare lightbulb. The
film told the story that the public was excluded.

The late 1960s and 1970s were an era when journalists around the
country chafed at some of the restrictions and inequities of their

profession. They petitioned employers to hire more minority journalists, and they met on their own to discuss their writing or production work. Journalists in Jackson were no exception. Saddler and Alexander were leaders of Project Media, a group of black journalists in Jackson radio, television, and newspaper work established in 1975. Alexander spearheaded the group, Saddler said. He was "politically ahead of his time. He was aggressive, gung ho, kind of pulled me along. . . . We wanted to make black journalists sensitive to the position they had and the role that they carried. For the first time we cut across station lines. There was a tendency for Channel 3 people to stick with Channel 3 people, 12 with 12, and so on. We had an opportunity to discuss work situations, job opportunities, key news stories that we were all covering, issues that were prevalent at that time, like race, equity, justice." They also helped their news organizations recruit minority journalists and technicians.[44]

Outside WLBT, the impact of the station's new outlook and additional black staff members was clear as well. Robert Clark, who in 1967 became the first black person elected to the state legislature since Reconstruction, said that the only time African Americans got any coverage, it was negative. "Even in 1967 when I first ran, I had to threaten to call the FCC to even get coverage of my campaign. After they lost the license and had a change of leadership, then it was at that stage when African Americans began to get other than negative coverage."

When Clark was first elected, "they didn't give me negative coverage or positive. They gave me no coverage. The newspapers then were negative. The only way I could get coverage was to call a press conference." He was working on such issues as education—compulsory school attendance, early childhood education—and economic development, areas in which TV viewers might be interested. "If you had a demonstration or a press conference, you could always get coverage. This was the way the message could get to the community."[45]

Reuben Anderson, a Jackson attorney who later became the first black justice on the Mississippi Supreme Court, encountered the same lack of coverage when he ran for Jackson city commissioner in the late 1960s. WLBT would cover those candidates it wanted in office. "Fairness was what we experienced after CII took over. They started to cover issues important to the minority community that had never been covered before." It wasn't that the new group would support candidates but, Anderson added, "they covered everybody. That hadn't happened before."[46]

Stories in long-uncovered areas or about people who never received coverage could have tangible benefits. Once Dilday sent Saddler and Alexander to the small Delta town of Mayersville to interview Unita Blackwell, who had just been elected as the first black female mayor in the nation. Long a civil rights activist, Blackwell was turning her considerable energy into improving her hometown, which suffered from the same poverty that stunted most Delta communities. "We were out front of the county courthouse—you know how they have you posed—and they were asking me what the town needed," Blackwell said. "I was telling them that we didn't have anything—that we needed a fire truck. Just then a fire broke out in somebody's house and the people were running around trying to save their house. It wasn't a canned thing; it was just a coincidence." But the fire was on film, and Mayersville received a government grant to buy its fire truck.[47]

Years after the interim operators were gone from the WLBT scene, I asked some of its personnel and local activists to sum up the results they thought this change in management and outlook had brought. Said former station manager William Dilday: "By covering the things that we did, we opened up a lot of politics to people. We showed them the things that happened in the state legislature. We gave people a knowledge of state government they'd never had. We gave people an understanding of what county governments did. We made people much more aware of their government and we made the elected officials more accountable."[48]

There were psychological results as well. Rims Barber, a white Presbyterian minister who had moved from Iowa to Mississippi in the 1960s, was working at the time for the Delta Ministry. It was affiliated with the National Council of Churches and sought social and economic change in the Delta, one of the state's poorest regions. Many Mississippians at that time would say they didn't want to get involved in "that mess," meaning civil rights activity. "Once it was on TV every evening at 6 or 10 P.M., it was no longer 'that mess,'" Barber said. "That was real. That was the significant impact" of the changes at WLBT.

"I'm not an expert on the sociology of it all but it does make a difference to how people react to each other in public. If there's a black candidate, it's not as scary because you watch a black anchor on TV," Barber added. Until WLBT's coverage of the black community changed, people saw life as something that happened to them rather than something they created, he said. "The job of an organizer was to help people see that they could make change. When there are cultural influences around that work against that—that's the old Channel 3— then the job is that much harder. With the changes, people could say, 'Yes, it is real. I can hope. I can believe. I can think that something will change.'"[49]

L. C. Dorsey also explained the meaning of the changes at WLBT in movement terms. She had grown up in a sharecropping family in the Delta and worked on a plantation herself. Later she enrolled her children in a Head Start program and found the encouragement there to earn a doctorate in social work. By the time she served on the CII board in the late 1970s, she was working with the Southern Coalition on Jails and Prisons trying to improve conditions for those who were incarcerated. Dorsey remembered the days when she had been, by her own description, a foot soldier in the civil rights movement, going from door to door, farm to farm, to get people to summon the courage to register to vote.

"The political struggle was dependent on communications to reach all of its factions," Dorsey recalled. Without any news on television, activists had to rely on mimeographing flyers that people carried in their cars—slow, tedious, and inefficient efforts. The only black newspaper, the *Jackson Advocate*, was struggling for survival. Civil rights workers in the Delta tried to buy time on the radio station but couldn't. "Once the news broadcasts changed, you were able to communicate with the people about the progress or lack thereof" on issues they cared about. "We watched the impact of access to communication on the political process—on schools, on housing."[50]

By the late 1990s Robert Clark, whose activities were so rarely covered when he first ran for office, had become the president pro tem of the Mississippi House of Representatives. One of the legislature's most senior members, he leaned back in his chair in his small office off the House floor and reflected on what the changes at WLBT had meant beyond politics. They "gave African Americans the assurance that they were somebody after having been taught for so long and for generations that they were inferior. They saw black folk on television speaking to issues that they had only heard white folk speak to. The only place they had heard blacks speak was in church. And there they were talking about going to heaven, wearing golden slippers and a white robe. They found out black folk could speak to issues here on Earth."[51]

Earle Jones, the businessman who had been on the CII board the entire time it ran WLBT, felt that there were two areas of particular achievement for its management, one specific, the other more general. "The epitome was to get the Peabody Award for *Probe*. We started with a small audience and built it. The second thing was participating in the hiring and proof that blacks can do the job. That was something larger than WLBT. That was the greatest part of it. That broke the barrier for a lot of businesses" in the area and showed them what black people could do.[52]

Walter Saddler, part of this evolution in news for so many years, put it another way. "We opened up the airwaves to a diversity of views and opinions. People may not have always agreed but we established some common ground and then we could build on that." They covered issues of equity, he said: "Why there were paved roads in the white community and dirt roads in the black community. Why should that be? . . . We served as the eyes and ears of the people who had to go to work during the day. You don't see a lot of that today. We pushed and prodded and put the answers out there to show what was and wasn't going on." In hindsight, Saddler said, the changes contributed to a climate of greater expectations. People started asking more of their politicians.

Without the license challenge, Saddler was asked, would all this have happened? "In time it would have happened" he replied, "but not as quickly and not as peacefully." Saddler saw a genuine relationship between the races in Jackson, unlike any he saw anywhere else. "What the media did in this town was help bridge that gap in understanding. We needed that intermediary. We could not have sat down and talked about these issues without it."[53]

For most of the 1970s, then, CII ran—and dramatically altered— WLBT. From a station that had editorialized against opening the University of Mississippi to a black student, WLBT ten years later declared itself against vetoing money that would have gone to a health center in an all-black town. The question remained whether the station could maintain this momentum when it changed hands again.

7. THE STRUGGLE FOR CONTROL

No matter how sweeping, the changes at WLBT in the 1970s could have become only a footnote, albeit a historic one. Maintaining the station's new look was by no means assured. That depended on who won the fight over the permanent license.

In the early 1970s when the new licensing effort began, Jackson was still divided racially. Groups that had the money to assemble experienced broadcasters and pay attorneys in order to apply for the license at the Federal Communications Commission often were not racially integrated. Groups that might maintain the station's integrated management and programming might not have had the money to sustain what would become a long, and at times nasty, battle to win at the FCC. One reporter described it as a "mudball fight in a small room."[1] The license battle would also occur in the context of changing national politics, that is, white backlash against civil rights gains for blacks. With a television license on the line, the financial and political stakes were high—everyone involved knew that—but no one had any idea that the fight they were entering would last almost a decade.

That Lamar Life Broadcasting would contend for the permanent license was a given. The land, building, and equipment it owned at

WLBT were worth more than $2 million by its own estimate—
perhaps as much as $20 million, others said.[2] WLBT consistently led
in ratings and ad sales. Lamar was a fixture in the community, and
its pride was at stake. The federal court of appeals had threatened
its existence—unfairly, Lamar officials felt. No one else might have
moved into the contest against Lamar had not Aaron Henry, one of
WLBT's challengers, and a group of fellow investors calling themselves Civic Communications Corporation sought the permanent
license. This group, which included blacks and whites, had strong civil
rights links that concerned more moderate whites. Civic's entry into
the license fight propelled others from Jackson to form groups to seek
the license—Democrats, Democrats about to become Republicans,
and Republicans, as one participant described them.

Consider, for instance, Channel 3, Inc., a group Robert Travis assem-
bled. A congenial man, Travis had grown up in Belhaven, an older section
of Jackson near Millsaps and Belhaven Colleges. R. L. T. Smith had
been the mail carrier in his neighborhood. Travis, a University of
Mississippi graduate and a lawyer, saw the possibilities WLBT offered.
From the language in the appeals court decision in 1969, it seemed
obvious to Travis and others that someone other than Lamar was
going to win the license. "None of our group would have pushed to
get Lamar removed. These were people who would not have gotten
involved in that. If I was going to be a part of taking something away
from Lamar, I wasn't going to do it," Travis said. But the entry of Civic
"spurred our group particularly—we felt, 'We are more representative
than they are.' We felt that the station would be in better hands with
us than it would be with Civic. Civic was the diametric opposite of
Lamar. Civic was definitely a civil rights group. That was not a popular thing with a lot of white people then." Civil rights activity "irri-
tated the hell" out of many white people, he added.

Everyone, Travis said, "knew that Lamar lost its license because
it didn't do the job required under the regulations. We had to do

something different. . . . We hoped to bring a representative group of blacks and whites together to run a business. There was no business like that in Jackson in that day."[3]

Five groups contested the license: Lamar; Civic; Channel 3; Dixie National Broadcasting, which included several prominent Mississippi Republican leaders; and Jackson Television, Inc. All had some black participation, although in several cases only token. Aaron Henry later expressed surprise at seeing so many groups come forward with minority members who had stood on the sidelines during the earlier challenge.[4]

Lamar remained a contender for the permanent license because it still ran the station, because of its status in Jackson, because it still had Arnold & Porter as counsel, and because its parent insurance company was by then headed by Robert Hearin, one of the wealthiest men in Mississippi. He had joined United Gas Company after graduating from the University of Alabama in 1939 and worked as a leasing agent in Alabama and Mississippi, then served with the navy during World War II. Later he became vice chairman of First National Bank in Jackson, then its president.[5] It was Hearin, according to Jackson attorney Reuben Anderson, who had directed that Fred Beard be fired and who wanted to improve the station. But, said Anderson, "that station was so bad, there was no way to cleanse it in our lifetime. No matter what Mr. Hearin did, he couldn't have changed the image. Too much damage was done."[6]

On January 29, 1970, Lamar, still running the station, filed its new application, saying that it would have 10.5 percent of its airtime devoted to news and 4.2 percent to public affairs. It had established a community advisory group in 1967 and had polled a variety of community members about local needs, people like Reuben Anderson, Hazel Brannon Smith, Ken Dean, Charles Evers, and author and professor Margaret Walker Alexander. It had six blacks in white-collar jobs, or 8.2 percent of those posts. That compared with 1.1 to 2.1 percent employed at the networks in New York, it pointed out. Lamar also pledged not to sidestep hot issues. "We could, as many do, simply avoid anything controversial—that's the safe way," its application said. "But it is also the blind way, for it ignores both reality and responsibility. There will always be differences of opinions, honest ones. That's what freedom is all about."[7]

The group that had motivated the others to contest the license— Civic Communications—was put together by Weyman H. D. Walker, a young white Texan who had long been fascinated by television. The medium had, as Warren Burger had written in his appeals court decision, infinite power in American life to change the way people think. Walker recognized that influence. His uncle, Paul Walker, had been an FCC member under Presidents Roosevelt and Truman from 1934 to 1953, the last fourteen months as commission chairman.[8] Even in his early twenties, Walker knew that he wanted to be in television and had considered seeking a license near Galveston but decided against it. By the late 1960s he was running a television station in Meridian, Mississippi, and had struck up a friendship with Charles Young, a black cosmetics manufacturer who was active locally in the NAACP. Through Young, he met the state NAACP president, Aaron Henry. Walker had aired an integrated children's program on his Meridian station well before *Our Playmates* debuted on WLBT. He had also invited many black and white leaders to appear on *Hot Line*, a call-in show.

"It wasn't that I went in there to put blacks on the air but they were out there and needed to be invited along with everybody else," Walker remembered. "I didn't go there as a social reformer. It was just the right thing to do . . . . Forty percent of the people in Mississippi were black. They had children who would like to be on TV, too."

Black Mississippians had modest aims as far as WLBT was concerned, simply wanting some changes made at the station, Walker said, but he thought that they could take it over. He and Charles Young drove to Clarksdale to see Aaron Henry about organizing a group to apply for the license, then left at 4 A.M. to see Charles Evers in Fayette. They had no money, just an idea.[9] To raise the money, Walker went to Walter Hall, a white banker in the Galveston area. Hall was conservative in his banking practices but liberal politically, supporting Democratic senator Ralph Yarborough and President Lyndon Johnson.

Together they sought guidance from Martin Firestone, a former FCC attorney who had earlier advised Walker against establishing the Galveston station. Firestone said that when he met Hall, the decision ordering new applications for the WLBT license had not yet been handed down, so they were talking about taking on an incumbent license holder. Firestone told Hall that it could take three or four years to go through a comparative hearing and gave him a dollar figure of about $150,000 to $175,000, exclusive of appeals.[10] Hall eventually spent far more than that. He normally did not invest outside his areas of expertise, which were banking, insurance, and real estate, or outside of Texas, but he agreed to back the group. "I put up the money because I was the one who had it," Hall said. "I thought it was wrong for that station to mistreat the blacks that way." Hall lent all the principals the money for their shares and also paid Firestone's legal fees for ten years.[11]

Civic Communications consisted of Walter Hall, Weyman Walker, Aaron Henry, Charles H. Young, Charles Evers, Hodding Carter III, and Patricia Derian, who had been active in keeping the Jackson public schools open as other whites resisted school desegregation orders. Like Aaron Henry, Young would later be elected to the state legislature.

Robert Travis and Reuben Anderson organized Channel 3, Inc. The group had nine whites and six blacks on its board. Included were

James E. Fowler of Jackson, who ran a Buick dealership and was active in insurance and real estate; Dr. John A. Peoples Jr., president of Jackson State University; Dr. A. B. Britton; Robert L. T. Smith Jr., supermarket owner and son of the Reverend R. L. T. Smith; and Mary Hendrick, wife of a Jackson doctor.

Hendrick said that she knew she had been selected to be in the group because its organizers needed a white woman with some civil rights activity. She had worked on keeping the public schools open and was president of the YWCA when it was desegregated. "It was very frightening here in those times," she recalled. She had also hosted a group created by the National Council of Negro Women in Washington that brought black and white women from the North to Jackson to show moral support for local women during Freedom Summer in 1964. Hendrick was a fifth-generation Mississippian, originally from Oxford, who had moved to Jackson in 1948 when her husband established a pediatrics practice. She had not expected to be involved in a TV station, but once she signed on she hoped that it would "be absolutely the best, most open TV station anywhere."[12]

Channel 3 proposed to run news and public affairs programming as almost 15 percent of its schedule. It had surveyed community leaders—making a special effort, it said, to contact the black community. That survey had, not unsurprisingly, shown that people considered school integration and race relations to be Jackson's most pressing problems.[13]

Dixie National's moving forces were William D. Mounger, an independent oil producer and real estate developer, and attorney Rubel Phillips, who had been the Republican candidate for governor in 1963 and 1967. The group also included Talmadge Portis Jr., an employee of the Mississippi Employment Security Commission who would help run the station if Dixie National won the license.[14] Phillips, a lawyer who represented Dixie National Life Insurance Company, said the broadcasting group was formed once it became likely that Lamar, run by a competing insurance company, wouldn't retain the WLBT license. "We thought our chances were as good as anyone else's."[15]

Mounger, a 1948 graduate of the U.S. Military Academy at West Point who served in the Air Force just after it was created, would be the president of WLBT if Dixie National won the license. "It was exciting because if you're head of the number one television station in an area, it gives you a role in the community," he said. He had already done well financially, and this was a new arena for him—and a chance to be part of the entertainment industry. Mounger, who had been deeply involved in Richard Nixon's presidential campaign, said that he wanted the station to have balanced policies—not have it fall over onto one side or another. "I didn't envision taking over to try to make it a right-wing station."[16]

Dixie National said it would use 5 percent of its airtime for news and another 2 percent for public affairs. As with Channel 3, Dixie said that its survey of community leaders and other Jackson residents had shown that communication between the races was the area's great problem. It proposed one program dealing exclusively with black culture, put on by black personnel.

The fifth group, Jackson Television, included businessman Alvin P. Flannes; Dr. Robert Smith; businessman Sydney Geiger; and the retired president of Jackson State University, Jacob L. Reddix. Flannes later played a key role in negotiations aimed at settling the case. Born in Wisconsin in 1917, he moved to Jackson in 1962 and started the Wholesale Industrial Pipe and Supplies company. He became actively involved in civic affairs, serving on the board of Goodwill Industries in Mississippi, working with the Natchez Trace Parkway Association, and helping determine how the state could establish a comprehensive mental health center in Jackson.[17] Jackson Television's format would devote 12.3 percent of its airtime to news and 5.7 percent to public affairs. School integration, race relations, and housing topped the list of concerns revealed in its community survey.[18]

Once the appeals court issued its decision in June 1969 requiring competition for the license, there was a flurry of legal action aimed at clarifying that ruling or heading off its mandate. On July 7 Lamar asked the court to rehear the appeal, arguing that the record did not support the court's apparent grounds for reversing the FCC, which had voted to renew Lamar's license. Furthermore, "if the court meant to direct the commission to deny the WLBT renewal license, its action would be a grossly unwarranted invasion of the administrative function, more than warranting a rehearing."[19] That same day, the FCC also asked for a rehearing or clarification, arguing, too, that the court had exceeded its authority.[20]

The court denied the petitions on September 5, 1969. Judges Carl McGowan and Edward Tamm wrote that the court had not inappropriately taken upon itself a decision that supposedly should lie only with the FCC, that is, the denial of the license renewal application. Had that been the court's purpose, the judges said, it would not have contemplated that the licensee could be one of the competing applicants. What the court had decided, they added, was that the proceedings had been "hopelessly bungled" and the public interest would be best served by getting on with a new hearing. The judges said that Lamar had not in over six years established that it should continue to hold a valuable public asset. The court put most of the blame for delays in the case on what it considered commission ineptitude.[21]

More skirmishes followed. On September 10, 1969, WLBT's lawyers asked the court to stay its mandate pending the station's request that the Supreme Court consider the case.[22] The Office of Communication of the United Church of Christ predictably opposed the motion, saying on September 16 that the public interest had already been harmed by the delays. "Thousands of small black children have become teenagers while government agencies have dragged out proceedings to give them equal access to this public channel. Meanwhile, Lamar has made profits in the hundreds of thousands of dollars."[23]

On September 17 Lamar withdrew its motion to stay the mandate, having decided not to appeal the case to the Supreme Court.[24] Lamar's attorneys may have decided it would be unwise to challenge Burger's appeals court opinion when he was then sitting as chief justice. Or it simply might have been clear that in an administrative proceeding such as this, the Supreme Court would not hear a case that had no pressing constitutional issue.

In December 1969 the FCC threw out its grant of the WLBT license to Lamar, inviting other groups to file applications to operate on Channel 3.[25] Once again Lamar protested, asking the commission to reconsider its requirement that it file a new application. Its protest went nowhere.[26]

On May 4, 1970, the FCC ordered a hearing on which of the five proposals to run WLBT would best serve the public. That FCC order opened the starting gate for a contest in which each applicant sought to raise the most questionable aspects of the others' proposed operations that it could. The lawyers kept busy trying to broaden the issues their opponents had to address while attempting to reduce their own clients' vulnerability.

Civic, for example, wanted to enlarge the issues by bringing up WLBT's performance between 1961 and 1964.[27] Another contender, Channel 3, Inc., asked the FCC to consider whether Civic actually had available a loan of $900,000 to operate the station, contending that Walter Hall did not have the legal authority to commit his bank to such a loan. Channel 3 attorney Forbes Blair also questioned Hall's proposed loans to Civic's other participants, loans apparently being made because they lacked sufficient resources to be involved otherwise. Channel 3 felt that with Hall a stockholder himself, his dealings with the other subscribers were not sufficiently at arm's length.[28] The next month, Hall filed an affidavit outlining how the $900,000 commitment would be met by restructuring the loan and offering it through five banks in which he was the controlling stockholder. What he had done was, in his experience, consistent with banking practices under Texas laws.[29]

Channel 3, Jackson Television, and Dixie National were all questioning how much financial control—and thus policy control—Hall would have. This question bothered the Reverend Everett Parker as well, although the United Church of Christ had no direct role in the comparative hearing. Parker said later that he didn't completely trust Hall. Told that many years afterward, Hall said he understood. Chuckling, he added: "I wouldn't have trusted me, either."[30]

The nature of the contest changed markedly on September 8, 1970, when the FCC selected Communications Improvement, Inc. (CII) to operate WLBT while it determined the permanent licensee. Not only was Lamar having to compete for the license that it had held since 1953, now it was no longer the incumbent. On December 24, 1970, an FCC review board agreed with Civic's argument that the federal court of appeals had in effect held that there had not been a proper resolution of the issues initially raised against WLBT. Therefore, it expanded the issues in the comparative hearing to determine whether WLBT: had afforded reasonable opportunity for discussion of conflicting views on issues of public importance between 1961 and 1964; had acted in good faith with respect to presenting programs dealing with racial discrimination; had misrepresented this programming to the public or the FCC; and had the qualifications to hold the license. These issues sounded remarkably like those the hearing examiner was supposed to resolve in 1967 but that the appeals court found he had not. No wonder this case went on and on.

Civic had also requested that the hearings consider how each group learned of the needs of the community and thus whether its programming would be responsive to those needs. The review board agreed to add such an issue. Civic had promised more locally produced public affairs programs than any other applicant, the board noted, in an attempt to explore topics such as race relations and school desegregation. Because the review board believed that this indicated unusual attention to local community matters, it said there should be further inquiry to determine any differences among the applicants.

The review board added that Hall's affidavit sufficiently clarified Civic's financial status by showing that he did have authority to commit his banks to the loans needed to operate the station. But the board added that Civic would have to show whether it had misrepresented to the FCC whether it in fact had a $300,000 mortgage loan commitment. This would later prove an important element in the case.[31]

Hearings began April 5, 1971, under the direction of administrative law judge Lenore Ehrig. Ehrig, who was born in New York City and whose family later moved to Baltimore, was a graduate of George Washington University and in 1951 had received her law degree there as well. She had been practicing before the FCC as part of a small law firm for about ten years. Then, with two young children, she decided that life in private practice required too many long hours, so she joined the FCC staff in the late 1960s. When she retired from the FCC, she was its chief administrative law judge.[32] Martin Firestone described Ehrig as "very businesslike." She had before her the example of the court's criticism of the way Jay Kyle handled the hearing, Firestone said, adding that "all the stuff Kyle didn't let in on WLBT, she let in."[33] Rubel Phillips called her "exceedingly intelligent, exceedingly fair."[34]

Among the first witnesses for Lamar Life was station manager Bob McRaney Jr., still at WLBT working for the interim operator. He talked about the programs he helped develop, especially for coverage of the black community. Over the next few days other station employees appeared, as did part-owner Robert Hearin, who said he had joined the station's board in 1960 and took a more active role after

1963. "We were conscious of criticism of the station and we wanted to respond to it," he said. "As a result, over this period of time we completely changed the board of the station and the management," naming McRaney to replace Beard.[35]

John D. Murchison, the wealthy Texan who was one of the majority owners, testified that he received reports on the broadcasting operation through Hearin or former president of the company P. K. Lutken, who had died in 1969. Murchison said he had attended the board meeting in 1970 when the station's new policy statement outlining its principles had been approved. Murchison's testimony was followed by a variety of local civic leaders, speaking, as others had done at the 1967 hearing, about their positive dealings with the station.

For the rest of the month, Jackson Television, Channel 3, and Dixie National witnesses testified about their backgrounds and the roles they might play if their group received the license. For example, Talmadge Portis Jr., who was black, would have been in top management had Dixie National secured the license. He said that he had no previous television experience. Margaret Walker Alexander, the noted black novelist who had written *Jubilee*, a Civil War novel about her grandmother, was also a member of the Dixie National group. Alexander, a professor of English at Jackson State University, said that she had suggested the group create a program called *Voices* about black history, drama, and "any phase of the black world which needs expression."[36]

On May 6, 1971, Rubel Phillips appeared at the hearing. His testimony would later play a pivotal role in the fight over the WLBT license and show how even what seemed the minutest of details could alter cases at the FCC. As part of Dixie National's application, he had submitted a statement of his business connections. Was there anything in that statement, Dixie National's attorney Joseph F. Hennessey asked, that Phillips wanted to change? Phillips had said that he was a vice president of Stirling Homex Corporation, a company that made modular housing. But he had not taken that office, he testified. "I do represent the company as an attorney, but I am not an officer."[37] This statement meant nothing to Civic's attorney Martin Firestone at the time, but later it would trigger an investigation that changed the case's outcome.

As the hearing continued, a bombshell burst on the Civic group, set off by one of its own members. Charles Evers published a memoir, *Evers*, in which he revealed that he had engaged in bootlegging and paying off the police when he lived in Chicago. And he had run a brothel while he was in the military in the Philippines. "The fellows wanted to see the young ladies and I tried to provide them with what they wanted," Evers wrote. "It was a good business." Evers also admitted to numbers-running when he lived in Chicago.[38] In an article in the *Washington Post*, Evers was quoted as saying that all of these activities had occurred long ago and that he had done nothing like that since. The statute of limitations had run out on all his self-confessed crimes, he insisted.[39]

But character matters, said the four other contending groups. They asked the FCC review board to add an issue against Civic because of Evers's admission of illegal conduct.[40] In July the FCC review board granted the request, saying that the commission was concerned with the past conduct of those to whom it entrusted broadcast licenses. The board added, however, that Civic should be allowed to refer to countervailing circumstances in Evers's background, including his "subsequent adherence to law and exemplary conduct."[41]

As Civic's attorneys were dealing with that self-inflicted wound, another critical question arose, one that would also affect the group's application, showing yet again the intricacy of concerns involved in FCC cases. Civic's opponents asked whether it indeed had a mortgage commitment when its application was being prepared. It did not,

Civic's organizer Weyman Walker testified. He had looked at the documents other groups had filed and saw that a Jackson bank had offered Channel 3 mortgage financing. He assumed that since the two groups were going to operate the same kind of network-affiliated station if either received the license, they would be given the same financing, which was not necessarily the case. When Civic laid out its financial plan in its application, it said in a footnote that it included payment on a mortgage. How that would be interpreted—whether it was saying it had a mortgage commitment or was simply planning for one—would prove critical.[42]

At times the attorneys were testy with one another. For example, Patricia Derian, a Civic shareholder, was being questioned by Reed Miller, Lamar's lawyer, when she started talking about the Freedom Bookstore that had been in WLBT's lobby. How, she was asked, had she known it was in the lobby? "I went there and looked at it. I went there and talked to Fred Beard about it. I was shocked it was there." She added that she had bought some items. Miller, who had objected to discussing the ultraconservative bookstore during the Jackson hearings, objected again. "A bookstore has many books and I am sure she could have gotten the same books at Brentano's or seen them at the Library of Congress if she went to look at them."

Civic's attorney Firestone countered that it was relevant that a station having problems with race relations had promoted such a store on its premises. "I think this is a little more than a generalized statement that the same books can be bought at Brentano's. Brentano's is not a licensee of the Federal Communications Commission."[43]

Firestone wanted to show that WLBT had not covered the news as fairly as it said it had in the early 1960s and that it had not used courtesy titles for blacks, an issue that kept cropping up but was of great importance to blacks offended by their omission. Firestone knew that this was a new proceeding with a new record in front of an examiner new to the case, and he was determined to score whatever points against Lamar that he could on this issue.

To back up his argument, he had requested copies of news articles read on the air. One afternoon at about 4:30, he said, Reed Miller dumped about three thick volumes of papers on the hearing-room table. The material included many years of news scripts. Leafing through the volumes later, Firestone found some material that he raised in questioning both WLBT's news director, David Mieher, and its former news director, Richard Sanders.

Mieher said WLBT announcers used the broadcast scripts as they came off the wires. If the copies that Firestone had contained penciled-in editing, then that was what had been read. One of these edited scripts referred to Aaron Henry only by his first name on second reference. "That was incorrect usage," Mieher said. "I would hope that whoever read it corrected it on the air."[44]

Later Firestone asked Sanders about the editing on news copy about Autherine Lucy's unsuccessful attempt to desegregate the University of Alabama in 1956. Demonstrations followed her arrival on campus after she had won a federal court case to try to become the first black student admitted. "Look at the last paragraph, for instance," Firestone said. "Can you read through the strikeout? What does it say in that portion that has been stricken?"

"It says, 'Miss Lucy's . . . ,' " Sanders replied.

"And what is the printed word above?" Firestone asked.

"Autherine."

"And that is the first name of Miss Autherine Lucy?"

"Yes, sir."

"And can you tell whether this editing was done at WLBT-TV?"

"Well, it came out of my files."

Several other stories were similarly edited. In addition, instead of "Miss Lucy," the words "the Negro" had been inserted. In another place, her name was removed and "the Negro woman" was inserted.[45]

The hearings moved into the fall of 1971 with testimony by Charles Evers, who had been a losing gubernatorial candidate in the Mississippi election that November. One of the attorneys asked him whether he realized the seriousness of the inquiry into Civic's character because of his illegal activities. "No, I really don't," Evers replied. "I am a great believer in the Bible. My momma taught me a long time ago that a man should be forgiven 70 times 7. I wrote this and I explained it. No one asked me to do this. I did this because I wanted to change and be a good man. If I am going to be beat over the head asking the country to forgive me, then I am guilty. That's all I can say." Asked why he thought the FCC should overlook his violations, Evers said, "I think that since 1960 my record speaks for itself. I have been in a legitimate business, and I have done all that I could to make it better for all of the races. And I am still doing that. And I don't know of anything I have done in violation since then."

Civic's attorney Firestone asked Evers how old he had been when he was in bootlegging. Young, Evers replied. He lost his restaurant and his taxi licenses—everything he had—because of his stand on registering and voting. He went to Chicago where he tried to find a job. He had a bachelor's degree in sociology from Alcorn, but people either discriminated openly or told him he was too qualified. Evers worked as a washroom attendant and carried sides of meat at a packing company, and he started finding prostitutes for customers at the hotel to make some money. He returned to Mississippi when his brother, Medgar, was killed. "It was the sort of thing that he and I had agreed upon. We would always keep fighting for the rights of our people in Mississippi. I went away and stayed for five years because I said I was going to make enough money in five years to come back and live without being pressured and put out of business. So my five years was just about up anyway. He was killed, and I came on back—the same day he was killed."[46]

Firestone put Evers's book into the record as evidence. "We believe," he said, "that the book provides the commission with information

concerning the nature of the times, other experiences of the witness," and would give the FCC a proper basis for evaluating Evers's
character.[47]

To counter questions about Evers's character, Civic's attorney
brought in Joseph Rauh, who had represented the Mississippi
Freedom Democratic Party in Atlantic City at the 1964 Democratic
convention. Rauh said Evers's speeches "are the greatest force for
peace and non-violence in the state of Mississippi today."[48] Civil rights
leader Fannie Lou Hamer came from Ruleville, Mississippi, to
Washington, testifying that she had worked with Evers on marches
and voter registration drives. Asked whether she would have continued her association with Evers had she known of the violations he
talked about in his book, Hamer answered: "As the person he is now,
that would have nothing to do with his past, with the way I feel about
him as a man now."[49]

The hearings ended, and early in 1972 all the groups filed their proposed findings. Basically, each argued that it should receive the
license, minimizing the importance of the issues on which it felt weak
and emphasizing what it considered the deficiencies in the other
groups' applications. Then, on April 20, 1973, Ehrig issued a 237-page
order recommending that Dixie National be awarded the license. She
stressed Dixie National's plan to integrate its ownership, black and
white, into operation of the station. She said the group deserved a dis-
tinct preference because of the importance the commission placed on
such operations in securing the best public service. Dixie National,
she said, was the only one of the applicants that would place a black—
Talmadge Portis Jr.—in a full-time, top management post.

No one else measured up in Ehrig's view. She believed that Civic
had misrepresented to the commission the availability of a $300,000
mortgage. She didn't think much of Weyman Walker's background,
either. Civic's application had indicated that he would run the station.

Ehrig wrote that Walker had been dismissed as general manager at the Meridian station after six months on the job "because of his manner of doing business and his failure to keep the other stockholders informed." She added that Walker's performance at that station and what she considered his misrepresentation to the commission about Civic's application did nothing to recommend him as a responsible manager of WLBT.[50] Civic also received a significant comparative demerit because of the character issues raised by Charles Evers's admissions. Although Ehrig said that his recent activities did demonstrate redemption, she still believed that his transgressions were not inadvertent or isolated instances. Furthermore, she said, Evers had flagrantly disregarded commission procedures in refusing to produce tax returns concerning his illegal income. The Internal Revenue Service indicated that he had not filed returns, although he said under oath that he had.[51] Based on these factors, Ehrig disqualified Civic as a prospective licensee.

Turning to Lamar, Ehrig wrote that the Murchison brothers, both Texas residents, were absentee owners whom she considered unresponsive to the needs and interests of the Jackson community. She added that while Lamar had emphasized that McRaney would be the station's general manager, he had left the station by this time, and there was no assurance that he would return to Jackson.[52]

As for the other two applicants, Jackson Television had said six of its stockholders would serve full time at the station, but Ehrig didn't consider that realistic. Two of them were over seventy years old, and the others held time-demanding jobs. Only one, who was not a local resident and had never been active in Jackson's civic life, had any broadcasting experience.[53] As to Channel 3, it had proposed no full-time integration of owners and management, so Ehrig placed its application at the bottom of the ladder in this category. Furthermore, she concluded that the broadcast experience of James Searer,

who would have been Channel 3's station manager, "appears to have
been puffed if not, in fact, misrepresented" at the hearings.[54]

Near the end of her lengthy opinion, Ehrig summed up why she
was awarding the license to Dixie National. "In the years to come,
the people of Mississippi will have to continue to deal with the issue
of racial integration and accommodation. The Dixie application
with Mr. Mounger and Mr. Portis at the station full time, and with
its other stockholders whose social sensitivity has resulted in a flood
of writings by them and the receipt of many awards, will afford the
commission the greatest assurance that the racial issue, as well as other
needs ascertained by the applicant, will be treated openly, forthrightly
and fairly."[55]

Some observers thought that it was no accident that the Republicans were in political power in the White House when the most
Republican of the applicants received the license. It seemed like "a
political fix," Earle K. Moore, the United Church of Christ attorney,
recalled.[56] Interviewed years later, Ehrig said that there had never
been any pressure, direct or indirect, brought to bear on how she
handled the case or decided it. She added that "never once while I was
there did I ever have any commissioner contact me about a case."[57]
Likewise, William Mounger said in an interview that his being a
prominent Republican had nothing to do with Dixie National's
selection.[58] Robert Travis of the Channel 3 group smiled on hearing
that assertion and said he thought it had everything to do with it.[59]

Despite the seeming finality of Ehrig's order, the case was far from
over. Martin Firestone searched for some flaw that would justify
reopening the proceedings, as did the United Church of Christ.

A navy veteran who had graduated from Columbia law school,
Firestone had more than ten years' experience in communications
law at this point. He had joined the FCC staff in November 1960 and
stayed until 1964. The commission then had what Firestone described

as an aggressive regulatory climate under chairmen Newton Minow, who pronounced television "a vast wasteland," and E. William Henry.

Firestone worked in the FCC's renewal branch, which handled licenses and enforced the Fairness Doctrine. He was the staff attorney, for example, on a case involving WRAL-TV in Raleigh, North Carolina, which he said had aired some "horrendous editorials on racial issues" by Jesse Helms, later a U.S. senator, when Helms was the station's executive vice president. Firestone's friend Mike Finkelstein worked on the WLBT case after the investigation by William Ray and John O'Malley turned up enough material to suggest commission action. A few years after both left the commission, Finkelstein and Firestone formed a law partnership.[60]

When Weyman Walker was putting the Civic group together, he wanted Firestone to meet Walter Hall. Firestone found Hall "brusque, abrupt, arrogant. He seemed more interested in what he had to say than in what I had to say. I formed a perception, erroneous, that he was acting like that because he was a big fish in a small pond. A lot of [his attitude] never changed, but I came to realize over time that he was truly committed to this thing. He was running a bunch of banks, yet he came to Washington several times and he was devoting a lot of time to this project."[61]

When I met Walter Hall in League City in 1999, he was almost ninety-two years old. He was in poor health but proved both crusty and a flirt. To all the couples who passed by us at the restaurant at a club he had helped found, Hall would say. "Why did this good lookin' woman marry a guy like you?" They clearly had heard his line many times. I had one more conversation with Hall, at his Clear Rock Ranch in the Texas Hill Country, in July 1999. He died the following March. Columnist Molly Ivins described him as "that wonderful citizen." He was a lovely man, she wrote. "Especially for a banker."[62]

The first question anyone has upon learning of Hall's involvement in the WLBT case is why? Why would a Texas banker finance a case about a Mississippi television station? What was it in his background that led to his concern for the underdog? Hall summed up the reasons: his mother's influence, his early work experience, and several of his courses at Rice University.

Walter Hall was born May 30, 1907, in Houston, the youngest of seven children. His father was a mechanic who worked for many years for the interurban rail line between Houston and Galveston. Hall's mother traded eggs and butter at a local store against the family's account for food purchases, and her analytical skills helped the family through financial crises during the Depression.[63]

Hall learned early about prejudice. When he was eight, he and his mother went to downtown Houston on the streetcar, which had a sign directing whites to the front of the car and "colored" to the back. The conductor was supposed to move the sign, depending on who got on, so that the most people possible could obtain seats. A number of black workmen got on the streetcar. There were empty seats for whites, but the conductor didn't move the sign so the men stood in the back of the streetcar. Young Walter piped up and asked, "Why doesn't that man change the sign?" His mother quietly explained the Jim Crow segregation laws. When they reached downtown, the conductor finally changed the sign. "That demonstrated to me, as an eight-year-old boy, that basic unfairness existed."[64]

Hall attended Rice University, starting in 1924, because it was close to home and tuition free. During the summer he worked for the Humble Pipeline Company as a laborer replacing pipes.[65] His work on the pipeline and later at a clay mine gave him respect for the hard work that many people did to earn a living.

At Rice, he was exposed to philosophy and the history of religions by his favorite professor, Radoslav A. Tsanoff. Tsanoff's courses taught

Hall the value of tolerance. He "was so objective that to this day I don't know what philosophy he espoused," Hall remarked, "nor do I know which religion he followed. As a country boy brought up in the Baptist church, this was a revelation to me."[66] From Tsanoff, Hall said he learned great men could have differences of opinion on important subjects and still be cooperative. "That has been the most important lesson that I learned at Rice."[67] Hall later endowed a public affairs professorship in Tsanoff's name.

During the late 1920s Hall became a Democrat because he said he had had a "bellyful" of President Herbert Hoover. Hall saw many people financially wiped out during the Depression. He had begun work on January 1, 1931, at Citizens State Bank in League City—its only employee. After Franklin D. Roosevelt was inaugurated as president in 1933, he ordered all banks closed to try to save the banking system. Hall did as directed, locking the front door but leaving the back door open because people desperately needed their money. "We cashed small checks for food and medicine all during the bank 'holiday.'" His bank survived because it was small and remained solvent.[68]

During the Depression the Red Cross asked Hall to store its flour for the needy in his bank vault because it was always dry (the Gulf Coast being notoriously damp). "Some of our citizens at first didn't want to be seen carrying Red Cross flour. Some people asked me from time to time to put sacks in the back of my car. I only lived about five blocks from the bank, and they would come by after dark to pick it up."[69]

Long a civic activist, Hall helped residents of Dickinson and League City obtain safe water, establish the local school district, and fight to equalize the tax structure in Galveston County. His determination in that case foreshadowed his tenaciousness in the WLBT fight. His lawyers looked into his concerns that big industries weren't paying a fair share of taxes. They told Hall that lawsuits would be long and difficult. But Hall was serious. When one of his opponents wanted to settle, Hall insisted he would withdraw his lawsuit only if the other side got a court order to equalize the county taxes—and did so with him and the press present. And that's what happened.[70]

Politics was a natural extension of his civic activity. "To tell you that it's pleasant to get out and organize precinct conventions day in and day out for a period of months, year in and year out during election years—that simply would not be true," Hall observed. But he saw no alternative because his community had problems. When he got into a contest, he said, "I don't want the man that I'm supporting or the issue that I'm supporting to come in second."[71]

"Walter didn't leave anything to chance—he was a good vote counter," said Chandler Davidson, retired professor of sociology at Rice University who has written books about Texas politics and who knew Hall well. "He knew what everyone was doing. He was sort of a small-scale Lyndon Johnson" in that respect. Active at the grass roots, Hall "rolled up his sleeves, got down in the mud and got involved in Texas politics." He knew politics from the bottom up rather than the top down and "liked nothing better than a fight."[72]

Hall backed candidates, such as Senator Ralph Yarborough, who he thought supported progressive Democratic programs. Yarborough, the only southern senator to vote for the Civil Rights Act of 1964, served in the Senate for fourteen years and helped expand health care, increase the minimum wage and job training programs, and extend education benefits to Cold War-era veterans. "In my campaigns," Yarborough said, "a $5,000 contribution was a huge contribution. There were only about 10 people who ever gave me that much. [Hall] was one of them."[73]

Being a Texas Democrat, Hall crossed paths often with Lyndon Johnson, backing him in many races. But Hall also disagreed with

Johnson on occasion. New to the Senate, Johnson sent Hall a copy of his first speech in which he supported the filibuster, often used to block civil rights legislation. Hall wrote on the bottom of Johnson's note to him, " 'Dear Lyndon, I'm sorry you think more of your right to speak without limit than you do another man's right to vote,' and I sent it back to him."[74] Hall remained close to the Johnsons once they reached the White House, however, and he and his wife attended several events there. Later he maintained his friendship with Johnson's widow, Lady Bird, whose Hill Country ranch was not far from his. That friendship would play a role in the WLBT case.

He couldn't be fired for his activism, Hall once said, because he owned 51 percent or more of every bank with which he had been connected, and he didn't let politics interfere with his business interests. "My basic concept was that I was a citizen first, a banker second."[75] He proved financially astute, moving his bank in the 1930s from League City to nearby Dickinson, where oil had been discovered. He also entered the real estate and insurance businesses. His wife, Helen, who had been his high school sweetheart, worked for several years as postmaster, so the couple accumulated some savings. In 1943 Hall and a group of other local people bought the Citizens State Bank serving the military's Camp Wallace, where 15,000 to 18,000 people were based. In 1953 Hall bought half of a bank in a nearby wealthy town with large oil and gas reserves. That bank had lent little money, and many of the oilmen used Houston banks as a result. Hall changed that, and the bank prospered. Later, Hall bought land for a shopping center, developed it, operated it for several years, then sold it at a profit. In 1956 he organized a bank again in League City. In 1961, seeing the prospects that the coming of a national space center would offer, he chartered another bank near Houston. (Some in Texas saw Hall's influence with LBJ helping change a bit of prairie into a booming space-industry town, but he always denied it.)[76]

Hall's successes as a capitalist provided the money to keep Civic's interests alive. He bankrolled an investigation Firestone wanted because of questions that arose about the Dixie National presentation to the FCC.

Ehrig's decision awarding the license to Dixie National had astounded everybody, Firestone said, because the other groups did not consider Dixie National the strongest applicant.[77] Others told *Washington Post* reporter William Greider that they considered the fight to be between Civic and Jackson Television. "When Civic became severely tarnished, many expected Jackson TV to win, partly because it has 30 percent black ownership and a balance of moderates," Greider wrote soon after Ehrig's decision. "The opposition assumed the Republican entry was a weak contender because of its heavy political coloring and its small ownership percentage for blacks," about 4 percent. "Everyone agrees that Dixie's three black directors, including novelist Margaret Walker Alexander, have impeccable credentials. But they fear that Mounger and Phillips and Dixie National Insurance Co., an all-white majority, will prevail and gradually the racial integration [at WLBT] would regress," Greider added.

Giving the license to Dixie National would be "like an awful lot of traveling to get back to where you started," said Patricia Derian.[78] Or as Charles Horwitz, a member of the Community Coalition for Better Broadcasting, told the *New York Times* at about the same time, "Dixie National isn't all that community minded. I know a lot of its stockholders and they're old-line Mississippians. If the FCC goes back to its old ways and Dixie gets the license, it might be a step backward, not only for broadcasting here but also for broadcasting all across the country."[79]

Firestone put aside all the material he had on the other groups and concentrated on Dixie National. He wanted to demonstrate to an FCC review board why he believed that Ehrig was in error. It was better to have something factual and definitive rather than to base his argument on a judgment call. In his written testimony for the FCC hearing, Rubel Phillips, a key member of the Dixie National team, said that at one time he was a vice president of Stirling Homex, but at the hearing itself, Phillips said he never took office as vice president but was an attorney for the firm. That change in testimony offered Firestone his opening. He wondered how Phillips could make a mistake in saying he was a vice president and then in another place say he wasn't. The FCC has a rule that applicants must maintain the truth and accuracy of their statements on an ongoing basis. Phillips had not done so, Firestone decided, and no one had looked into it.

He called Walter Hall. "It doesn't look very good for us," Firestone told Hall. "I'm probably grasping at straws." Civic's best hope was to try to maintain the litigation. Hall said what he always said: "Do what you want to do and send me the bill."[80] Firestone knew that although Civic had been disqualified, it could remain involved in the case because it still held the possibility that it could appeal that decision—first to a review board, then to the full FCC, then to the court of appeals, possibly up to the Supreme Court. It could tie the case up in litigation for years. "That was the leverage I had. It was one of the few times in my life that I had real money, money that could finance the case."[81]

The details involved in the legal work that followed may seem arcane, but they are important to understanding the outcome of the case. On such details do station licenses turn—and millions of dollars, dozens of dreams.

Firestone obtained the 1971 annual report for Stirling Homex, a publicly traded company. In it there was a picture of Rubel Phillips, and under his name it said, "vice president, southern operations." Firestone also learned that Stirling Homex had been a high flier on the stock exchange, seeing its stock go from $16.50 a share in February 1970 to $55 before bankruptcy proceedings began in July 1972.[82] Firestone thought the discrepancy about Phillips's relationship with Stirling Homex provided him with sufficient basis to ask the FCC review board, as he did on July 20, 1973, to send the case back to Ehrig.[83] The FCC always took seriously any misrepresentation, Firestone said. It didn't matter so much what was lied about, rather the fact that there was a lie.

The Office of Communication was also in the hunt and had been investigating Phillips's connection to Stirling Homex. Andrew Schwartzman, then a young associate of the church's attorney, Earle K. Moore, did the legwork. He thought that Moore wanted to keep the case alive to give the interim operators of WLBT more time to carry out reforms at the station and to prevent or at least delay what the church considered any "bad guys" from obtaining the permanent license.[84] A month after Civic filed its petition, the church, too, asked that the case be reopened. Its petition discussed a variety of complex securities and loan issues, many of them involving Phillips. It concluded that there was evidence that some Dixie National officials had improperly exploited their political affiliations to obtain favored treatment from government agencies. There was also evidence, the church claimed, that Phillips had participated in deception of investors in Stirling Homex. If that were true, it could disqualify him from being involved with a broadcast licensee. The church's petition stated that in 1971 the Mississippi office of the federal Farmers Home Loan Administration (FHLA) had approved a $15 million loan for the Gulf Coast Housing Development Corporation, a nonprofit group that Phillips had set up and that would have used Stirling Homex's modular housing. A copy of the FHLA commitment letter, signed by W. T. Richardson Sr., the deputy state director, was marked in evidence in the Stirling Homex bankruptcy hearing. Moore was clearly raising his eyebrows at how a nonprofit organization could get such a commitment when his petition said its board had never met.[85]

Firestone had found that, under federal law, regional offices couldn't commit the FHLA to loans in excess of $300,000. What, he asked himself, was going on? He went back through the bankruptcy records and found a copy of the loan commitment, which had been signed by W. T. Richardson. Deposing Richardson, he asked him to produce his document. He couldn't. The only one he had was an old application that was not for $15 million. Firestone called Hall, telling him that it looked like major fraud. "Can we get handwriting and document experts in to analyze this document?"

"Do what you have to do," Hall replied, "and send me the bill."

The expert couldn't do much with the handwriting, saying that in all possibility it was a forgery but he couldn't say for sure, Firestone recalled. "It looked like it had been traced from another document."[86]

The FCC review board reopened the case January 11, 1974, saying that Civic had raised serious questions concerning Dixie National's qualifications. Ehrig should hear evidence on whether Dixie National had failed to report fully the relationship of Rubel Phillips with Stirling Homex and whether Dixie National should be disqualified. The board would not, however, reopen the part of the case concerning Weyman Walker's qualifications as Civic had also requested; Firestone considered Ehrig overly harsh on this point. The review board dismissed the church's petition because it was not a party to the case at hand.[87]

Meantime, Civic's partners bought out Evers. He wanted his stock divided between Aaron Henry and Charles Young, so Walter Hall loaned them the money to buy it. "When we won the case," Young said, "we would repay him plus the interest." If they lost, Hall said he would forgive the debt but added that "he had no intention of losing the case." Once again, Everett Parker was skeptical of Hall's role, Young added, and was watching developments closely.[88] As the case dragged on over the next several years, Hodding Carter and Patricia

Derian left Civic's ranks. President Jimmy Carter had named them to posts in the State Department.

Hearings resumed and would grind on for years. Lenore Ehrig granted Firestone's request to take depositions from Rubel Phillips; three government officials from the FHLA, including W. T. Richardson; and Stirling Homex officials. In his deposition that summer, Richardson testified that the signature on the letter approving the $15 million loan was not his "and is, in fact, a forgery," Firestone said in a letter reporting to Ehrig.[89] Firestone was still trying to unravel Phillips's connection with Stirling Homex, and Dixie National's hold on the WLBT license was weakening.

The mudball fight continued, with another issue emerging. The United Church of Christ and the Jackson-based Community Coalition for Better Broadcasting wanted the FCC to investigate charges that William Mounger, president of the Dixie National group, was associated with a private school, Jackson Academy, that discriminated against blacks. They thought this role might reflect badly on Dixie National's ability to operate a TV station. Petitions were filed, denied, and appealed in the chain of legal maneuvering that so often earmarked this case. The commission itself got involved in June 1975, voting to continue keeping the church and the coalition out of the case. Benjamin L. Hooks, the first black member of the FCC, dissented, indicating that he believed the majority had no sense of the national mood or legal precedent. If the United Church of Christ was not entitled to intervene or if the segregated Jackson Academy issue was not ripe for commission attention, Hooks wrote, "then the year is really 1965 and we are all caught in an odious administrative time warp."[90]

The church eventually was permitted to intervene. In February 1976 an FCC review board decided that its charges should be examined. The board found substantial indications that the Jackson

Academy had a racially discriminatory admission policy for which Mounger might be presumed responsible as a board member. Fairness in dealing with racial and religious groups, the board said, was a well-recognized consideration in assessing qualifications to hold a license.[91]

The focus remained on the connection between Rubel Phillips and Stirling Homex because on July 28, 1976, the U.S. District Court in Manhattan indicted Phillips, David Stirling Jr., William G. Stirling, and several others. They were accused of scheming to defraud Stirling Homex shareholders in connection with the sale of securities. One of the charges in which Phillips was named asserted that in 1971 the parties had falsely inflated Stirling Homex's sales and earnings by arranging for a sale of housing modules for $15 million based on "a forged commitment letter."[92]

The pieces fell into place for Firestone. With this indictment, he thought that for all intents and purposes Dixie National was dead. "Now we had the overriding motivation for why Phillips did what he did—and he did it under oath." Firestone believed that Phillips had wanted to distance himself from Stirling Homex's business dealings and so had said he was not a vice president.[93] (Years later, Phillips told me that was not the case—that he had originally told Stirling Homex that he would be a company officer and that he would be available to move to another city. Between the time of the deposition and the time of the testimony, he had changed his mind, and thus changed his statement.)[94]

Civic's opponents' financial interests dictated that they continue to participate in the reopened case, but they were becoming aware that Firestone and Hall weren't going to let the litigation end. "Hall would pay for it all, even if it took seven or eight years," Firestone said.[95]

The case was taking its toll. Lawyers had wrangled over big points—and little—and earned big money for six years. Some of the people in Jackson were tiring of the fight and began to think that the public good, and their own, might be better served by a settlement. Even that effort took years. Talks among several of the groups had occurred as early as 1972, according to Alvin Flannes, president of Jackson Television.[96] A compromise had appeared possible during the summer of 1975. Two of the competing groups—Dixie National and Jackson Television—said that they would join forces so that WLBT would have 25 percent black ownership. Rubel Phillips would not be part of the new organization, removing, as *Broadcasting* magazine put it, a major source of controversy in the case.[97] The possible compromise fell apart by that October out of fears—doubtless justified—that the United Church of Christ would battle any settlement resulting in Dixie National and Jackson Television running WLBT.[98]

By October 1976 there was another attempted settlement, one in which the percentage of black ownership only inched up, dooming it from the start. The five applicants asked the FCC to give the license to a new corporation, TV-3. Blacks would have 31 percent ownership in the new group; there would also be seven black board members. Six women would be stockholders and three on the board of directors. The principal owners would be Alvin Flannes, who would also be president; Dixie National Life Insurance; and William D. Mounger. No members of Civic Communications would own stock. TV-3 proposed to maintain the WLBT staff that was operating the station under CII. Rubel Phillips would not be involved.[99]

Both the FCC's Broadcast Bureau and the United Church of Christ opposed the proposal. The Broadcast Bureau said that there were still issues to be resolved and there was no basis for thinking that granting the petition would shorten the case.[100] The Office of Communication claimed that TV-3 had done little more than parrot the existing public affairs programs being offered by CII. "TV-3 offers at best the same service offered by CII and, at worst, the risk of losing the current level of service."[101]

Dixie National remained the object of its opponents' disaffection. In January 1977 Civic asked the FCC to enlarge the issues in the case to determine whether Phillips had testified falsely in his deposition as part of the WLBT case and whether he had suborned perjury to get W. T. Richardson Sr. to testify falsely in his own deposition. In that FCC deposition, Richardson said that he had no knowledge about who signed the commitment letter. But during Phillips's fraud trial, Civic's attorneys wrote, "Richardson testified that he had lied in his deposition before the FCC and in previous sworn testimony before other governmental bodies on at least five separate occasions." Richardson also testified that Phillips had admitted to him his responsibility for the purported $15 million government loan commitment letter and that his secretary "had perpetrated the forgery by tracing Richardson's signature."[102]

It was Ken Dean who got Richardson to change his story, Phillips said early in 2003, referring to discussions between Dean and Richardson before Phillips's trial. "He [Richardson] said I had told him I had put his signature" on the commitment letter. That, Phillips said, was not true. He had not seen the loan document.[103] Did Phillips attribute his legal problems to the FCC license proceeding, I asked him, or had there been other investigations ongoing? The Securities and Exchange Commission was investigating, Phillips replied, but "there is no question in my mind that the competition over this license caused my legal problems." What, with the perspective of almost three decades, was his view of his role in the case? "I wish I had not gotten myself or my company involved. I had never been in a proceeding like this where the object is to find something wrong with the other guy. I call it a 'gotcha' proceeding." It was the United Church of Christ and Ken Dean that caused his problems, he said.

"Marty Firestone may have been clapping his hands but they caused my problems."[104]

Meantime, the settlement proposed in 1976 was coming unraveled. Civic had agreed to participate because at the time of the negotiations, it had been unable to connect Phillips with the fraudulent loan document since he had denied any knowledge of it. Civic had also decided that it didn't even have substantial evidence to prove that Phillips had failed to disclose properly that he was a Stirling Homex officer. For these reasons, Civic's lawyers decided the group had little choice but to agree to the TV-3 settlement proposal. However, since that agreement, Phillips had been indicted, and at his trial in January Richardson had admitted his false testimony and said that Phillips had orchestrated the cover-up. Later that month Phillips was convicted. He was sentenced to ten months, of which he served eight at the federal prison camp at Eglin Air Force Base in Florida, and fined $5,000. Civic's attorneys said their group would not have been willing to settle the case had it known Phillips and Richardson had committed perjury.

Civic had wanted to bring its own stockholders into the operation of the station and, most important, to have 51 percent of the stock be held by Mississippi blacks, creating, as far as it was aware, the first black-controlled VHF television station in the United States. The other applicants did not accept that proposal, and so Civic withdrew from the proposed settlement.[105] Within a few days, Jackson Television, Dixie National, and Channel 3 filed a breach of contract suit in the chancery court in Jackson against Civic.

"I have never seen a more savage fight in my life over anything," said Tom Royals, a Jackson attorney who worked with Civic on matters requiring a Mississippi lawyer. Royals has an aw-shucks, I'm-just-a-country-boy manner, but that shouldn't fool anyone. He's smart and keenly analytical about the Jackson scene. "The way these hearings play out, you can defeat another group if you come up with what is called an issue. An issue can be anything. So everybody starts digging into everybody else. They were savagely throwing everything that they had at the other groups. I have always thought Rubel Phillips, a good man, was a victim of that."

Civic had asked Royals, who had been prosecuting criminal cases, to handle the local lawsuit against it. Royals had done legal work for Mississippi Action for Progress, an agency that sponsored Head Start in a number of counties and in which Aaron Henry and Charles Young were central figures. "I had done some civil rights work. I was a free thinker, and they felt that I would not be subject to the pressures" of all those powerful people involved in the case in Jackson.

A graduate of Millsaps College and the University of Mississippi law school, Royals moved to Jackson in 1957. He said that Henry and Young knew he wouldn't be intimidated by the establishment. "I was a member of the establishment in some way, but I saw my law practice as representing the people who hired me." Royals went to Washington to meet Walter Hall, who asked him if he was worried about losing business because his participation on Civic's side might anger powerful people in Mississippi. Royals admitted that he knew these were people who might send him business—or might not—but that he would fight hard for his case.

Hall was "the most striking individual I'd ever met in my life," Royals said. "Frankly, I didn't understand the use of money and the use of power at that time, which was what this whole suit was about. It was all about the use of money, the use of power, the use of lawyers who had the staying power, who could be more creative and live it out."[106]

The WLBT case was "a fight that ought to be fought," Hall told Royals. " 'You need to quit thinking little, Royals,' " the attorney recalled Hall saying, and that he should do whatever he needed to do, hire whomever he needed to hire, to accomplish his goal.[107]

"I remember after I'd been working on the suit for a little while, he met with me and he said, 'Tom, tell me about our adversaries.' I said, 'Oh, Mr. Hall, they're very rich people.' He said, 'Tell me about that. How rich are they?' And I got to telling him about these people and I said, well, this one's worth five or six million dollars. This one's worth $15 million. This one's worth $20 million and so forth and I finished and he said, 'Tom, that ain't rich.' I said, 'Well, Mr. Hall, I thought that was rich.' And he said, 'No sir, Tom, that's not rich. I don't want you to be intimidated by that.' "[108]

The case had to be settled, Royals said. "There were going to be so many casualties nobody would be left." Hall told him that they would not be money-whipped—that he had enough money in a trust to cover the case and had put instructions in his will that his heirs were to continue it. They were to spare no reasonable expense. While economics rang the bell in the WLBT case, Royals said, "you had to handle those egos, too. These were all people who were very successful in some way, either through money or politics and very successful people have big egos and they want to win—whether they're playing poker or basketball or TV-station getting."[109] With Hall's backing, Royals was able to stand up to the powerful figures involved, he said, and discovered that they were looking at him in a new light. "I said to myself, 'This is what Mr. Hall was trying to tell me, that I needed to learn the resources that I had at hand.' "[110]

"Hall was a tank. You may have thirty or forty soldiers walking down a road firing rifles but if you bring in a tank, it makes a difference. Hall wouldn't go away. He couldn't be scared. He couldn't be embarrassed out of it. He couldn't be bought out of it. He was there for the duration. With very rich people like Hall, the deal is the thing. They've got to have projects. It's lucky for the people of Mississippi" that someone with his power wanted to do good, Royals said. "Once he got addicted to that deal, there was to be no quitting without winning."[111]

Royals recalled talking to friends who were close to Senator James O. Eastland, then Mississippi's premier power broker, and they said Eastland wanted to see the case settled. Royals called Hall and suggested that he contact Eastland. "I thought the thing was starting to ruin people's lives. It was so nasty." But Hall didn't know Eastland and wondered whether Eastland would see a Texas banker, a liberal to boot. Hall did, however, know Lady Bird Johnson, whose late husband had served for years in the Senate with Eastland. Hall contacted her to see if she would tell Eastland who he was and ask the senator to meet with him. She did so in late 1977 or early 1978, and Eastland agreed to see Hall.[112] Hall flew to the Mississippi Delta, where Eastland lived, and evidently convinced Eastland that he was in the fight to stay.

Afterward, Eastland may have suggested to some of the people involved that they were getting into a war of attrition that wasn't doing the state of Mississippi any good and that the case should be settled, Royals said. "I don't think he got directly involved in how to settle it. I think the main emphasis coming from him was, please, try to get this thing settled and I think that probably had some influence on people."[113]

Having CII, a group totally separate from the applicants, running the station day-to-day had taken the pressure off the FCC. But the case went on for so long that a lot of people got tired of putting up the money, said Robert Travis of the Channel 3 group. They all said that they were only "funneling money to Washington to support lawyers."[114]

Reuben Anderson, another member of the Channel 3 group, agreed with Travis about the motivation for the final settlement. "Our biggest challenge was resources. We all had law firms in D.C. and that cost money," Anderson said during an interview in the conference room at his Jackson law firm. Both Travis and Anderson credited Alvin Flannes with understanding the politics and economics of the situation.

Flannes brought some of the key people together, and the first few negotiating sessions were mainly posturing—everybody talking about how strong their group was, Anderson said. He added that the key players in the settlement, at least those at the negotiating table, were Flannes, Travis, Mounger, Aaron Henry, Charles Young, and himself. Each group still thought it would win—Dixie because of its political influence, others because of their black representation or money. Civic, too, always believed it would win, Anderson said. "Aaron felt that right always won—and he thought he was always right."[115]

When it came down to it, "Aaron assisted in softening the positions," Anderson observed. Hall was adamant that there should be a black majority owning the station, and he was also insisting that Henry be chairman of the board. "I wanted that prestige for Aaron," Hall said.[116]

Hall must have spent $500,000, Anderson said. "We always thought their money would dry up. It never did. He just got stronger. If it wasn't for Hall and the strong position they were in—that essentially weakened the others. Dixie and our group caved. They had right and the resources. That means a lot." At the outset, Anderson noted, "Nobody understood how Civic could have any resources"—people like Aaron Henry simply were not wealthy. But "this guy Hall's commitment was stronger than the rest of us."[117]

Hall "had a vision that most of the rest of us didn't have," Royals said. Many of the people in the fight saw it as one about an investment because a TV station, Royals had heard, "was sort of like owning an oil well or a money-producing factory." But Hall didn't need the money. Hall thought he was contributing by trying to get that TV station in black hands.[118]

But in addition to his desire to see that blacks were treated more fairly on one television station, Hall did believe that money might be made. Long before the final agreement was reached, Hall commented to a friend by letter on his reasons for becoming involved. "I have always felt we had far from an even chance in this," Hall wrote, "but while the odds were long against us, the earnings would have been so great, it was worth the gamble. By earnings, I not only mean the money to have a well run, fair and decent nondiscriminating TV station (the largest and strongest in Mississippi) but one that would have provided a real bucket of funds."[119]

Hall told his friend Chandler Davidson that he felt black people had been treated outrageously. "I felt that something dramatic had to be done on a statewide level, and that TV station was the largest, most powerful in Mississippi." The fight proved very costly. "I looked upon it as providing two things. If we succeeded, it would be notice to the nation that blacks could not be mistreated, maligned, and lied about with impunity by an important thing like a TV station. And, secondly, as I'm not at all opposed to making money, and I knew something of the value of a big TV station, that if we succeeded, it would make some money. But whether we succeeded or not, the effort to bring into focus the deplorable situation in Mississippi was in order."[120]

Even as settlement talks moved along in Jackson, Ehrig continued the case in Washington during the summer of 1978, hearing testimony from William Mounger and board members from Jackson Academy. Mounger said in an affidavit that he had been elected to the academy's board of directors in 1963 and was especially interested in the school's emphasis on reading. To the best of his knowledge, he said, the academy did not have a policy based on racial exclusion. Sometimes decisions were made not to accept potential students who might cause discipline problems, he said, adding that as far as he knew, "no black child ever applied for admission to Jackson Academy. Had there applied a black child who had the educational potential and the ability to pay the tuition, I would have voted to admit any such applicant that came to my attention."[121]

Ehrig had often expressed her belief that the public interest would be best served by settling such a protracted proceeding.[122] On October 25, 1978, she started to get her wish—she received a letter saying the groups had reached a final settlement in which TV-3 would have 51 percent black stockholders. Dixie National and Jackson Television's participants would each own 25 percent of the stock, and Channel 3's stockholders, 20 percent. Unlike the earlier version of TV-3, Civic's participants would own 30 percent of the new corporation. The civil action against Civic was postponed, and the following January all five of the original applicants asked that their settlement agreement be approved. This time, it would take. The mudball fight could end.

TV-3 would purchase the WLBT facilities from Lamar and agreed to reimburse the groups that had applied for the license for their provable expenses. Those expenses had been the highest for Dixie National and Civic, $450,000 each. In Civic's case, virtually all of that came from Walter Hall. The bulk of Civic's costs had been more than $375,000 in legal fees and related expenses to Firestone and predecessor law firms, plus $47,125 to Tom Royals, the Jackson counsel. The agreement spelled out the membership of the board of directors, which would include Walter Hall, Aaron Henry, and Charles Young from Civic; William Mounger and a representative from Dixie National Life Insurance; Alvin Flannes from Jackson Television; one director from Channel 3, with the understanding that would be one of its black stockholders; and a final director selected by a majority vote of the black stockholders in TV-3.[123]

In an affidavit accompanying the settlement papers, Flannes indicated that he and Hall had met in Dickinson, Texas, on July 26, 1978, to discuss a settlement that would include participation by some of Civic's stockholders and the concept of black ownership. In September 1978 Hall, Flannes, Mounger, Travis, and Robert Neal of Dixie National Life Insurance met in Jackson and reached the understanding that resulted in the settlement.[124] On October 5, 1979, the Office of Communication and the Community Coalition for Better Broadcasting supported the settlement agreement because of its commitment to minority ownership and control.[125]

After wading through all the legal filings, Ehrig conferred with the attorneys in Washington on November 13, 1979. She set a firm deadline for her final action within ten days or two weeks, because "constitutionally I am unable to enter another year with this case still pending."[126]

In a decision released December 3, 1979, Ehrig awarded the license to TV-3. "The public interest cries out for such action," she said, adding that "the history of this proceeding has been long and tortuous." WLBT had been a matter of controversy at the FCC for approximately twenty-five years—starting with complaints against the station in 1955. Ehrig's opinion said that the preeminent feature of TV-3 was that 51 percent of its stock would be owned by black stockholders. The black stockholders, Ehrig wrote, "constitute a virtual Who's Who in the political, economic, professional, educational and artistic leadership in the station's service area." With broad community representation in the TV-3 ownership, "the diversity of opinions and viewpoints likely to be available in Jackson will be increased." Heavy minority employment by the interim WLBT operator led the station's audience to accept and expect the representation of minority interests and views, she observed, and this agreement assured that those needs would continue to be met. The settlement also "will at long last conclude this protracted litigation which has yo-yo'd back and forth between the courts and the commission for a generation."[127]

Ehrig also addressed the issues involving Rubel Phillips and William Mounger. She ruled that there was insufficient evidence to conclude that anyone with Dixie National other than Phillips intended to mislead the commission and that none of the others from Dixie National who would participate in WLBT had been tainted by Phillips's involvement with the Stirling Homex matter. Concerning Mounger, she said that there was no evidence indicating that he would act in a discriminatory manner as a broadcaster, accepting his word that when he was a board member of Jackson Academy, no black student had sought or was denied admission to the school.[128]

"After eleven years of effort," Hall remarked, "we were finally called upon to either join with those who felt somewhat like we did, or face many more years of costly struggle. We made a compromise settlement," and the actions of the group that emerged "have shown that blacks and whites can work together effectively, both in running a decent, objective TV station, and also a profitable one . . . . Of course, I take some satisfaction in the fight because I was putting up the money. The others were not people of substantial means." But they were leaders in Mississippi and knew their state well.[129]

Early in 1980 CII, which had been running WLBT, bowed out. It had brought enormous change to the station and to broadcasting in the South. Aaron Henry, once turned down in an effort to obtain airtime for a political message because of his race, became the new chairman of the board of WLBT.

8. NATIONAL IMPACT

The WLBT case was a landmark in communications law. In the end, almost sixteen years of fighting yielded results that affected not only Jackson but also the entire nation. The challenge and the subsequent court decisions helped change the face of television and its regulation. At a critical time in U.S. history, federal regulators had to listen to citizens, not just to broadcasters. What Warren Burger had seen as the need for "audience participation" led to a new approach to regulation—one that allowed public pressure on the Federal Communications Commission and on broadcasters to improve content and reduce commercials on children's programs, for example, as well as to increase hiring of minorities and women at a time when few were employed in key media jobs. People started to think differently about how television affected their lives, and young attorneys established public interest communications law firms to help community groups "talk back to their television sets," to use Nicholas Johnson's phrase. The spirit of protest was well under way through the civil rights, antiwar, and women's movements, and the legal precedent established in the WLBT case allowed activists to train their sights on broadcasters.

That this era has ended in no way lessens its importance. The changes that occurred in that era underscore how much citizens

have lost today in a wave of deregulation and the creation of communications megalopolies. Deregulation in turn has shifted the focus
of those public interest groups that remain onto broader communications policy issues.

The WLBT case had significant impact in two other areas as well.
First, it buttressed the Fairness Doctrine. Using the Fairness Doctrine,
for example, a young attorney named John Banzhaf won favorable decisions from the FCC and the U.S. Court of Appeals in 1968
requiring that television stations airing cigarette commercials inform
their audiences of the other side of a controversial public health issue.
These decisions—and public health findings—helped put the skids
under cigarette advertising on television, which Congress banned in
1969.[1] Second, the WLBT case put broadcasters on notice that they
needed to hire and promote more minorities. As an outgrowth of the
WLBT case, the United Church of Christ asked the FCC to require
stations to take affirmative action to diversify their staffs. To some
extent, the FCC did so. The Fairness Doctrine and the FCC's affirmative action rules are dead or much weaker now—like the large-
scale public participation fostered by the appeals court decision in the
WLBT case—but that case figured prominently in their histories.
Surveying the fights to maintain each of these policies underscores
the powers arrayed against them and the difficulty maintaining them,
no matter how hard won.

Increasing public participation in FCC matters was the most
immediate major impact of the WLBT decision. Black residents of
Texarkana, Texas, with concerns about the lack of local coverage their
community received from television station KTAL, were the first to
use this new standing. The United Church of Christ helped a coalition of local groups, including the NAACP, challenge KTAL's license
renewal at the FCC in January 1969. Their grievances included failure to include any black leaders in Texarkana in the station's survey

of community needs—even though more than a quarter of the city was black. The station covered news of concern to white citizens of Texarkana but not that involving the black community. For example, the challengers said that during a rainstorm KTAL reported on the difficulty motorists had getting through high water on one street while neglecting flooding of homes and high water blocking the only access to a black neighborhood. "This is an example of KTAL's practice of covering a minor inconvenience to white residents and disregarding a perilous disaster in the Negro community," the groups said.[2]

That May the station indicated that it was ready to negotiate.[3] The Reverend Everett Parker announced on June 10 that the station and the groups had reached agreement. KTAL pledged to recruit a staff more representative of the community, including at least two full-time black reporters; air discussions of controversial issues with black and white participants; make no nonessential references to people's race; and meet regularly with community representatives to discuss program policies.[4] Given the agreement, the FCC renewed KTAL's license on July 29, 1969. The commission was changing its tune from the WLBT case, saying now that the cooperation that had led to this agreement "should prove to be more effective in improving local service than would be the imposition of strict guidelines by the commission."[5]

But the case was not closed; another legal precedent was about to be set. Once the FCC approved the KTAL agreement, the attorney for the citizens' groups—Earle K. Moore, once again—filed a request that it also approve the station owners' plan to reimburse the United Church of Christ for its legal expenses. Reimbursement had figured in the talks, but the church had said that the substantive issues came first, so the settlement submitted to the FCC made no mention of payment. KTAL's lawyers said that the station would reimburse the church provided that the commission approved the settlement first and later the payment.

Almost a year after Moore submitted his request—the reimbursement claimed was $15,137.11—the FCC rejected it. The commission majority considered that the potential for abuse—that is, frivolous cases—if reimbursement were allowed outweighed any benefit to the public interest in paying to help community groups. However, such reimbursement was common among commercial broadcasters. FCC chairman Dean Burch and Nicholas Johnson dissented on grounds that the FCC had previously allowed reimbursement where it helped public interest goals, adding that the commission could set rules to prevent abuse.

The Office of Communication took the case to the U.S. Court of Appeals, where it was argued November 2, 1971. The Justice Department intervened on the side of the Office of Communication, arguing that public groups couldn't be expected to make large-scale efforts to reform broadcasting unless they believed that their lawyers could win reimbursement. On March 28, 1972, the court overturned the FCC's ruling, saying that the commission could not make a flat prohibition against reimbursement.[6] That decision allowed other public interest groups, especially environmentalists, to become involved in cases at other regulatory agencies, such as the Federal Power Commission. They brought cases they might not otherwise have been able to file and made substantial gains because they could obtain good legal counsel with the hope of winning reimbursement of legal fees.

A new player had entered the game in the reimbursement case—Citizens Communications Center, founded by a young attorney named Albert H. Kramer, a Stanford law school graduate. The Robert F. Kennedy Memorial encouraged the center's establishment, and several foundations, including the Stern Fund and the Ford Foundation, supported its work. Other public interest communications firms established during this period included the Stern Community Law Firm, whose first director was Tracy Westen, a former aide of Nicholas Johnson. A third group was the Media Access Project, whose first director was Tom Asher. It is the only one of the three still in existence as a free-standing entity and has been headed for many years by Andrew Schwartzman, who as a young attorney worked with Earle K. Moore in the latter days of the WLBT case. Taking cases to the FCC was enormously complex. These firms gave the public the expertise to use the WLBT precedent in order to pursue their broadcast reform goals.

License renewal time in the 1970s became, in the words of *Broadcasting* magazine, "triennial high noon."[7] Initially, the strongest activity geared toward improving television stations' performance came from the black community. Within a few years, American Indian, Latino, and Chinese American groups also were involved, as was the National Organization for Women (NOW). By 1971—just two years after the KTAL agreement—the United Church of Christ was aiding about a hundred community groups across the country in their negotiations with the industry, according to *Broadcasting*. Backed by Ford Foundation grants, the Office of Communication provided legal and technical advice and help in monitoring stations.[8] The Field Foundation and the AFL-CIO also supported the Office of Communication efforts.[9] Between 1971 and 1973 more than 340 stations had petitions filed against them to deny their license renewals.[10]

Anger and frustration motivated many people to become involved in broadcast reform issues. As longtime *Broadcasting* correspondent Leonard Zeidenberg wrote, "Broadcasting, they seem to feel, is letting them down; it is not serving *their* interests, reflecting *their* needs, expressing *their* points of view. . . . To a growing number of groups across the country, it is clear, broadcasting is too important to be left to the broadcasters. They are determined to make their impact."[11] For some of the activists, broadcasting was a personal issue. It affected how they felt about themselves. Zeidenberg quoted one NOW member as saying, "I feel I'm being derogated by television, by the news, entertainment, and public affairs shows. By the commercials, too. Women are patronized as stupid. No grown woman goes into a paroxysm of delight over a clean floor."[11]

In Texas, a coalition of black, Latino, Native American, and white organizations joined to monitor five television and radio stations in Dallas and Fort Worth. In July 1971 the Dallas–Fort Worth Coalition for the Free Flow of Information won concessions from the stations. These included promises to hire more minorities for on-air jobs such as reporting and anchoring as well as public affairs positions in which they might advise stations about programs of interest to their communities.[12]

Citizens' groups trying to block the sale of television and radio stations also started raising fair employment and other issues. For example, Citizens Communications Center represented minority groups that negotiated an agreement with Capital Cities Broadcasting (Capcities) in late 1970. Capcities had sought to buy three television and six radio stations from Triangle Publications, Inc., but minority groups opposed the sale. Capcities agreed to set up a $1 million fund for minority-interest programming on the television stations in Philadelphia; New Haven, Connecticut; and Fresno, California. In exchange, the citizens' groups withdrew their objections. The FCC approved the sale, citing the unprecedented agreement as a factor in its decision.[13]

Also in 1971, Time-Life Broadcasting sought to sell its television stations to McGraw-Hill Book Company for $69.3 million. Citizens' groups filed petitions to deny the assignment of the licenses to McGraw-Hill for stations in Bakersfield and San Diego, California; Grand Rapids, Michigan; Denver; and Indianapolis. Basically, the groups objected to the transfer because it would contribute to what they considered a growing concentration of media ownership. They said it would violate a commission policy that prohibited acquisition of more than two VHF stations in the top fifty markets without a compelling public interest showing. The coalition also considered that neither Time-Life nor McGraw-Hill had made an adequate effort toward achieving equal employment opportunity.[14]

The commission voted 4-2 in March 1972 to approve the sale, with Nicholas Johnson and Robert Bartley dissenting. The commission majority said that McGraw-Hill had made the required public interest showing and that it would bring new viewpoints to the five communities involved. It added that the transfer would also promote the diversification goals of the FCC's cross-ownership policy.[15]

The citizens' groups filed suit at the U.S. Court of Appeals in Washington, D.C., seeking to overturn the FCC decision. As in the Capcities deal, McGraw-Hill faced costly litigation if it did not reach agreement with the citizens' groups, giving the latter their leverage. Thus in May 1972 McGraw-Hill agreed to buy only four of the five television stations and made extensive commitments involving programming, citizen advisory committees, employment, and training. Dropping the Grand Rapids television station from the package clearly was part of the price McGraw-Hill was required to pay to persuade the groups to drop their suit, according to *Broadcasting*. That meant that McGraw-Hill would have two, not three, TV stations in the top fifty markets, in line with the FCC's own rules. Albert Kramer, representing the coalition, said that forgoing acquisition of the Grand Rapids station was the real significance of the agreement, calling it "the private enforcement of a public law."[16]

Commercial stations were not the only targets. In 1970 the FCC had dismissed complaints that the Alabama Educational Television Commission (AETV) had preempted a number of black-oriented programs distributed over the national public television network.

The FCC renewed AETV's public television station licenses, saying that a licensee had wide latitude in its programming. Two University of Alabama students and a local priest asked the FCC to reconsider. They charged that the stations not only failed to serve Alabama's black viewers but also discriminated against them in employment and programming. In 1975 the commission voted 4-2 that AETV had followed a racially discriminatory policy in its employment and overall programming practices during the 1967–1970 license period and denied the licenses. It permitted AETV to reapply for the licenses because it had corrected some of its problems. Six of the license renewals were unopposed, and a settlement was reached between citizens' groups and three others in January 1980.[17]

Many of the encounters between broadcasters and citizens' groups had positive effects as each side learned from the other. But some were confrontational, and some groups represented few members of the public. The industry was unhappy about the reform efforts, with a spokesperson for the National Association of Broadcasters (NAB) saying that responsible stations welcomed suggestions or complaints from their audience. "But *these* people—they want to set themselves up as super-censors . . . super-program directors. And they want to do it over night. Change takes time—that's the price we pay for a democracy."[18]

In response to the industry concern, Senator John O. Pastore of Rhode Island, the influential chairman of the Senate communications subcommittee, proposed legislation in 1969 designed to insulate broadcasters from irresponsible applications for their stations at renewal time. His bill required the FCC to determine that granting renewal to a station would not serve the public interest before it could consider competing applications. Pastore told the NAB convention that year that it was his "deep-seated conviction that public service is not encouraged nor promoted by placing the sword of

Damocles over the heads of broadcasters at renewal time. The broadcaster must have reasonable assurance that if he does his job—and does it well—he's going to remain in business and not have his investment go down the drain."[19]

The black community and other groups opposed the Pastore bill, organizing a groundswell of publicity against it. With chances for passage of the bill diminishing, the FCC in January 1970 adopted a policy statement to try to alleviate the situation (and avoid defeat for Pastore). On a 6-1 vote, it said that it would favor an incumbent broadcaster over rival applicants if the station owner could show in a hearing that the station's programming had been substantially attuned to the needs and interests of the community.[20]

In dissent, Nicholas Johnson prophesied what would come when the broadcast industry won deregulation some years later. Congress and the FCC had shown themselves relatively powerless to do anything more than spar with the mass media, Johnson wrote. "Effective reform, more and more, rests with self-help measures taken by the public. Recognizing this, the broadcasters now seek to curtail the procedural remedies of the people themselves. The industry's power is such that it will succeed, one way or another." Once the government concedes, there is no turning back, he added. "Not only can the industry win every ball game, it is now in a position to change the rules."[21] That has been the case almost from that day to this.

Black Efforts for Soul in Television and the Citizens Communications Center asked the FCC to reconsider its policy. It would not. Johnson again dissented, echoing his words in the WLBT case. By refusing to listen to the groups opposing the policy, the FCC had "reached a new low in its self-imposed isolation from the people; once again we closed our ears and minds to their pleas." And once again the U.S Court of Appeals overruled the FCC. On June 11, 1971, the judges said that their action would restore competition by repudiating a commission policy unreasonably weighted in favor of the stations it was supposed to regulate. Thereafter, the FCC approached the issue of comparative renewal standards on a case-by-case basis because neither the commission nor Congress could agree on a policy.[22]

The WLBT case made itself felt in other areas of television. Establishment of the principle that the public had a right to participate in FCC matters also enabled action by parents concerned about the lack of quality television programming for children and overcommercialization on the programs that did exist. In 1968, two years after the precedent-setting first court decision in the WLBT case, Peggy Charren of Newton, Massachusetts, and others formed Action for Children's Television (ACT). Over the next two decades ACT led efforts to increase public awareness of the influence of television and its commercials on children, improve programs aimed at youngsters, and gain support from the FCC and Congress for their concerns. ACT later spurred passage of the Children's Television Act of 1990, which required that children's programs reduce commercials by almost two minutes an hour and that the FCC consider as one of its guiding factors in renewals whether broadcasters were serving the educational needs of children.[23]

In addition to helping set in motion this public interest movement, the WLBT case also gave added weight to the Fairness Doctrine. In its first opinion in the WLBT case, the appeals court in 1966 pointed out that even though the FCC said it had accepted all of the United Church of Christ's allegations that the station had violated the Fairness Doctrine, it still had renewed the license because it hadn't wanted to remove from the air one of Jackson's only two TV stations at the time. The court said the public might be as well or better served "with only one TV outlet acutely conscious that adherence to the Fairness Doctrine is a *sine qua non* of every licensee."[24]

By 1969 the WLBT case was back in court, on appeal from the second FCC decision renewing the station's license. The appeals court reversed the FCC again, basing much of its decision on what it considered the indifference of the commission and its hearing examiner to the court's message that the public should be heard. But the judges also reemphasized the Fairness Doctrine, saying that it "plays a very large role in assuring that the public resources granted to licensees at no cost will be used in the public interest."[25]

This support of the Fairness Doctrine should have been no surprise. In 1967 the appeals court had upheld the doctrine in a case involving WGCB in Red Lion, Pennsylvania. Edward A. Tamm, one of the judges in the WLBT case, wrote in the Red Lion decision that the Fairness Doctrine was not "unconstitutionally vague, indefinite or uncertain." The WGCB case involved the refusal of an ultraconservative station owner to allow response time to author Fred Cook, whose character had been attacked on the air by the Reverend Billy James Hargis on a 1964 Christian Crusade broadcast. The FCC had said the station should provide Cook with response time; the owner refused and appealed the decision. Saying that "the American people own the broadcast frequencies," Tamm wrote that Cook should receive time to respond to Hargis's attack.[26]

Again the owner appealed, to the chagrin of many others in the industry, who considered his case a weak one on which to hang their pleas to overturn the Fairness Doctrine. Broadcasters brought several other suits that ultimately were joined with the Red Lion case. A quirk of timing put these cases before the Supreme Court just as the appeals court was reaching its 1969 decision on WLBT's license.

On June 9, 1969, the Supreme Court emphatically upheld the Fairness Doctrine. Justice Byron White wrote: "We need not and do not now ratify every past and future decision by the FCC with regard to programming. There is no question here of the commission's refusal to permit the broadcaster to carry a particular program or to publish [his] own views. . . . Such questions would raise more serious First Amendment issues. But we do hold that Congress and the Commission do not violate the First Amendment when they require a radio or television station to give reply time to answer personal attacks and political editorials."[27] Eleven days later the appeals court issued its decision in the WLBT case.

This opinion was by no means the last word on the Fairness Doctrine. The mood to curtail government regulation grew in the late 1970s and intensified after the 1980 election of Ronald Reagan as president. In 1981 Reagan named Mark S. Fowler, no fan of the Fairness Doctrine, as FCC chairman. The commission wrestled with the issue for six years, uncertain whether it had the authority to kill the doctrine or whether Congress had written it into law and so would have to be the body to eliminate it.

In 1985 the FCC said it believed the doctrine was unconstitutional and called upon Congress to repeal the measure. Congress was not inclined to do so, not wanting to be seen attacking fairness. By August 1987 the FCC voted 4-0 that the doctrine was no longer needed and therefore no longer in effect. "We seek to extend to the electronic press the same First Amendment guarantees that the print media have enjoyed since our country's inception," said Dennis R. Patrick, the new FCC chairman. Enforcing the doctrine had meant that broadcasters "shied away from covering controversial issues in news, documentaries and editorial advertisements," FCC general counsel Diane S. Killory maintained.

Asked about the impact of the decision, consumer advocate Ralph Nader said broadcasters would be able to ignore critical issues or present only one side. Issues like women's rights, the health effects of smoking, and the safety of nuclear power plants would have received far less attention had the Fairness Doctrine not been in effect, Nader asserted.[28]

In February 1989 the D.C. Circuit Court of appeals—the same court that in 1966 and 1969 had accepted the Fairness Doctrine as

an obligation of broadcasters but now with different judges—backed
its repeal by the FCC. The court agreed with the FCC that the doctrine was no longer needed and that it actually discouraged broadcasters from covering controversial topics.[29]

Some have argued that the Fairness Doctrine itself has never
been declared unconstitutional and should be enforced. Andrew
Schwartzman of the Media Access Project pointed out that the court
of appeals had reversed the part of the FCC's 1987 decision that the
Fairness Doctrine was unconstitutional. It allowed the commission
to stop enforcing the doctrine on grounds that it was discretionary
rather than mandatory. "While broadcasters run around complaining
that the Fairness Doctrine is unconstitutional, [the 1969 Red Lion]
decision has never been disturbed." Just as failure to heed the Fairness Doctrine tripped up WLBT in the 1960s, it could still have a
role today, Schwartzman said. Groups backing civil rights, women's
rights, and gay and lesbian issues should remain interested in the
Fairness Doctrine, he noted, adding that it is "especially important for
groups who are not part of the mainstream debate. It could still be a
legal tool for getting some broadcasters to pay attention to important
issues, and for assuring that coverage is 'fair.' "[30]

The Fairness Doctrine remains on the agenda of the Media Access
Project and like-minded groups, said Schwartzman. "The principle
is as important as ever. We are not done with it." The FCC under
former chairman William Kennard had been considering trying to
rejustify the doctrine, but commission interest died when the new
chairman, Michael Powell, was appointed by President George W.
Bush in 2001. Nonetheless, Schwartzman said, the two court decisions
in the WLBT case stressing the importance of the Fairness Doctrine
"materially advanced the reform movement" because broadcasters
became more conscious of their obligations. "The standard that we
still expect today is much, much higher than it would have been"

absent the WLBT case. This was not about networks and their news, Schwartzman added, but about presentation of controversial issues at local levels.[31]

Finally, the outcome of the WLBT license challenge influenced integration efforts at other broadcasting stations. Not only had the case sent a message to broadcasters that they risked losing their licenses for discriminating, it contributed to the atmosphere that led the FCC to direct radio and TV stations to hire more minorities.

In April 1967—while preparing for the Jackson hearing in the WLBT case—the Office of Communication asked the FCC to require broadcasters to report each year on actions they were taking to promote employment and programming aimed at minority groups. Joining the Office of Communication in this request were the church's Board of Homeland Ministries and Committee for Racial Justice Now. Many southern stations unfairly discriminated against blacks in employment, said the Reverend Everett Parker, adding that an appropriate commission rule might get northern stations' attention as well.[32]

The United Church of Christ was laying at the FCC's door an issue it could not avoid. Commissioners might wish the question would go away, but they were going to have to vote on it, and given the times, they must have felt that they could not vote against establishing such policies.

The FCC received comments on the petition from thirty-five groups and individuals, all of which supported it save one, the NAB, which said it was sympathetic to the goals of the proposal but had some reservations about its reporting procedures and enforcement powers. The NAB contended that the commission did not have regulatory power over civil rights, a function it said Congress had given to the Equal Employment Opportunity Commission (EEOC) under the 1964 Civil Rights Act.[33]

In July 1968 the commission proposed a rule requiring stations to take affirmative action to increase minority hiring and to report regularly to the FCC on their efforts. It said that there was a national policy against discrimination in hiring and that the Civil Rights Act did not reserve the power to regulate employment practices exclusively to the EEOC.

Asked for legal guidance, the Justice Department weighed in on the policy considerations. Stephen J. Pollak, assistant attorney general in charge of the civil rights division, wrote the commission that "because of the enormous impact which television and radio have upon American life, the employment practices of the broadcasting industry have an importance greater than that suggested by the number of its employees. The provision of equal opportunity in employment in that industry could therefore contribute significantly toward reducing and ending discrimination in other industries."[34]

The FCC also said that licensees had a responsibility of conscience in the employment area. "The nation is confronted with a serious racial crisis. It is acknowledged that the media cannot solve that crisis," the FCC stated, "but on all sides it has been emphasized that the media can contribute greatly in many significant respects, particularly to understanding by white and black of the nature of the crisis and the possible remedial actions." The commission noted that the report of the National Advisory Commission on Civil Disorders, also known as the Kerner Commission, convened after a wave of race rioting shook the country in the mid-1960s, had said that the media had not communicated to their white audience the difficulties and frustrations of being black in America. The Kerner Commission report also made clear, the FCC said, that "of all the media, broadcasting is the most important in this respect because it is most turned to by the ghetto."

The FCC stressed that saying "We can't find qualified Negroes" was not enough; greater commitment was required. It pledged to back up its policy by denying license renewal to any station found to have discriminated in employment.[35]

The new affirmative action proposal followed by just one week the FCC's seemingly contradictory 1968 decision to renew the WLBT license despite the ongoing challenge. *New York Times* reporter Eileen Shanahan asked FCC general counsel Henry Geller at a briefing on the new policy "why, in view of the Mississippi decision, any station owner should believe he would actually lose his license if he followed discriminatory employment practices." Dodging the implication, Geller replied that the WLBT case turned on a determination of the facts and that any case under the new policy would also depend on the facts. The commission majority had not accepted as true the allegations of discrimination against WLBT.

The *New York Times* article underscored the key role of the United Church of Christ in precipitating the new policy. "The antidiscrimination policy announced by the commission today," wrote Shanahan, "could have been adopted at any time subsequent to the passage of the 1964 civil rights bill, Mr. Geller said. But the FCC simply did not look at the issue of discrimination in employment, he said, until it received the petition of the United Church of Christ. If the church had not brought the matter to the commission's attention, he said, presumably some other complainant would have, in time."[36]

In addition to pressure from the civil rights community for the rules, there was sentiment within the FCC staff about taking a stand, but opposition as well. As Geller recalled, he had attended a Kerner Commission meeting and left it charged up to have the FCC make its contribution to alleviating the racial problems facing the nation. His office got behind the Office of Communication petition, as he would have liked the FCC to have done concerning the church's challenge of WLBT in 1964. William Ray of the Broadcast Bureau—one of the investigators sent to Mississippi in 1962—argued that his bureau did not have the resources to handle the workload that would result from issuing the rules; the question should be left to agencies that generally handled such matters. Geller maintained that broadcasting "constituted the most important informational medium and was required to serve the public interest, that we couldn't deal with content, and that affirmative action to employ minorities would be the only and most effective way to insure that broadcasting did make the necessary contribution to healing the nation." Even if resources kept the FCC from fully implementing the decision, Geller said, "it was important to make a beginning. I won in a close decision."[37]

Almost a year later—June 4, 1969—the FCC issued its final rule, saying that it had a responsibility independent of other agencies to set down a strong policy against discrimination. Originally, the commission had indicated that it would act against bias on the basis of complaints against a station. But in announcing the rules, the FCC said that stations had an affirmative duty to seek out minority employees and to report to the commission. Each station with five or more full-time employees would have to develop an equal opportunity program involving training, hiring, promotion, pay scales, and work assignments.[38]

Parker remained skeptical of the commission's ability to police its own rule. In February 1970 he accused the FCC of "dawdling" by doing nothing to make sure its rule was being obeyed. People cannot wait for disinterested agencies to protect their rights, he said, announcing a plan to monitor stations' employment practices. Joining with Parker in the effort, Jean Fairfax of the NAACP Legal Defense and Education Fund said that "the communications industry has been selected because it sets the stage for other industries to obey or defy the law." She added that her organization would organize local groups to study employment practices and monitor programming. The Office of Communication would train the citizens' groups to

interview station managers and help petition the FCC if the groups
so desired.

Such an effort was under way in Atlanta. Early in 1970 the NAACP
and the Community Coalition on Broadcasting joined in an effort to
negotiate reforms with every broadcaster in Atlanta. The black groups
charged radio and TV stations in the city with racial discrimination
in programming and hiring. They wanted the stations to increase
their efforts to learn the needs and interests of the black community—
at that point, 47 percent of Atlanta's population—and to serve those
needs better. Attorneys from the Office of Communication and
Citizens Communication Center helped train local people how to
do the research needed for their case and what to expect in negotiations with station managers. Within a few months, the black groups
had negotiated agreements with most of the stations, many of which
agreed to hire black employees and to provide training for them.
They also pledged to increase public affairs programming dealing with
issues of interest to the black community. Neither the church nor the
NAACP fund was looking to revoke broadcasters' licenses, Parker
insisted. "Revocation is a poor way to get what we want. We want
to bring change by negotiation."[39]

That summer the Ford Foundation announced its second grant to
permit Parker's staff to expand efforts to train local groups to negotiate with broadcasters. "Television and radio can be peculiarly vicious
in trampling on the dignity of minority citizens who are at the bottom of the economic heap and are not greatly valued as consumers,"
Parker said as his office released a report called "Racial Justice in Broadcasting." Television and radio, he went on, had "glorified material
standards and creature comforts" and raised the expectations of the
poor but had done little to help them achieve the prospects "it dan-
gles before them so alluringly. On the contrary, radio and television
have avidly reported the turbulence, violence, destruction, frustration

and despair of America's deprived people, but not their hopes and aspirations." Broadcasting's inability to communicate with minorities stemmed from the industry's reluctance to employ them, he added.[40]

The FCC issued its first study of broadcasting industry employment practices in 1973, finding that in 1972 African Americans were 6.6 percent of broadcasting employees. Only a few months earlier, however, the Office of Communication reported a different story. Its own survey, using FCC reports, found that full-time and part-time minority employees made up 4.081 percent of the broadcast workforce in 1971 and 4.781 percent in 1972. Calling the broadcasters' record "dismal," Everett Parker also said that one in five of all commercial stations had no minority employees. About a third of the 609 stations surveyed had no minority employees in the four upper categories of jobs—management, professional, technical, and sales.[41]

In 1977 the U.S. Commission on Civil Rights issued its report, *Window Dressing on the Set: Women and Minorities in Television.* Its title revealed its message. Employment of minorities and women had indeed increased between 1971 and 1975, the civil rights commission said, but they weren't being promoted. White males held the vast majority of decision-making posts in the industry, the commission noted, and network news programs were no better. White males outnumbered both minority and female correspondents by almost nine to one on ABC, CBS, and NBC broadcasts. Moreover, the minorities and women tended to cover stories related to minorities' and women's interests.[42]

Minorities and women wrestled with these assignments. As a female print journalist, I know I did. If I didn't cover the stories that I knew existed about women trying to break into politics or later about the quality of child care available to working parents, no one else would be likely to do so on a male-dominated staff. But I also wanted to cover presidential politics or perhaps be a foreign correspondent.

As Ed Bradley put it: "I'm a reporter who happens to be black. It's too easy to paint yourself in a corner. On '60 Minutes' I want to break down doors and interview Bette Davis, the same as Mike Wallace. Or do a piece on the Muppets, like Morley Safer. Did Morley do that because he was a Muppet?"[43]

Broadcasting magazine raised questions about diversity in a 1971 article about the pressures on television stations to hire more women and minorities. "Is it impossible for a white reporter to report, say, on developments in the inner city with sensitivity and perception?" it asked. "Can only a black—and a home-grown one, at that—do the job properly? And what of the likelihood that a black's background would impair his ability to do an objective job? These are fair questions. But some blacks and Chicanos and Chinese and Latinos seem to feel that they have seen too many straight-nosed, blue-eyed reporters talking into a camera about a world that bears little relationship to their own."[44] Minorities and women were covering more beats and even starting to occupy the coveted anchor spots on local news broadcasts. They did it slowly—program by program, station by station, network by network. It is all too easy today, when the 6 P.M. news regularly features men and women on anchor teams—blacks, whites, Latinos, and Asian Americans—to forget the sea of white male faces that predominated not only among the newsmakers but also among news gatherers just a few decades ago. It was not true, as some white males would whine, that minorities and women were the only people being hired, but slowly people like Randall Pinkston, Max Robinson, Ed Bradley, Bernard Shaw, Connie Chung, Carole Simpson, and others began to show what they could do. But as one network newsman said, "There is still a tendency to hire the average white guy and look for the superblack."[45]

Even with the progress that they made, by the late 1990s minorities still made up less than 20 percent of broadcast employees. Yes,

Carole Simpson had sat in for Peter Jennings on ABC's evening news and regularly anchored the network's Saturday evening newscast. Yes, Bernard Shaw anchored CNN news for many years. But the three principal network news anchors still were white males as the new millennium began.

One cannot with any precision tie the presence of more women, African Americans, Latinos, and Asian Americans on broadcast news staffs to changes in the news that is covered. In a country increasingly diverse, where these groups are stepping into the mainstream in politics, business, education, and other fields, the news itself has changed. But if all the news executives or broadcast reporters live in a white-dominated suburb or on the edge of a polyglot city, they won't hear of the trends and the tensions of the other members of the community when they go to church, to the grocery store, or to their children's school. If all the executives and reporters are male, they may not see the impact of economic and social change on the lives of women, either. Race and gender can and do matter in news coverage, and the WLBT case directly and indirectly hastened change in this area.

During the presidency of Jimmy Carter, the climate of opinion started to change about government regulation. Moves toward reducing regulation accelerated under President Ronald Reagan. That in turn led to changes in both the politics of affirmative action and the level of citizen participation at the FCC. Some of these changes were a backlash against the social movements of the 1960s and early 1970s that had produced much of the energy for broadcast reform efforts. And by the 1980s and 1990s some of the people in those movements were gone. Some who had been active had seen doors open for them at broadcast stations, law firms, or universities, and they stepped through them to work—for change or not—from the inside. Some had gotten tired. Some had moved on to other issues. Others remained active but found that less regulation—and thus the absence of meaningful relief—made efforts to challenge local licenses unproductive. The focus of the Media Access Project and newer organizations such as the Center for Digital Democracy and the Minority Media and Telecommunications Council, for example, turned to broader national policy issues, such as media ownership and affirmative action.

It has been hard to get people to focus even on programming, let alone issues one or two levels removed, such as ownership, said David Honig of the Minority Media and Telecommunications Council, which represents a coalition of national groups in various proceedings at the FCC. The issues are critical and influence the diversity of programs people will see on their TV sets, but building a movement around them is difficult, and financial resources are hard to find, he added. Today's regulations will be determined less by thousands of people writing to the FCC and more by whom the president nominates as regulators and who wins confirmation.[46]

By 2003 the FCC under chairman Michael Powell was easing the rules on ownership of television stations and other communications properties, but not without resistance from the public interest media groups. "A greater number of owners means more competition and a wider variety of individuals making decisions about what the American people can see and hear," according to the Media Access Project. In addition, if control of broadcast stations were not so concentrated, stations might not be so prohibitively expensive, and minorities and women, underrepresented in ownership, might be able to raise the capital to purchase a media company.[47]

FCC action, community pressure, and simple common sense in the face of shifting demographics led to changes in the complexion of broadcasting staffs from the 1970s onward. Even as that occurred, some Americans were changing their attitudes about affirmative action. The movement toward curbing affirmative action programs gathered steam in California in the mid-1990s. University of California

Board of Regents member Ward Connerly led an effort that resulted in the repeal of the university's affirmative action program in 1995. He also sponsored a ballot proposition to end such programs in all state agencies, which passed in 1996.

By April 1998 this trend caught up with the FCC. The federal appeals court overturned the FCC's affirmative action program. In this case, the NAACP had challenged the license renewal of two stations in Clayton, Missouri, owned by the Lutheran Church–Missouri Synod. The NAACP said that the stations were deficient in hiring blacks. The FCC agreed that the stations had not made adequate efforts to hire minorities but had renewed the licenses. It ordered regular affirmative action reports. The church appealed, going before a changed appeals court. Gone were Judges Burger, McGowan, and Tamm. In an opinion written by Laurence H. Silberman, appointed by President Reagan, the court ruled that the agency's program did not serve a compelling public interest, like eradicating racial discrimination, and brought undue pressure on broadcasters to hire minorities.

At the time that the court ruled, nearly 20 percent of television and radio employees were minority-group members. That was double the percentage in 1971, not long after the rules were adopted. "The main reason for that has been this program," that is, the FCC's affirmative action rules, Andrew Schwartzman of the Media Access Project told the *New York Times*.[48]

The FCC set about revising its rules to try to meet the court's concerns. In January 2000 it adopted rules explicitly stating that a broadcaster's record in hiring women and minorities was not to be used as a factor in deciding whether to renew the station's license. The new rules also required broadcasters to undertake various outreach activities when they had job openings. The FCC policy required that license holders continue to file reports on their efforts, but these records would be used only to monitor industry employment trends and prepare reports to Congress.[49]

Even so, a year later the federal appeals court struck down the new FCC rules, saying that they still created pressure to recruit women and minorities. Commission chairman William Kennard called the decision outrageous, adding, "We're at a time when there is a troubling disconnect between images people see on television and the realities of our multicultural society. One way the FCC has tried to bridge this divide is by trying to get the broadcasters to be sensitive to recruiting broadly. This decision says you can't do that, in effect."[50]

In November 2002 the FCC approved new equal employment opportunity rules that did not specifically target women and minorities. The new rules required only that stations publicize vacancies and participate in job fairs and similar activities, with no obligation to focus on any particular category of people. The rules were tame ones, designed to try to pass court muster. The president of the NAB complained, however, that the new rules seemed to have done nothing to alleviate the burden of paperwork generated by "over-regulatory EEO rules." Broadcasters feared that civil rights groups might use any required annual reports as a basis for lawsuits. They would have preferred using tax credits to encourage minority and female hiring.[51]

Thus the FCC at the beginning of the twenty-first century was geared toward less regulation to enforce fair portrayal of issues by the media and to enhance employment opportunities for minorities and women in broadcasting. It was allowing increased concentration of ownership of the media. These trends made it more difficult for members of the public to exercise effectively their right to participate in FCC matters that had been won in the WLBT case. Despite the efforts of those coalitions still working in these areas, a chapter in broadcasting history had undeniably ended, one that had nonetheless had a transformative effect on how Americans thought about television and its impact on their lives.

EPILOGUE

By the beginning of the twenty-first century, WLBT remained the market leader in Jackson, especially dominating news broadcasting with forty-seven half hours a week. But the universe of television had changed, just as Jackson and Mississippi had changed. No longer were there just two channels serving the Mississippi capital. Cable stations abounded. To be sure, there were more roles for blacks on national television—but they seemed to be in situation comedies with only a few starring roles in dramas.[1] At WLBT, the staff was about 40 percent minority. Jackson had a black mayor and a black police chief. The Mississippi House of Representatives was almost 30 percent black and the state Senate almost 20 percent black. When this case began, there were no black state legislators.

Dan Modisett, vice president and general manager of WLBT, expressed pride that his station's workforce was well integrated in terms of equal responsibility and pay. African Americans filled the jobs of program director, chief engineer, and general sales manager, added Modisett, who is white.[2]

TV-3, the product of the agreement between the contending applicants, had taken control of WLBT in 1980 after the FCC awarded it the permanent license. Early in 1984 a new company formed by several TV-3 stockholders joined with Buford Television Corporation of Tyler, Texas, to buy the station. They brought in Frank Melton of Houston as chief executive officer. Aaron Henry remained chairman of the board. There clearly wasn't room at WLBT for two men of the firm wills of Melton and William Dilday, who had been station manager under interim operator Communications Improvement, Inc., and then TV-3. Melton fired Dilday. Civic Communication, a resurrection of the name of the Walter Hall–backed contender, was established as the holding company for WLBT and in 1986 bought Buford out.[3] Aaron Henry was still board chairman, and Melton, who is black, continued running the station.

Henry, one of the original WLBT challengers, was elected to the Mississippi legislature in 1979. He served there almost until his death in 1997. In his role at WLBT, Henry said he always thought the station "had to maintain the opportunities for blacks and other minorities to have access to the station because that was the basis on which we won the license from the FCC."[4] The Reverend R. L. T. Smith, the other Mississippi challenger, died in 1993. The Reverend Everett Parker retired as head of the Office of Communication of the United Church of Christ in 1983 but remained a communications activist.

Melton, who exuded self-confidence, drew local headlines in the early 1990s as "the angriest man in Mississippi" for his crusade against drug dealers in Jackson. He named names of drug dealers on the air and kept prodding the police department and local political leaders to get them off the streets.[5] He worked actively with youths through the YMCA in Jackson. In 2002, after another sale of WLBT, he was named executive director of the Mississippi Bureau of Narcotics, the state's enforcement and prevention agency.

In 2000 WLBT and two other stations owned by Civic merged with Cosmos Broadcasting, a subsidiary of Liberty Corporation. The move gave Cosmos—today known simply as Liberty Corp.—fifteen television stations. Melton said consolidation in the industry led to the deal. If a syndicator came to Jackson to sell programs, he said, he couldn't compete because he had only three stations and the others in town were part of larger organizations such as Media General that could pay more. The majority of the station's owners would thus be white, Melton said, adding that that was a fact of life in publicly traded companies.[6] Mergers such as this one became possible as the FCC relaxed its rules on how many stations any group could own. Earlier concerns about media concentration seem almost quaint today.

The merger squared with a drop in the number of minority-owned television stations in this country. The most recent figures, from a Commerce Department report in January 2001, show that minority ownership of television stations has declined to the lowest point since the government began collecting data in 1990. Minorities owned twenty-three full-power commercial television stations, or 1.9 percent of the licensed stations. In 1995 and 1996, minorities owned as many as thirty-eight TV stations. The report showed the effects of mergers and limited access to investment capital.[7]

With WLBT in new corporate hands, with the television industry increasingly deregulated, with affirmative action programs dormant if not dead, with the Fairness Doctrine no longer enforced, with the public interest movement a shell of its former self, what then is the lasting legacy of this sixteen-year legal struggle? No one can erase history—the impact that the WLBT case had on the industry and on the political dialog in Jackson. As WLBT manager Dan Modisett said, "It was a sea change in the whole industry. It woke an industry up."[8]

To summarize:

- The case created the precedent that allowed the public to participate in FCC issues concerning the powerful medium of broadcasting. Nothing has altered that standing, as it is called, although public participation often has limited effect today because of ongoing deregulation of broadcasting. Perhaps as important in the long run was the idea that this case made people think in new ways about the impact of television on their own lives.

- The appeals court decisions buttressed the controversial Fairness Doctrine, saying in effect that stations should know that presenting controversial issues and allowing response time to those who disagreed were part of their obligation as public licensees. Other groups were able to use that doctrine to try to win access to airtime for their concerns for more than a decade thereafter. And as one public interest lawyer said, the standard of fairness is higher for local television stations now than it was at the outset of this case.
- When WLBT lost its license, the case sent an earthquake through the industry. Under petition by the same group that launched the WLBT case, the FCC had to confront the issue of employment discrimination in broadcasting. It required, for nearly three decades, affirmative action by broadcasters to hire and promote more women and minorities. These rules, with the U.S. government standing behind them, prodded broadcasters to diversify their staffs.
- A television station with one of the potentially largest black audiences for local news intensified its coverage of that community at a time of immense political and social turmoil in Mississippi. That, remember, had been the original aim of the challenge.

Some may remember the WLBT case for the courage and doggedness of the challengers and for the impact they had on both the industry and the community around Jackson, Mississippi. Others will doubtless damn the challengers for singling out one broadcaster for the practices of many at the time and for pushing the FCC to examine programming content. But the case was indeed historic. It changed lives and perceptions, and it remains an example of what can happen when the public not only cares but also acts.

CAST OF CHARACTERS

ANN ALDRICH—Attorney who worked with the WLBT challengers, especially on the FCC hearing in Jackson in 1967.

TOM ALEXANDER—One of WLBT's first black cameramen and directors.

REUBEN ANDERSON—Jackson attorney, first black member of state supreme court, member of Channel 3, Inc., group seeking permanent license.

FRED BEARD—Station manager of WLBT from 1953 to 1965.

WARREN BURGER—Head of the three-judge federal court of appeals panel that, first, ruled that the FCC had to let the public participate in regulatory matters and, second, blistered the FCC and in effect took the license from Lamar Life Broadcasting; later chief justice of the United States.

HODDING CARTER III—Editor of the *Delta Democrat-Times*, member of the Civic Communications Corporation that sought permanent license.

KENNETH COX—FCC member who dissented in both WLBT decisions.

KENNETH L. DEAN—President of the board of Communications Improvement Inc., the interim management of WLBT.

PATRICIA DERIAN—One of the white monitors trained by Everett Parker to check WLBT programming, member of Civic Communications Corporation.

WILLIAM DILDAY—First black TV station manager in the South, hired by the interim management of WLBT.

LENORE EHRIG—FCC administrative law judge who presided over the comparative licensing hearings in the 1970s.

CHARLES EVERS—NAACP official in Mississippi, mayor of Fayette, member of original Civic Communications Corporation group, author of controversial memoir.

MEDGAR EVERS—Mississippi field secretary for the NAACP, filed complaints against WLBT starting in 1957, appeared on the station just weeks before he was killed from ambush in front of his home.

MARTIN FIRESTONE—Attorney for Civic Communications Corporation.

ALVIN FLANNES—Jackson businessman; member of Jackson Television, which competed for permanent license; instrumental in final settlement negotiations.

HENRY GELLER—FCC general counsel.

WINIFRED GREEN—One of the WLBT monitors in 1964.

J. HEWITT GRIFFIN—Longtime WLBT program director and acting manager between Robert McRaney's firing and William Dilday's hiring.

WALTER HALL—Texas banker who bankrolled Civic Communications Corporation's fight for WLBT license, instrumental in settlement.

ROBERT HEARIN—President of Lamar Life Insurance Company, active as WLBT prepared for 1967 hearings.

GORDON AND MARY ANN HENDERSON—White Jacksonians who helped organize local monitors.

AARON HENRY—Clarksdale pharmacist and one of the black Mississippians who helped challenge the WLBT license, president of the state NAACP, and later state legislator and chairman of the board of WLBT.

E. WILLIAM HENRY—Chairman of the FCC at the time of the first WLBT decision, from which he dissented.

HARRY HUGE—Arnold & Porter attorney who worked with WLBT staff as it prepared for 1967 hearing.

ROSEL HYDE—FCC member during first WLBT decision, chairman at the time of the second, voted for license renewal both times.

NICHOLAS JOHNSON—FCC member who dissented from the second FCC decision renewing the WLBT license after the Jackson hearing.

EARLE JONES—Jackson businessman, board member of Communications Improvement Inc.

ORRIN JUDD—Prominent Baptist and attorney to whom Everett Parker turned for legal representation when communications law specialists wouldn't touch the WLBT challenge.

WILLIAM A. KEHOE JR.—FCC attorney, questioned Beard at 1967 FCC hearing.

REV. EDWIN KING—White Mississippian who was Tougaloo College chaplain, testified at the FCC hearing in Jackson about WLBT news coverage.

JAY KYLE—FCC hearing examiner for Jackson hearings, recommended that the license be renewed.

MARY ANN LINDSEY—One of WLBT's early black employees, now program director.

P. K. LUTKEN—President of Lamar Life Broadcasting when WLBT license was challenged.

CARL MCGOWAN—Federal appeals court judge who twice overruled FCC on WLBT renewals.

ROBERT MCRANEY JR.—WLBT station manager from 1965 to 1972.

FRANK MELTON—WLBT top executive from mid-1980s to 2000, when station was sold; fired Dilday.

REED MILLER—Arnold & Porter attorney, represented Lamar at 1967 hearings and in fight for permanent license.

EARLE K. "DICK" MOORE—New York attorney, represented the Office of Communication of the United Church of Christ in its challenge of WLBT, later represented other public interest groups.

WILLIAM MOUNGER—Chief stockholder in Dixie National Broadcasting, which initially won the permanent WLBT license.

CLINT MURCHISON JR. AND JOHN MURCHISON—Wealthy Texans, owners of Lamar Life Insurance Company, retained Arnold & Porter to represent WLBT.

JOHN O'MALLEY—FCC staff member sent to Mississippi in 1962 along with William Ray to investigate complaints after WLBT editorialized against entry of James Meredith as the first black student at the University of Mississippi.

REV. EVERETT PARKER—Head of the Office of Communication of the United Church of Christ who conceived the challenge and trained the monitors who documented WLBT's programming; later helped with other license challenges and petitioned FCC for equal employment rules.

RUBEL PHILLIPS—Key figure in Dixie National Broadcasting and twice Republican gubernatorial candidate in Mississippi; investigation into his role with a company involved in stock fraud effectively killed Dixie's application.

RANDALL PINKSTON—First regular black anchor on WLBT's prime-time evening newscasts, later joined CBS News.

PAUL PORTER—Attorney for WLBT, former FCC chair, and cofounder of the Washington law firm of Arnold & Porter.

WALTER SADDLER—Early black anchor at WLBT under interim management.

RICHARD SANDERS—WLBT news director from 1954 to 1965.

AARON SHIRLEY—Jackson pediatrician, vice president of the board of Communications Improvement, Inc.

HAZEL BRANNON SMITH—Mississippi newspaper editor who won the Pulitzer Prize for editorials on racial issues; testified at 1967 Jackson hearing.

REV. R. L. T. SMITH—One of the black Mississippians who helped challenge the WLBT license; initially denied purchase of airtime for a congressional campaign in 1962.

EDWARD A. TAMM—Federal appeals court judge who twice ruled against FCC on WLBT license renewals.

ROBERT TRAVIS—Jackson attorney who organized Channel 3, Inc.

WEYMAN H. D. WALKER—Organized Civic Communications Corporation, connected Martin Firestone with Walter Hall.

REV. ANDREW YOUNG—Civil rights worker who testified at FCC hearing in Jackson; later became a member of Congress, U.S. ambassador to the United Nations, and mayor of Atlanta.

CHARLES YOUNG—Meridian businessman, member of Civic Communications Corporation, later state legislator.

TIMELINE

1955—Complaints filed with FCC charge WLBT with violations of Fairness Doctrine on racial issues.

1959—FCC grants license renewal to WLBT despite findings of Fairness Doctrine violations.

1962—FCC receives complaints about Mississippi broadcasters after disturbances surrounding enrollment of James Meredith at University of Mississippi; FCC sends two investigators to Mississippi.

1963—FCC requests that WLBT and other stations submit detailed factual reports in response to critical investigation findings.

1964—WLBT files its renewal application; United Church of Christ, Aaron Henry, and the Reverend R. L. T. Smith file a petition to deny WLBT license.

MAY 19, **1965**—FCC grants a one-year renewal of WLBT's license on a 4-2 vote, although finding that serious issues regarding public interest had been raised.

JUNE 10, **1965**—United Church of Christ appeals to federal court of appeals in Washington, D.C., asking for standing in the case and claiming the FCC should have held a hearing.

MARCH 25, **1966**—Federal court of appeals rules that the FCC had erred in not granting a hearing and says the public must be allowed to participate.

MAY 26, **1966**—FCC orders a hearing.

MAY 1, **1967**—FCC begins hearing conducted by Jay Kyle, in Jackson, Mississippi.

OCTOBER 13, **1967**—Hearing examiner decides that renewal of WLBT's license would serve the public interest.

JUNE 27, 1968—FCC renews WLBT license, with Nicholas Johnson and Kenneth Cox dissenting. United Church of Christ appeals to federal appeals court.

JUNE 20, 1969—U.S. Court of Appeals reverses FCC and directs it to conduct new proceeding to determine a permanent licensee.

SEPTEMBER 8, 1970—FCC names Communications Improvement, Inc., as interim operator of WLBT.

APRIL 5, 1971—Hearings conducted by administrative law judge Lenore Ehrig open to determine licensee among five competing groups.

APRIL 1971—Charles Evers's book discussing his earlier prostitution and gambling operations is published, eventually contributing to disqualification of the group of which he is part, Civic Communications Corporation.

APRIL 20, 1973—Administrative law judge Ehrig awards permanent license to Dixie National Broadcasting group.

JANUARY 11, 1974—FCC review board reopens the case after investigations reveal new information about Rubel Phillips, one of the Dixie National stockholders; he was later convicted of stock fraud.

MAY 1977—Attempted settlement fails.

OCTOBER 25, 1978—Contending organizations agree to a settlement creating a majority-black–owned station; it is approved by administrative law judge Ehrig December 3, 1979.

1980—Communications Improvement, Inc., turns station over to the group created by the settlement, TV-3, with Aaron Henry as the chairman of the board.

NOTES

INTRODUCTION

1. All the material in the Introduction concerning Randall Pinkston comes from an interview with Pinkston by the author on March 11, 1999, in New York and from several subsequent telephone conversations.
2. J. Hewitt Griffin interview, July 7, 1999, Jackson, Miss.
3. Steven A. Holmes, "FCC Requirement on Minority Hiring Is Voided by Court," *New York Times*, April 15, 1998.
4. Neil A. Lewis, "FCC Revises Rule on Hiring of Women and Minorities," *New York Times*, January 21, 2000; John Schwartz, "FCC Unveils New Rules on Hiring," *Washington Post*, January 21, 2000; Stephen Labaton, "Court Rules Agency Erred On Mandate for Minorities," *New York Times*, January 17, 2001; Doug Halonen, "FCC OKs Rules on Equal Employment," *Electronic Media*, November 11, 2002, p. 4; Edmund Sanders, "FCC Is Expected to Readopt Rules on Equal Employment," *Los Angeles Times*, November 7, 2002.

1. SEEKING A VOICE

1. *Report of the National Advisory Commission on Civil Disorders* (New York: Bantam, 1968), p. 366.
2. Pete Daniel, *Lost Revolutions: The South in the 1950s* (Chapel Hill: University of North Carolina Press, 2000), pp. 179–305.
3. Lamar Life Insurance Co. records, box 24, folder 52, Mississippi Department of Archives and History, Jackson.
4. Junior League of Jackson, *Jackson Landmarks* (Jackson, Miss.: Calvin Hale Advertising, 1982), p. 42.

5. Lamar Life Insurance Co. records, box 24, folders 47–57.

6. Fred Beard interview, April 17, 2000, Columbus, Miss.

7. Richard Sanders interview, September 14, 2001, Scottsdale, Az.

8. Maurice Thompson, "Through These Portals," November 1968, Lamar Life Insurance Co. records, box 24, folder 53.

9. Hodding Carter, statement attached to "Reply to Opposition to Petition to Intervene and to Deny Application for Renewal," Office of Communication of the United Church of Christ, July 14, 1964, Docket 16663, Vol. 2, FCC files, National Archives, College Park, Md.

10. John Dittmer, *Local People: The Struggle for Civil Rights in Mississippi* (Urbana: University of Illinois Press, 1994), p. 46.

11. Fred Beard testimony, FCC hearing, Jackson, Mississippi, May 8, 1967, p. 810, Docket 16663, Vol. 5, FCC files.

12. NAACP letter to the FCC, October 27, 1955, referenced in a November 16, 1957, letter from J. Francis Pohlhaus, NAACP Washington counsel, to John C. Doerfer, FCC chairman, Docket 16663, Vol. 3, FCC files.

13. Fred Beard to the FCC, December 8, 1955, Docket 16663, Vol. 14, FCC files.

14. Sanders interview, September 14, 2001.

15. Associated Press, "Bayonet Rule Opens Little Rock School to Nine Negro Students; Soldiers Club, Stab Foes of Integration," *Jackson Daily News*, September 25, 1957.

16. Sanders interview, September 14, 2001.

17. Charles Evers and Andrew Szanton, *Have No Fear: The Charles Evers Story* (New York: John Wiley and Sons, 1997), p. 31.

18. Other background material on Medgar Evers's life and work comes from Evers and Szanton, *Have No Fear*; Myrlie Evers and William Peters, *For Us, the Living* (New York: Doubleday, 1967); Myrlie Evers-Williams with Melinda Blau, *Watch Me Fly* (Boston: Little, Brown, 1999); Adam Nossiter, *Of Long Memory: Mississippi and the Murder of Medgar Evers* (Reading, Mass: Addison-Wesley, 1994); and Maryanne Vollers, *Ghosts of Mississippi: The Murder of Medgar Evers, the Trials of Byron de la Beckwith and the Haunting of the New South* (Boston: Little, Brown, 1995).

19. Evers and Peters, *For Us, the Living*, pp. 72–73.

20. Ibid., p. 89.

21. Ibid., p. 79.

22. Vollers, *Ghosts of Mississippi*, p. 43.

23. Medgar Evers, Monthly Report to the NAACP, September 27, 1956, NAACP files, Manuscript Division, Library of Congress, Box C243; Evers and Peters, *For Us, the Living*, p. 165.

24. Telegram from the Mississippi NAACP to President Eisenhower, NAACP files, Library of Congress, Box C243.

25. Fred Friendly, *The Good Guys, the Bad Guys and the First Amendment: Free Speech vs. Fairness in Broadcasting* (New York: Vintage Books, 1977), pp. 21–25; Les Brown, "Fairness Doctrine," *The New York Times Encyclopedia of Television* (New York: Times

Books, 1977). The 1949 clarification was necessary because an equivocal FCC decision in 1941 about political broadcasts on several New England radio stations had led the industry and others to believe that the commission was forbidding editorializing. The FCC waded back into the issues in 1949, denying that its 1941 decision had meant that stations could not editorialize.

26. Medgar Evers to the FCC chairman, October 17, 1957, Docket 16663, Vol. 3, FCC files.

27. J. Francis Pohlhaus, NAACP Washington counsel, to John G. Doerfer, FCC chairman, November 16, 1957, Docket 16663, Vol. 3, FCC files.

28. Mary Jane Morris to Medgar Evers, November 19, 1957, Docket 16663, Vol. 3, FCC files.

29. Fred Beard to Mary Jane Morris, July 17, 1958, Docket 16663, Vol. 3, FCC files.

30. Dittmer, *Local People*, pp. 79–91.

31. WLBT news special script, May 24, 1961, personal files of Richard Sanders.

32. WLBT special report script, May 26, 1961, personal files of Richard Sanders.

33. Report on WLBT coverage of the civil rights movement in Mississippi in the 1960s, submitted as a Lamar exhibit, personal files of Richard Sanders.

34. Hugh Morgan, "Mississippi's Gentle Democrat," *Jackson Capital Reporter*, June 5, 1980, R. L. T. Smith file, Mississippi Department of Archives and History.

35. Evers and Peters, *For Us, the Living*, pp. 237–238.

36. Ibid.

37. R. L. T. Smith to FCC chairman, January 16, 1962, R. L. T. Smith Papers, Tougaloo College, Tougaloo, Miss.

38. R. L. T. Smith to Robert F. Kennedy, January 18, 1962, R. L. T. Smith Papers.

39. Fred Beard telegram to FCC, February 1, 1962, and letter to FCC, February 1, 1962, Docket 16663, Vol. 8, FCC files.

40. R. L. T. Smith to Robert F. Kennedy, February 2, 1962, R. L. T. Smith Papers.

41. Ben F. Waple, acting secretary of the FCC, to R. L. T. Smith, February 8, 1962, Docket 16663, Vol. 8, FCC files.

42. Eleanor Roosevelt, "Serenity through Strength" column, March 1962, R. L. T. Smith Papers.

43. James A. Wechsler, "A Quiet Man," *New York Post*, March 20, 1962.

44. Fred Beard to Ben F. Waple, April 12, 1962, Docket 16663, Vol. 8, FCC files.

45. James A. Wechsler, "Southern Gag," *New York Post*, April 17, 1962.

46. Ben F. Waple to Lamar Life Broadcasting, April 17, 1962, Docket 16663, Vol. 8, FCC files.

47. R. L. T. Smith to Burke Marshall, April 23, 1962, R. L. T. Smith Papers.

48. Sanders interview, September 14, 2001.

49. United Press International, May 4, 1962, DOCKET 16663, Vol. 9, FCC files.

50. R. L. T. Smith to Eleanor Roosevelt, April 24 and May 8, 1962, R. L. T. Smith Papers.

51. R. L. T. Smith notes about Eleanor Roosevelt, R. L. T. Smith Papers.

52. L. M. Sepaugh, quoted in Inter-Office Memorandum to the FCC from the chief of its Broadcast Bureau summarizing the FCC investigation into broadcasting concerning the entry of James Meredith to the University of Mississippi, July 11, 1963, pp. 12–13, FCC meeting agenda files, National Archives.

53. Medgar Evers to Fred Beard, June 28, 1962, and Beard to Evers, July 12, 1962, Docket 16663, Vol. 12, FCC files.

54. Medgar Evers to Fred Beard, July 16, 1962, Docket 16663, Vol. 13; Russell Rowell to W. C. Wells Jr., July 20, 1962, Docket 16663, Vol. 9, FCC files.

55. Material prepared by WLBT for FCC, personal files of Richard Sanders.

56. WLBT editorial delivered by Fred Beard, September 12, 1962, Docket 16663, Vol. 8, FCC files.

57. Ross Barnett, "A Statewide Address on Television and Radio to the People of Mississippi," September 13, 1962, Docket 16663, Vol. 8, FCC files.

58. WLBT editorial delivered by Fred Beard, September 14, 1962, Docket 16663, Vol. 8, FCC files.

59. WLBT editorial delivered by Fred Beard, September 17, 1962, Docket 16663, Vol. 8, FCC files.

60. AFL-CIO Labor Council, Petition Protesting Grant of Application Requesting Hearing and Other Relief, June 1, 1964, Docket 16663, Vol. 1, FCC files.

61. Fred Beard memorandum on interview with William Ray and John O'Malley, November 21, 1962, p. 1, Docket 16663, Vol. 8, FCC files.

62. WLBT editorial delivered by Fred Beard, September 21, 1962, Docket 16663, Vol. 8, FCC files.

63. WLBT Comment, broadcast by Richard Sanders, October 4, 1962, personal files of Richard Sanders.

64. Inter-Office Memorandum to the FCC summarizing the FCC investigation, July 11, 1963, p. 20, FCC files.

65. William B. Ray, *FCC: The Ups and Downs of Radio-TV Regulation* (Ames: Iowa State University Press, 1990), pp. x–xi.

66. Interview with John O'Malley, May 17, 1999, Fredericksburg, Tex. All subsequent quotes from O'Malley are from that interview.

67. Inter-Office Memorandum to the FCC summarizing the FCC investigation, p. 17.

68. Fred Beard memorandum, p. 3, Docket 16663, Vol. 8, FCC files.

69. Inter-Office Memorandum to the FCC summarizing the FCC investigation, p. 14.

70. Fred Beard memorandum, p. 2, Docket 16663, Vol. 8, FCC files.

71. Inter-Office Memorandum to the FCC summarizing the FCC investigation, pp. 12–13.

72. NAACP, "Background Information on New Desegregation Drive in Jackson, Miss.," May 28, 1963, p. 2.

73. Mayor Allen C. Thompson speech, WJDX and WLBT, May 13, 1963, R. L. T. Smith Papers.

74. Dittmer, *Local People*, p. 160.

75. Evers and Peters, *For Us, the Living*, pp. 267–268.

76. Nossiter, *Of Long Memory*, p. 30.

77. Medgar Evers speech on WLBT, May 20, 1963, Docket 16663, Vol. 10, FCC files. See also Adam Nossiter, *Of Long Memory*, p. 58; John Salter, "Medgar Evers Speaks—May 1963," in *Freedom Is a Constant Struggle: An Anthology of the Mississippi Civil Rights Movement* (Montgomery, Ala.: Black Belt Press, 1999), pp. 36–37.

78. Evers and Peters, *For Us, the Living*, p. 269.

79. Evers-Williams, *Watch Me Fly*, pp. 74–76.

80. Ibid., p. 77.

81. Inter-Office Memorandum to the FCC summarizing the FCC investigation, p. 26.

82. Ben F. Waple to Lamar Life Broadcasting Co., July 25, 1963, Docket 16663, Vol. 8, FCC files.

83. P. K. Lutken to Ben F. Waple, FCC secretary, October 29, 1963, Docket 16663, Vol. 8, FCC files.

84. Howard Monderer to Ben F. Waple, FCC secretary, January 21, 1964, Docket 16663, Vol. 8, FCC files.

2. SERVING WHOSE PUBLIC INTEREST?

1. Carolyn Martindale and Lillian Rae Dunlap, "The African Americans," in *U.S. News Coverage of Racial Minorities: A Sourcebook*, ed. Beverly Ann Deepe Keever, Carolyn Martindale, and Mary Ann Weston (Westport, Conn.: Greenwood Press, 1993); Jannette L. Dates and William Barlow, eds., *Split Image: African Americans in the Mass Media* (Washington, D.C.: Howard University Press, 1990).

2. *Report of the National Advisory Commission on Civil Disorders* (New York: Bantam, 1968), p. 383.

3. Dr. Martin Luther King Jr.'s life and work have been featured in many books, including David J. Garrow, *Bearing the Cross: Martin Luther King, Jr., and the Southern Christian Leadership Conference* (New York: W. Morrow, 1986); Adam Fairclough, *To Redeem the Soul of America: The Southern Christian Leadership Conference and Martin Luther King, Jr.* (Athens: University of Georgia Press, 1987); Taylor Branch, *Parting the Waters: America in the King Years 1954–63* (New York: Simon and Schuster, 1988); Taylor Branch, *Pillar of Fire: America in the King Years 1963–65* (New York: Simon and Schuster, 1998); and Marshall Frady, *Martin Luther King, Jr.* (New York: Viking, 2002).

4. Andrew Young, *An Easy Burden: The Civil Rights Movement and the Transformation of America* (New York: Harper Collins, 1996).

5. So many years later, it is difficult to date this meeting. Parker remembers that it occurred perhaps as early as 1956–1957, the date cited by Robert B. Horwitz in his paper on the case, "Broadcast Reform Revisited: The Reverend Everett C. Parker and the Standing Case" (distributed by the Office of Communication of the United Church of Christ) or perhaps as late as 1961. In any event, King wanted Andrew Young, who had been employed by the National Council of Churches in New York in 1957, to work on his staff at the SCLC. In August 1961 Young went to work at Dorchester for an SCLC program financed through a grant from the Field Foundation routed through the United Church of Christ. Young became executive director of the SCLC in 1963, about the time it organized marches in Birmingham that were met with fierce official resistance, including use of fire hoses and police dogs on demonstrators.

6. Unless otherwise indicated, all information concerning Everett Parker comes from interviews by the author with Parker, December 9, 1997, and October 1, 1998, White Plains, N.Y., and a telephone interview, December 19, 2002. Similar and useful material can be found in interviews conducted with Parker by George Korn in 1990 and by Les Brown in 1996.

7. Everett Parker interview by Les Brown, August 30, 1996.

8. Erwin G. Krasnow, Lawrence D. Longley, and Herbert A. Terry, *The Politics of Broadcast Regulation* (New York: St. Martin's, 1982), pp. 10–15.

9. Fred Friendly, *The Good Guys, the Bad Guys, and the First Amendment: Free Speech vs. Fairness in Broadcasting* (New York: Vintage, 1977), p. 15.

10. Krasnow, Longley, and Terry, *The Politics of Broadcast Regulation*, p. 40.

11. Nicholas Johnson and John Jay Dystel, "A Day in the Life: The Federal Communications Commission," *Yale Law Journal* 82, No. 8, (July 1973), p. 1576.

12. Friendly, *The Good Guys, the Bad Guys and the First Amendment*, pp. 45–54; Les Brown, "Red Lion Decision," *The New York Times Encyclopedia of Television* (New York: Times Books, 1977), p. 359.

13. Douglas H. Ginsburg, Michael H. Botein, and Mark D. Director, *Regulation of the Electronic Mass Media: Law and Policy for Radio, Television, Cable and the New Video Technologies*, 2nd edn. (St. Paul, Minn.: West, 1991), p. 324.

14. David R. Colburn, "Florida Politics in the Twentieth Century," in *The New History of Florida*, ed. Michael Gannon (Gainesville: University Press of Florida, 1996); Michael Gannon, *Florida: A Short History* (Gainesville: University Press of Florida, 1993); Tom R. Wagy, *Governor LeRoy Collins of Florida: Spokesman of the New South* (University: University of Alabama Press, 1985).

15. Quoted in Donald P. Ranly, "The Challengers: Social Pressures on the Press, 1965–1975" (Ph.D. diss., University of Missouri–Columbia, 1976), p. 184.

16. Everett Parker interview by George Korn, May 28, 1990, as part of Korn's dissertation research at Southern Illinois University, personal files of Everett Parker.

17. All material about Gordon and Mary Ann Henderson in this chapter comes from a telephone interview by the author with Gordon Henderson on February 28, 2000, and correspondence from Henderson on February 23, 2000.

18. Edwin King interview, April 1, 1998, Jackson, Miss.

19. Instructions to monitors, Office of Communication of the United Church of Christ, Attachment B, exhibit 1, joint appendix of stipulations and exhibits in the U.S. Court of Appeals for the District of Columbia, Docket 19409, Library of Congress, Washington, D.C.

20. Gordon Henderson described the monitoring arrangement in testimony before the FCC hearing, May 1, 1967, Jackson, Miss., pp. 121–129, Docket 16663, Vol. 5, FCC files, National Archives, College Park, Md.

21. William Greider, "TV Reform Slowing; Miss. Case May Be 1st, Last," *Washington Post*, July 17, 1973.

22. Winifred Green interview, July 7, 1999, Jackson, Miss.

23. "Report of Local Programming Station WLBT-TV, Jackson, Miss., March 1–7, 1964," Office of Communication of the United Church of Christ, joint appendix of stipulations and exhibits, pp. 3467–3482, Docket 19409, Library of Congress.

24. Ibid.

25. John Dittmer, *Local People: The Struggle for Civil Rights in Mississippi* (Urbana: University of Illinois Press, 1994), p. 180.

26. Edward Hudson, "Judge Orrin G. Judd Dies; Cited Willowbrook Abuse," *New York Times*, July 8, 1976.

27. Petition to Intervene and to Deny Application for Renewal, Office of Communication of the United Church of Christ, April 15, 1964, p. 3, Docket 16663, Vol. 1, FCC files.

28. Arthur Whitman, "The Ordeal of Reverend Smith," *Saga, The Magazine for Men* 24, no. 6 (September 1962), p. 92.

29. "Negroes Hear Barnett," *Jackson Daily News*, January 4, 1962; "Negro Raps Gallery Pass Legislation," *Jackson Clarion Ledger*, January 7, 1962.

30. Whitman, "The Ordeal of Reverend Smith," p. 92.

31. R. L. T. Smith testimony, FCC hearing, Jackson, Miss., May 2, 1967, p. 242, Docket 16663, Vol. 5, FCC files.

32. Everett Parker interview, December 9, 1997, White Plains, N.Y.

33. Aaron Henry with Constance Curry, *Aaron Henry: The Fire Ever Burning* (Jackson: University Press of Mississippi, 2000).

34. Robert Smith, oral history, "Staying the Course," in Henry, *Aaron Henry*, p. 215.

35. Everett Parker interview, December 9, 1997.

3. ENTER WARREN BURGER

1. Memorandum opinion and order, FCC, May 19, 1965, Pike & Fisher, 5 RR 2d, Vol. 105.

2. E. William Henry interview, July 10, 1999, Memphis, Tenn.

3. Les Brown, "Richard A. Mack," *The New York Times Encyclopedia of Television* (New York: Times Books, 1977), p. 255, and "John Doerfer," p. 121.

4. WLBT's Opposition to Petition to Intervene and to Deny Application for Renewal, filed May 15, 1964, pp. 7–8, Docket 16663, Vol. 1, FCC files, National Archives, College Park, Md.

5. Memorandum opinion and order, FCC, May 19, 1965, pp. 21–22.

6. "Short Renewals in Mississippi," *Broadcasting*, May 24, 1965, p. 68.

7. E. William Henry interview, July 10, 1999.

8. Henry Geller interview, January 6, 1999, Washington, D.C.

9. Les Brown, "Lee Loevinger," *The New York Times Encyclopedia of Television*, p. 249.

10. Les Brown, "Robert Bartley," *The New York Times Encyclopedia of Television*, pp. 35–36; "Robert E. Lee," p. 240; "Rosel H. Hyde," p. 202.

11. E. William Henry interview, July 10, 1999.

12. Kenneth Cox interview, March 1, 1999, Washington, D.C.

13. E. William Henry interview, July 10, 1999.

14. Dissenting Statement of Chairman E. William Henry in Which Commissioner Kenneth A. Cox Joins, Memorandum opinion and order, FCC, May 19, 1965, pp. 25–27, 40.

15. E. William Henry interview, July 10, 1999.

16. John Herbers, "FCC Tells Southern Stations to Halt Radio-TV Racial Bias," *New York Times*, May 21, 1965; Richard K. Doan, "Mississippi TV Station—Bias Rap," *New York Herald Tribune*, May 21, 1965.

17. Walter Pincus, "Discriminating TV in Mississippi," *New Republic*, June 5, 1965, pp. 7–8.

18. Memorandum opinion and order, FCC, May 19, 1965, p. 12.

19. Christopher Banks, *Judicial Politics in the D.C. Circuit Court* (Baltimore: Johns Hopkins University Press, 1999), p. 1.

20. Notice of Appeal, Office of Communication of the United Church of Christ, Aaron Henry, Robert L. T. Smith and United Church of Christ at Tougaloo, Appellants, v. Federal Communications Commission, Appellee, Lamar Life Broadcasting Company, Intervener, filed June 10, 1965, pp. 4–7, Docket 19409, U.S. Court of Appeals files, Federal Records Center, Suitland, Md.

21. Brief for Appellants in the U.S. Court of Appeals, District of Columbia Circuit, Office of Communication et al., pp. 20–21, 30–31, 40–44, Docket 19409, Court of Appeals files, Library of Congress.

22. Brief for Appellee in the U.S. Court of Appeals, District of Columbia Circuit, Federal Communications Commission, pp. 21–22, 38–53, 55, Docket 19409, Court of Appeals files, Library of Congress.

23. Fred Beard interview, April 7, 2000, Columbus, Miss.

24. Susanne Beard interview, April 7, 2000, Columbus, Miss.

25. John T. McQuiston, "Paul A. Porter, Capital Lawyer, Who Held New Deal Posts, Dies," *New York Times*, November 27, 1975; Kenneth Crawford, "Lawyer Paul A. Porter

Dies at 71," *Washington Post*, November 27, 1975; Les Brown, "Paul A. Porter," *The New York Times Encyclopedia of Television*, pp. 339–340.

26. Transcript, Paul A. Porter oral history interview, October 2, 1970, by Joe B. Frantz, tape 1, pp. 2–3, Lyndon B. Johnson Library, Austin, Tex.

27. Transcript, Paul A. Porter oral history interview, October 2, 1970, by Joe B. Frantz, tape 1, pp. 9, 18.

28. Everett Parker interview, December 9, 1997.

29. Richard Pearson, "U.S. Appeals Court Judge Edward A. Tamm, 79, Dies," *Washington Post*, September 23, 1985.

30. Bart Barnes, "Appeals Court Judge Carl McGowan, 76, Dies," *Washington Post*, December 22, 1987.

31. Ann Aldrich interview (telephone), December 29, 1998.

32. Joan Biskupic, "Ex-Chief Justice Warren Burger Dead at Age 87; Court Helped Define Major Social Changes," *Washington Post*, June 26, 1995; Linda Greenhouse, "Warren Burger Is Dead at 87; Was Chief Justice for 17 Years," *New York Times*, June 26, 1995; David G. Savage, "Former Chief Justice Warren Burger Dies at 87," *Los Angeles Times*, June 26, 1995.

33. Lisa Grace Lednicer, "Community Took Pride in Hometown Achiever," *St. Paul Pioneer Press*, June 26, 1995.

34. Savage, "Former Chief Justice Warren Burger Dies."

35. Henry Geller interview, January 6, 1999.

36. Brief for Appellants in the U.S. Court of Appeals, p. 23.

37. 359 F.2d 994 (1966), pp. 994–1009.

38. Ibid., p. 1005.

39. Albert Kramer interview, July 11, 1998, Washington, D.C.

4. THE FCC HEARS NO EVIL

1. Earle K. Moore interview, September 30, 1998, New York.

2. Robert McRaney Jr. interview, April 7, 2000, Columbus, Miss.

3. Robert McRaney Jr. interview (telephone), October 2, 2002.

4. "In the Wings: WLBT Hearing, FCC Votes to Schedule Court- Ordered Renewal Hearings on Race Issue," *Broadcasting*, May 30, 1966, p. 59; FCC order in reapplications of Lamar Life Broadcasting Co., May 25, 1966, Docket 16663, FCC files, National Archives, College Park, Md.

5. Statement of Commissioner Kenneth A. Cox concurring in part and dissenting in part, FCC order of May 25, 1966, Docket 16663, Vol. 4, FCC files.

6. Petition for reconsideration, Office of Communication of the United Church of Christ, June 17, 1966, Docket 16663, Vol. 4, FCC files.

7. Opposition to petition for reconsideration, Lamar Life, July 12, 1966, Docket 16663, Vol. 4, FCC files.

8. Memorandum opinion and order, FCC, September 27, 1966, Docket 16663, Vol. 4, FCC files.

9. Statement of Commissioner Kenneth A. Cox concurring in part and dissenting in part, Memorandum opinion and order, FCC, September 27, 1966.

10. Henry Geller interview, January 6, 1999, Washington, D.C.

11. Earle K. Moore, 1967 office calendars, Earle K. Moore Papers, New York Law School, New York.

12. Earle K. Moore memorandum to Everett Parker, March 17, 1967, Earle K. Moore Papers.

13. Everett Parker memorandum to Orrin Judd and Earle K. Moore, March 23, 1967, Earle K. Moore Papers.

14. Earle K. Moore memorandum to Orrin Judd, April 11, 1967, Earle K. Moore Papers.

15. Earle K. Moore interview, September 30, 1998; William Greider, "TV Reform Slowing; Miss. Case May Be 1st, Last," *Washington Post*, July 17, 1973.

16. Facsimile transmission from Washburn Law School, Office of the Dean, to the author.

17. Prehearing conference transcript, December 13, 1966, Washington, D.C., p. 2, Docket 16663, Vol. 4, FCC files.

18. Motion to designate place of hearing, Lamar Life, December 14, 1966, Docket 16663, Vol. 4, FCC files.

19. Opposition to motion to designate place of hearing, Office of Communication of the United Church of Christ, December 22, 1966, Docket 16663, Vol. 4, FCC files.

20. Memorandum opinion and order by James D. Cunningham, chief hearing examiner, December 27, 1966, Docket 16663, Vol. 4, FCC files.

21. "Challenge in the South," *Newsweek*, May 29, 1967, p. 63.

22. Office of Communication of the United Church of Christ news release, April 10, 1967.

23. Harry Huge interview, August 22, 2000, Washington, D.C.

24. Harry Huge, "Inquest at Jackson State," *New South* 25, no. 2 (summer 1970), p. 66.

25. Harry Huge interview, April 11, 2002, Washington, D.C.

26. Robert McRaney Jr. interview, October 2, 2002.

27. Harry Huge interview, April 11, 2002.

28. Robert McRaney Jr. interview, October 2, 2002.

29. Henry Geller, "Making the System Work," *Access*, March 1985, p. 7.

30. Joel Berson, "Senior Partner in Charge of Wisdom," *Access*, March 1985, p. 1.

31. Ann Aldrich interview (telephone), December 29, 1998, and "Resume: The Honorable Ann Aldrich," author's files, courtesy of Ann Aldrich.

32. Everett Parker testimony, FCC hearing, Jackson, Mississippi, May 1, 1967, pp. 110–114, Docket 16663, Vol. 5, FCC files.

33. Mary Ann Henderson testimony, FCC hearing, May 1, 1967, pp. 153–156, Docket 16663, Vol. 5, FCC files.

34. Gordon Henderson testimony, FCC hearing, May 1, 1967, pp. 121–129, Docket 16663, Vol. 5, FCC files.

35. Colloquy of Earle K. Moore, Reed Miller, and Jay Kyle, FCC hearing, May 1, 1967, pp. 129–132, 134–135, Docket 16663, Vol. 5, FCC files; also Vernon Guidry, Associated Press, "UCC Director Refuses to Identify Monitors," *Jackson Clarion-Ledger*, May 2, 1967.

36. R. L. T. Smith testimony, FCC hearing, May 2, 1967, pp. 307–308, Docket 16663, Vol. 5, FCC files.

37. Colloquy of Earle K. Moore and Reed Miller, FCC hearing, May 2, 1967, pp. 249–250, Docket 16663, Vol. 5, FCC files.

38. R. L. T. Smith testimony, FCC hearing, May 2, 1967, p. 341, Docket 16663, Vol. 5, FCC files; John M. Pearce, Associated Press, "Witnesses Differ at FCC Hearing," *Jackson Clarion-Ledger*, May 3, 1967.

39. Pearce, "Witnesses Differ at FCC Hearing."

40. A. D. Beittel testimony, FCC hearing, May 3, 1967, pp. 429–430, 476, Docket 16663, Vol. 5, FCC files.

41. George Owens testimony, FCC hearing, May 3, 1967, pp. 558, 567, Docket 16663, Vol 5, FCC files.

42. Ruth Owens testimony, FCC hearing, May 4, 1967, pp. 595–597, 611–614, Docket 16663, Vol. 6, FCC files.

43. Andrew Young testimony, FCC hearing, May 4, 1967, pp. 622–635, Docket 16663, Vol. 6, FCC files.

44. Wendell Taylor testimony, FCC hearing, May 4, 1967, pp. 644–645, 652–655, FCC files.

45. Edwin King testimony, FCC hearing, May 4, 1967, pp. 673–676, 678–686, Docket 16663, Vol. 6, FCC files.

46. Colloquy of Jay Kyle and Ann Aldrich, FCC hearing, May 5, 1967, pp. 686–687, Docket 16663, Vol. 6, FCC files.

47. Everett Parker interview by Les Brown, August 30, 1996, personal files of Everett Parker.

48. Harry Huge interview, April 11, 2002.

49. Hodding Carter testimony, FCC hearing, May 4, 1967, pp. 695–703, Docket 16663, Vol. 6, FCC files.

50. Richard Sanders interview, September 14, 2001, Scottsdale, Az.

51. Edwin King testimony, May 4, 1967, pp. 708–715.

52. FCC hearing, May 4, 1967, p. 721, Docket 16663, Vol. 6, FCC files.

53. Fred Beard testimony, FCC hearing, May 8, 1967, pp. 794–795, Docket 16663, Vol. 6, FCC files.

54. Ibid., pp. 796–804.

55. Ibid., pp. 809–810.

56. Ibid., pp. 812–814.

57. Ibid., p. 816.

58. Ibid., pp. 816–837.

59. Ibid., p. 834.

60. Ibid., pp. 837–842.

61. Ibid., pp. 870–873.

62. Ibid., pp. 875–878.

63. Ibid., pp. 883–886.

64. Ibid., pp. 900–910.

65. Richard Sanders testimony, FCC hearing, May 9, 1967, pp. 1022–1023, Docket 16663, Vol. 6, FCC files.

66. Ibid., pp. 1054–1056.

67. Ibid., p. 1079.

68. Ibid., pp. 1091–1092.

69. Ibid., pp. 1095–1096.

70. Hazel Brannon Smith testimony, FCC hearing, May 11, 1967, p. 1244, Docket 16663, Vol. 7, FCC files.

71. Ibid., pp. 1247–1250.

72. Ibid., p. 1254.

73. Harry Huge interview, August 22, 2000.

74. Jane M. Schutt testimony, FCC hearing, May 15, 1967, pp. 1553–1555, Docket 16663, Vol. 7, FCC files.

75. L. H. Newsome testimony, FCC hearing, May 12, 1967, p. 1365, Docket 16663, Vol. 7, FCC files.

76. Cecil J. Jaquith testimony, p. 1270; James C. Maloney testimony, pp. 1286–1287; James K. Child Jr. testimony, p. 1306; Dr. Samuel B. Johnson testimony, p. 1306; Dr. Benjamin B. Graves testimony, pp. 1275–1276; George Van Zant testimony, pp. 1279–1281; Joel McNinch testimony, p. 1298; John F. Pate testimony, pp. 1301–1303, FCC hearing, May 11, 1967, Docket 16663, Vol. 7, FCC files.

77. Kenneth L. Dean testimony, FCC hearing, May 10, 1967, pp. 1124–1126, 1135, 1139, Docket 16663, Vol. 7, FCC files.

78. Robert McRaney Jr. testimony, FCC hearing, May 12, 1967, p. 1402, Docket 16663, Vol. 7, FCC files.

79. Ibid., pp. 1440, 1446, 1447.

80. Ann Aldrich interview, December 29, 1998.

81. Charles Evers testimony, FCC hearing, May 15, 1967, p. 1478, Docket 16663, Vol. 7, FCC files.

82. Ibid., p. 1497.

83. FCC hearing transcript, May 17, 1967, pp. 1704–1705, Docket 16663, Vol. 8, FCC files.

84. Harry Huge interview, April 11, 2002.

5. ONCE AGAIN, A VERDICT

1. Henry Hampton and Steve Fayer, *Voices of Freedom: An Oral History of the Civil Rights Movement from the 1950s through the 1980s* (New York: Bantam, 1990), pp. 400–401.

2. Proposed findings and conclusions, Office of Communication of the United Church of Christ et al., July 28, 1967, Docket 16663, Vol. 12, FCC files, National Archives, College Park, Md.

3. Proposed findings of fact and conclusions of law, Lamar Life Insurance Co., July 28, 1967, Docket 16663, Vol. 13, FCC files.

4. Proposed findings and conclusions of law, FCC Broadcast Bureau, July 28, 1967, Docket 16663, Vol. 12, FCC files.

5. Earle K. Moore interview, September 30, 1998, New York.

6. Initial decision of hearing examiner Jay Kyle, October 13, 1967, Docket 16663, Vol. 13, FCC files.

7. Earle K. Moore to Everett Parker, November 24, 1967, Earle K. Moore Papers, New York Law School, New York.

8. Les Brown, "Rosel Hyde," *The New York Times Encyclopedia of Television* (New York: Times Books, 1977), p. 202; White House press release on appointment of Rosel H. Hyde, June 18, 1966, Lyndon Baines Johnson Library, Austin, Tex.

9. "Now It's the Hyde Era at the FCC," *Broadcasting*, June 27, 1966, p. 29.

10. *Variety* article quoted in Hal Humphrey column in *Los Angeles Times*, undated, from memorandum from Robert E. Kintner to President Johnson, White House files, Lyndon Baines Johnson Library.

11. "Logic Not Emotion," *Broadcasting*, June 27, 1966, p. 32.

12. White House press release on appointment of Nicholas Johnson, June 18, 1966, Lyndon Baines Johnson Library.

13. "Logic Not Emotion," p. 32.

14. Quoted in John Greenya, "Where Are They Now?" *Washington Lawyer*, May/June 1999, online version.

15. Les Brown, "Nicholas Johnson," *The New York Times Encyclopedia of Television*, pp. 218–219.

16. Kenneth Cox interview, March 1, 1999, Washington, D.C.

17. Earle K. Moore statement for United Church of Christ, oral argument, pp. 1710–1720, Docket 16663, Vol. 14, FCC files.

18. Ann Aldrich statement for United Church of Christ, oral argument, pp. 1720–1722, Docket 16663, Vol. 14, FCC files.

19. Paul A. Porter statement for Lamar Life Insurance Co., oral argument, pp. 1722–1740, Docket 16663, Vol. 14, FCC files.

20. Everett Parker to Earle K. Moore, June 5, 1968, Earle K. Moore Papers.

21. Colloquy of Nicholas Johnson and Paul Porter, oral argument, pp. 1749–1753, Docket 16663, Vol. 14, FCC files.

22. Colloquy of Kenneth Cox and William Kehoe, oral argument, pp. 1759–1760, 1765, Docket 16663, Vol. 14, FCC files.

23. Colloquy of Nicholas Johnson and William Kehoe, oral argument, pp. 1771–1774, Docket 16663, Vol. 14, FCC files.

24. ". . . And Station Licensing," *New York Times*, July 19, 1968.

25. Decision, Federal Communications Commission, in re Application of Lamar Life Broadcasting Co., June 27, 1968, FCC 68-689, 14 FCC 2d, pp. 431–442.

26. Dissenting opinion of Commissioners Kenneth A. Cox and Nicholas Johnson, WLBT license renewal, FCC 68-689, 14 FCC 2d, pp. 442–474.

27. Statement by Commissioner Robert T. Bartley, WLBT license renewal, p. 484.

28. Further statement by Commissioners Hyde, Lee, and Wadsworth, WLBT license renewal, p. 484.

29. "A Farce at the FCC," *Washington Post*, July 9, 1968.

30. Robert Lewis Shayon, "FCC on the Carpet," *Saturday Review*, August 24, 1968, pp. 54–55.

31. Office of Communication of the United Church of Christ news release, July 5, 1968.

32. Earle K. Moore interview, September 30, 1998.

33. "Another Court Date for WLBT," *Broadcasting*, February 24, 1969, p. 66.

34. Earle K. Moore interview, September 30, 1998.

35. Earle K. Moore videotaped interview by Steve Scheuer and Les Brown for the UCLA Oral History Project, November 26, 1996.

36. Earle K. Moore videotaped interview, November 26, 1996.

37. *Office of Communication of the United Church of Christ v. FCC, United States Court of Appeals, District of Columbia Circuit*, 425 F.2d 543 (1969), pp. 543–550.

38. Earle K. Moore videotaped interview, November 26, 1996.

39. In January 1969 the FCC had denied a license renewal to station WHDH in Boston, but in that case there was a competing applicant and the case, begun in 1954, was tainted by an ex parte scandal. WHDH's president had made off-the-record, and therefore improper, contacts with the FCC chairman during the proceedings. "FCC Closes Door on WHDH," *Broadcasting*, May 26, 1969, pp. 42–44.

40. "The Public's Airwaves," *New York Times*, June 25, 1969.

41. "WLBT Loses License, FCC Its Dignity," *Broadcasting*, June 30, 1969, p. 21.

42. Harry Huge interview, August 22, 2000, Washington, D.C.

43. Harry Huge interview, April 11, 2002, Washington, D.C.

44. Richard Sanders interview, September 14, 2001, Scottsdale, Az.

6. EXIT LAMAR LIFE, ENTER WILLIAM DILDAY

1. Phil Gailey, "Opening the Airways," *Washington Post*, February 12, 1973.

2. Communications Improvement, Inc., application for interim operation of WLBT, Earle K. Moore Papers, New York Law School, New York.

3. Aaron Shirley interview, March 30, 1998, Jackson, Miss.

4. United Methodist Church news release, April 22, 1974.

5. Board of directors for Communications Improvement, Inc., listed in Edwin Meek, "WLBT: Interim Operation, An Historical and Analytical Study" (Ph.D. diss., University of Mississippi, 1973), pp. 38–43.

6. Kenneth Dean memo to CII board of directors, July 28, 1971, quoted in Meek, "WLBT," pp. 73–77.

7. Kenneth Dean interview, November 1, 1999, Rochester, N.Y.

8. Robert McRaney Jr. interview (telephone), October 2, 2002.

9. J. Hewitt Griffin interview, July 2, 1999, Jackson, Miss.

10. Bob McRaney Jr., management report to CII board, February 22, 1972, WLBT interim operations archives, Box 43, Special Collections Department, Mitchell Memorial Library, Mississippi State University, Starkville.

11. Kenneth Dean interview, November 1, 1999.

12. Michael Schudson, *The Power of News* (Cambridge: Harvard University Press, 1995), p. 8.

13. Kenneth Dean interview, November 1, 1999.

14. United Press International article in WLBT interim operations archives, Box 1.

15. Viewer calls to WLBT, WLBT interim operations archives, Box 3.

16. Robert McRaney Jr. interview, April 17, 2000, Columbus, Miss.

17. Robert McRaney Jr. interview, October 2, 2002.

18. Earle F. Jones interview, April 19, 2000, Jackson, Miss.

19. John Milton Wesley interview (telephone), October 12, 2000.

20. Kenneth Dean interview, November 1, 1999.

21. William Dilday interview, April 2, 1998, Jackson, Miss.

22. Kenneth Dean interview, November 1, 1999.

23. William Dilday interview, April 2, 1998.

24. Viewer calls to WLBT, WLBT interim operations archives, Box 3.

25. WLBT 3 editorial, August 4, 1972.

26. William Dilday interview, April 2, 1998.

27. Phil Gailey, "He Acts—and Switchboard Lights Up," *Miami Herald*, January 28, 1973; William Dilday interview, April 2, 1998.

28. Minutes of the board of directors, CII, November 23, 1971, cited in Meek, "WLBT," p. 86.

29. Aaron Shirley interview, March 30, 1998.

30. Gailey, "He Acts—and Switchboard Lights Up."

31. William Dilday interview, April 2, 1998.

32. Minority group employees memo to Bob McRaney and Hewitt Griffin, February 21, 1972, WLBT interim operations archives, Box 3.

33. Mary Ann Lindsey interview, April 20, 2000, Jackson, Miss.

34. Minority employees letter to FCC, June 14, 1972, WLBT interim operations archives, Box 3.

35. Minority employees letter to William Dilday, June 28, 1972, WLBT interim operations archives, Box 3.

36. William Dilday response to minority employees, June 29, 1972, WLBT interim operations archives, Box 3.

37. William Dilday's first annual report to the CII board, May 31, 1973, WLBT interim operations archives, Box 43.

38. Kenneth Dean interview, November 1, 1999.

39. J. Hewitt Griffin interview, July 2, 1999.

40. John Milton Wesley interview, October 12, 2000.

41. William Dilday interview, April 2, 1998.

42. "Burgin "Probe" Show Wins Peabody Award," *Reporter*, April 28, 1977; Jeff Edwards, "'Probe' Enters Second Decade of Rare Success," *Jackson Daily News*, October 31, 1984.

43. William Dilday interview, April 2, 1998.

44. Walter Saddler interview, April 2, 1998, Jackson, Miss.

45. Robert Clark interview, March 31, 1998, Jackson, Miss.

46. Reuben Anderson interview, March 30, 1998, Jackson, Miss.

47. Unita Blackwell interview (telephone), March 31, 1998.

48. William Dilday interview, April 2, 1998.

49. Rims Barber interview, April 1, 1998, Jackson, Miss.

50. L. C. Dorsey interview, April 1, 1998, Jackson, Miss.

51. Robert Clark interview, March 31, 1998.

52. Earle F. Jones interview, April 19, 2000.

53. Walter Saddler interview, April 2, 1998.

7. THE STRUGGLE FOR CONTROL

1. William Greider, "TV Reform Slowing; Miss. Case May Be 1st, Last," *Washington Post*, July 17, 1973.

2. License application, Lamar Life Broadcasting, January 29, 1970, Docket 18845, Vol. 1, FCC files, National Archives, College Park, Md.; Greider, "TV Reform Slowing."

3. Robert Travis interview, October 6, 2000, Jackson, Miss.

4. Aaron Henry interview by Weyman Walker, February 23, 1996, Jackson, Miss.

5. Jerry Mitchell, "Jackson Multimillionaire Robert Hearin Dies of Heart Attack," *Jackson Clarion-Ledger*, November 29, 1990; "Hearin's Wealth Estimated at $100 million," *Jackson Clarion-Ledger*, July 29, 1988; "Bob Hearin," *Capitol Reporter*, September 24, 1981.

6. Reuben Anderson interview, October 4, 2000, Jackson, Miss.

7. License application exhibits, Lamar Life Broadcasting, Docket 18845, Vol. 2, FCC files.

8. Les Brown, "Paul A. Walker," *Les Brown's Encyclopedia of Television* (Detroit: Gale Research, 1992), p. 600.

9. Weyman H. D. Walker interview, July 24, 1999, Clear Rock Ranch, near Johnson City, Tex.

10. Martin Firestone interview, July 24, 1999, Clear Rock Ranch, near Johnson City, Tex.

11. Walter Hall interview, May 19, 1999, League City, Tex.

12. Mary Hendrick interview, October 6, 2000, Jackson, Miss.

13. "Five Groups Vie for WLBT (TV)," *Broadcasting*, February 9, 1970, p. 52.

14. Dixie National's 1970 license application identified Portis as employed by the Mississippi Employment Security Commission. However, William Greider's article in the *Washington Post* in 1973 identified him as a local General Motors executive.

15. Rubel Phillips interview (telephone), January 7, 2003.

16. William Mounger interview, October 5, 2000, Jackson, Miss.

17. Grace Simmons, "Alvin P. Flannes, Philanthropist," *Jackson Clarion-Ledger*, April 2, 1989.

18. "Five Groups Vie for WLBT (TV)."

19. Intervenor's petition for rehearing and for clarification of opinion, Lamar Life Broadcasting, July 7, 1969, Docket 19409, U.S. Court of Appeals, Federal Records Center, Suitland, Md.

20. Petition for rehearing or clarification, Federal Communications Commission, July 7, 1969, Docket 19409, U.S. Court of Appeals, Federal Records Center.

21. U.S. Court of Appeals decision of September 5, 1969, Docket 19409, Federal Records Center.

22. Motion to stay mandate, Lamar Life Broadcasting, September 10, 1969, Docket 19409, U.S. Court of Appeals, Federal Records Center.

23. Opposition to intervenor's motion to stay mandate, Office of Communication of the United Church of Christ et al., September 16, 1969, Docket 19409, U.S. Court of Appeals, Federal Records Center.

24. Motion for leave to withdraw motion to stay mandate, Lamar Life Broadcasting, September 17, 1969, Docket 19409, U.S. Court of Appeals, Federal Records Center.

25. "WLBT(TV) Now Up for Grabs," *Broadcasting*, December 8, 1969, p. 47.

26. "Another Round for WLBT(TV), *Broadcasting*, January 5, 1970, p. 39.

27. Petition to enlarge issues, Civic Communications Corp., May 22, 1970, Docket 18845, Vol. 7, FCC files.

28. Petition to enlarge issues, Channel 3, Inc., May 25, 1970, Docket 18845, Vol. 7, FCC files.

29. Affidavit of Walter G. Hall, June 15, 1970, Attachment A to petition for leave to file supplemental material, Civic Communications Corp., Docket 18845, Vol. 8, FCC files.

30. Walter Hall interview, May 19, 1999.

31. Memorandum opinion and order, FCC review board, December 31, 1970, copy in Patricia Derian Papers, Box 13, Mitchell Memorial Library, Mississippi State University, Starkville.

32. Lenore Ehrig interview, April 12, 2002, Washington, D.C.

33. Martin Firestone interview, March 4, 1999, Frederick, Md.

34. Rubel Phillips interview, January 7, 2003.

35. Robert Hearin testimony, FCC hearing, April 8, 1971, p. 1203, Docket 18845, Vol. 12, FCC files.

36. Margaret Walker Alexander testimony, FCC hearing, May 4, 1971, p. 2982, Docket 18845, Vol. 15, FCC files.

37. Rubel Phillips testimony, FCC hearing, May 6, 1971, p. 3236, Docket 18845, Vol. 15, FCC files.

38. Charles Evers, *Evers*, ed. Grace Halsell (New York: World Publishing, 1971), pp. 83–84.

39. Philip D. Carter, "Evers' Confessions Add to Campaign Hurdles," *Washington Post*, April 12, 1971.

40. Joint petition to enlarge issues, Lamar Life Broadcasting, Dixie National Broadcasting, Jackson Television, Inc., and Channel 3, Inc., May 11, 1971, Docket 18845, Vol. 16, FCC files.

41. Memorandum opinion and order, FCC review board, July 6, 1971, Docket 18845, Vol. 19, FCC files; "Evers's Past Steps into WLBT Present," *Broadcasting*, July 12, 1971, p. 10.

42. Weyman Walker testimony, FCC hearing, May 13, 1971, pp. 3983–3988, Docket 18845, Vol. 17, FCC files.

43. Patricia Derian testimony, FCC hearing, May 20, 1971, pp. 4559–4560, Docket 18845, Vol. 18, FCC files.

44. Martin Firestone interview (telephone), April 20, 2001; David Mieher testimony, FCC hearing, July 12, 1971, p. 5384, Docket 18845, Vol. 20; Lamar exhibits, p. 486, Docket 18845, Vol. 36, FCC files.

45. Richard Sanders testimony, FCC hearing, July 21, 1971, pp. 5920–5924, Docket 18845, Vol. 21, FCC files; Lamar exhibits, p. 251, Docket 18845, Vol. 36, FCC files.

46. Charles Evers testimony, FCC hearing, November 16, 1971, pp. 6810–6835, Docket 18845, Vol. 23, FCC files.

47. Martin Firestone statement, FCC hearing, November 16, 1971, p. 6841, Docket 18845, Vol. 23, FCC files.

48. Joseph Rauh testimony, FCC hearing, November 17, 1971, p. 6878, Docket 18845, Vol. 23, FCC files.

49. Fannie Lou Hamer testimony, FCC hearing, November 17, 1971, pp. 6884–6896, Docket 18845, Vol. 23, FCC files.

50. Memorandum opinion and order, Administrative Law Judge Lenore Ehrig, April 20, 1973, pp. 213, 224, Docket 18845, Vol. 48, FCC files.

51. Ibid., pp. 214–215.

52. Ibid., pp. 221–222.

53. Ibid., pp. 228–230.

54. Ibid., p. 231.

55. Ibid., p. 237.

56. Earle K. Moore interview, September 30, 1998, New York.

57. Lenore Ehrig interview, April 12, 2002.

58. William Mounger interview, October 5, 2000.

59. Robert Travis interview, October 6, 2000.

60. Martin Firestone interview, March 4, 1999.

61. Martin Firestone interview, April 20, 2001.

62. Molly Ivins, "A Wonderful Fellow, Especially for a Banker," *Fort Worth Star-Telegram*, May 13, 2000.

63. A. Pat Daniels, *Citizen First, Banker Second: History of a Texas Community Bank and Stories About Its Politically Liberal Leader* (Houston: A. Pat Daniels, 1995), p. 6.

64. Walter Hall interview, May 19, 1999.

65. Walter Hall interview by Chandler Davidson, Walter Buenger, and Louis Marchiafava, July 24, 1979, League City, Tex., p. 4, Walter G. Hall Papers, Woodson Research Center, Fondren Library, Rice University, Houston.

66. Walter Hall interview, May 19, 1999.

67. Walter Hall interview by Chandler Davidson, Walter Buenger, and Louis Marchiafava, July 24, 1979, p. 3.

68. Daniels, *Citizen First*, p. 20.

69. Ibid., p. 21.

70. Walter Hall interview by Chandler Davidson, December 27, 1982, Clear Rock Ranch, near Johnson City, Tex., pp. 11–12, Walter G. Hall Papers.

71. Walter Hall interview by Chandler Davidson, December 27, 1982, p. 17.

72. Chandler Davidson interview, July 20, 1999, Houston.

73. Steven Long, "Walter Hall: Can a Conservative Country Banker (Who May Be Texas' Oldest) Find Happiness as a Die-hard Liberal Democrat (Who Some Say Should Have Been Governor of Texas?)" *TEXAS, Houston Chronicle Magazine*, March 26, 1989, p. 5.

74. Walter Hall interview by David G. McComb, June 30, 1969, Dickinson, Tex., p. 13, Oral Histories, AC 75-29, Lyndon Baines Johnson Library, Austin, Tex.

75. Walter Hall interview by Chandler Davidson, December 27, 1982, p. 45.

76. Long, "Walter Hall," p. 4.

77. Martin Firestone interview, March 4, 1999.

78. Greider, "TV Reform Slowing."

79. B. Drummond Ayres Jr., "Burger Ruling Spurs Drive for TV Racial Equity," *New York Times*, July 16, 1973. The Ayres and Greider stories, which ran on successive days in the *New York Times* and the *Washington Post*, respectively, generated a little "mudball fight" of their own between Dixie National and the Office of Communication of the United Church of Christ. On October 11, 1973, Joseph F. Hennessey, Dixie National's lawyer, wrote the FCC to complain about several items, among them a charge that the United Church of Christ was using the *New York Times* as a vehicle "to float news leaks" unfavorable to Ehrig's decision awarding WLBT's license to Dixie National. Dixie National had previously attached the Ayres and Greider articles to an FCC filing in August. In response, Earle K. Moore wrote the FCC on October 16, 1973, that the United Church of Christ believed it was "highly desirable to keep the public fully informed about everything that is occurring" in selection of a licensee for Channel 3. "We repudiate the suggestion of covert activity implied by the word 'leak.' The reports in the *Times* and *Washington Post* about the Channel 3 contest were based on interviews 'on the record.' If Dixie National cannot accept the idea of public accountability, it ought not to apply for a public trust."

80. Martin Firestone interview, March 4, 1999.

81. Martin Firestone interview, April 20, 2001.

82. Arnold H. Lubasch, "5 in Sterling [*sic*] Homex Convicted of Fraud," *New York Times*, January 30, 1977.

83. Petition to remand proceeding, Civic Communications Corp., July 20, 1973, Docket 18845, Vol. 48, FCC files.

84. Andrew J. Schwartzman interview (telephone), December 16, 2002.

85. Petition to reopen hearing to receive additional evidence of decisional significance, Office of Communication of the United Church of Christ, August 15, 1973, Docket 18845, Vol. 48, FCC files.

86. Martin Firestone interview, July 24, 1999.

87. Memorandum opinion and order, FCC review board, January 11, 1974, Docket 18845, Vol. 50, FCC files.

88. Charles Young interview, July 5, 1999, Meridian, Miss.

89. Martin Firestone to Administrative Law Judge Lenore Ehrig, July 19, 1974, Docket 18845, Vol. 51, FCC files.

90. Memorandum opinion and order, dissenting opinion of Benjamin Hooks, June 10, 1975, Docket 18845, Vol. 52, FCC files.

91. Memorandum opinion and order, FCC review board, February 19, 1976, Docket 18845, Vol. 52, FCC files.

92. *United States of America v. David Stirling, Jr., William G. Stirling, Harold M. Yanowitch, Edwin J. Schultz, Rubel L. Phillips*, Attachment A to opposition to submission of Dixie National Corporation concerning "Stirling Homex" Issues, Office of Communication of the United Church of Christ and the Community Coalition for Better Broadcasting, December 3, 1976, Docket 18845, Vol. 55, FCC files.

93. Martin Firestone interview, July 24, 1999.

94. Rubel Phillips interview, January 7, 2003.

95. Martin Firestone interview, July 24, 1999.

96. Affidavit of Alvin P. Flannes in support of settlement, attachment to Lamar Life Broadcasting et al. letter to Administrative Law Judge Lenore Ehrig, June 3, 1976, Docket 18845, Vol. 53, FCC files.

97. "Compromise Looms in Jackson, Miss.," *Broadcasting*, July 28, 1975, p. 26.

98. James R. Searer to Al Flannes, September 26, 1975, Docket 18845, Vol. 52, FCC files; "WLBT Agreement Falls Apart," *Broadcasting*, October 27, 1975, p. 42.

99. Joint petition for approval of settlement agreement, Lamar Life Broadcasting, Civic Communications, Dixie National Broadcasting, Jackson Television, and Channel 3, Docket 18845, Vol. 53, FCC files.

100. Opposition to joint petition for approval of settlement agreement, FCC Broadcast Bureau, December 3, 1976, Docket 18845, Vol. 55, FCC files.

101. Petition to deny, Office of Communication of the United Church of Christ and the Community Coalition for Better Broadcasting, December 3, 1976, Docket 18845, Vol. 55, FCC files.

102. Petition to enlarge issues, Civic Communications, January 19, 1977, Docket 18845, Vol. 55, FCC files.

103. Rubel Phillips interview, January 7, 2003. Also DNBC opposition to UCC motion to quash notice of deposition served on Earle K. Moore, February 22, 1978, Docket 18845, Vol. 58, FCC files. In that filing, Dixie National's lawyers said that Richardson changed his testimony "because of an unsigned memorandum by Kenneth L. Dean." At a meeting between Richardson and Dean, the lawyers said, Richardson adopted a suggestion by Dean that Phillips had been implicated in the alleged forgery. "The testimony shows that Dean, through an attorney, Earle K. Moore, transmitted his unsigned memorandum" to the U.S. district attorney's office. Asked about the memo during the FCC hearings, Dean said that he had met Richardson while running for Congress. Asked if he suggested to Richardson that Phillips was involved in the forgery, Dean said, "My recollection is that he mentioned it to me, not that I mentioned it to him." Then he wrote up the conversation in a memo to protect himself and gave it to Moore, who was the lawyer for CII. See Kenneth Dean testimony, FCC hearing, June 19, 1978, pp. 8018, 8034–8035, Docket 18845, Vol. 60, FCC files.

104. Rubel Phillips interview, January 7, 2003.

105. Martin Firestone and Sydney Arak to Administrative Law Judge Lenore Ehrig, May 23, 1977, Docket 18845, Vol. 57, FCC files.

106. Tom Royals interview, April 20, 2000, Jackson, Miss.

107. Tom Royals interview by Weyman Walker, February 24, 1996.

108. Ibid.

109. Tom Royals interview, April 20, 2000.

110. Tom Royals interview by Weyman Walker, February 24, 1996.

111. Tom Royals interview, April 20, 2000.

112. Betty Tilson letter for Mrs. Lyndon Johnson to the author, January 25, 2000.

113. Tom Royals interview by Weyman Walker, February 24, 1996.

114. Robert Travis interview, October 6, 2000.

115. Reuben Anderson interview, October 4, 2000.

116. Walter Hall interview, July 24, 1999, Clear Rock Ranch, near Johnson City, Tex.

117. Reuben Anderson interview, October 4, 2000.

118. Tom Royals interview by Weyman Walker, February 24, 1996.

119. Walter Hall to Fagan Dickson, October 2, 1974, Walter G. Hall Papers.

120. Walter Hall interview by Chandler Davidson, December 27, 1982.

121. William Mounger affidavit, DNBC supplement to application for review, August 4, 1976, Docket 18845, Vol. 53, FCC files.

122. Memorandum opinion and order, Administrative Law Judge Lenore Ehrig, January 6, 1978, Docket 18845, Vol. 58, FCC files.

123. Joint petition for approval of settlement agreement, Lamar Life Broadcasting, Civic Communications, Dixie National Broadcasting, Jackson Television, and Channel 3, Inc., January 22, 1979, Docket 18845, Vol. 62, FCC files.

124. Further affidavit of Alvin P. Flannes, Joint petition for approval of settlement agreement, Lamar et al., Attachment E, Docket 18845, Vol. 62, FCC files.

125. Comments of public intervenors re qualifications to participate in ownership and reimbursement, Office of Communication of the United Church of Christ and Community Coalition for Better Broadcasting, Box 120, Aaron Henry Papers, Tougaloo College, Tougaloo, Miss.

126. Lenore Ehrig statement, FCC hearing, November 13, 1979, p. 9007, Docket 18845, Vol. 63, FCC files.

127. Memorandum opinion and order, Chief Administrative Law Judge Lenore Ehrig, December 3, 1979, p. 17, Docket 18845, Vol. 64, FCC files.

128. Ibid., pp. 7–9.

129. Walter Hall interview by Chandler Davidson, December 27, 1982, p. 57.

8. NATIONAL IMPACT

1. Fred Friendly, *The Good Guys, the Bad Guys and the First Amendment: Free Speech vs. Fairness in Broadcasting* (New York: Vintage, 1977), pp. 103–108.

2. Reply to opposition, Texarkana Organization et al., April 5, 1969, Earle K. Moore Papers, New York Law School, New York.

3. Report to the Ford Foundation, September 30, 1969, personal files of Everett Parker.

4. Statement of policy of station KTAL-TV in Texarkana, Texas, adopted as an agreement with twelve community organizations of Texarkana, Texas, June 9, 1969, Earle K. Moore Papers.

5. In re application of KCMC Inc., Texarkana, Texas, for renewal of license of station KTAL-TV, Federal Communications Commission, July 29, 1969, Earle K. Moore Papers; "Passing Marks Are Given KTAL-TV," *Broadcasting*, August 4, 1969, p. 36.

6. *Office of Communication of the United Church of Christ v. Federal Communications Commission*, 465 F. 2d 519 (1972), pp. 519–528. Also "Flat Ban on Reimbursements Vetoed," *Broadcasting*, April 3, 1972, p. 117.

7. "Sign of Changing Times in Renewals," *Broadcasting*, May 17, 1971, p. 34.

8. "Ford Funds for Black TV, Radio Interests," *Broadcasting*, July 6, 1970, p. 23.

9. "How the United Church Stirs Up the Cats," *Broadcasting*, October 6, 1969, p. 37.

10. Willard D. Rowland Jr., "The Illusion of Fulfillment: The Broadcast Reform Movement," *Journalism Monographs* (December 1982), p. 14.

11. "The Struggle Over Broadcast Access," *Broadcasting*, September 20, 1971, p. 32.

12. Maryln Schwartz, "5 Stations to Boost Minorities," *Dallas Morning News*, July 2, 1971; "5 Ft. Worth–Dallas Stations Support Minority Upbeat," *Variety*, July 7, 1971.

13. "A Spurt in the Price of Pacification," *Broadcasting*, January 11, 1971, pp. 20–22.

14. Office of Communication of the United Church of Christ, "A Program to Combat Racial Discrimination in Broadcasting," report to the Ford Foundation, December 13, 1971, Attachment G.

15. "Time's $59-million Sale Clears FCC," *Broadcasting*, March 13, 1972, p. 32.

16. "McGraw-Hill Sets Record for Concessions to Minorities," *Broadcasting*, May 15, 1972, pp. 25–26.

17. "Stars and All Fall on Alabama," *Broadcasting*, February 14, 1972, pp. 39–40; "Alabama's ETV's Lose License for Lack of Service to Black Audience," *Broadcasting*, January 13, 1975, pp. 23–24.

18. Steve Millard, "A Look at Those Broadcast Reformers," *Broadcasting*, May 5, 1969, p. 42.

19. Erwin G. Krasnow, Lawrence D. Longley, and Herbert A. Terry, *The Politics of Broadcast Regulation* (New York: St. Martin's, 1982), p. 210.

20. "FCC Dumps WHDH as Renewal Precedent," *Broadcasting*, January 19, 1970, p. 21; Krasnow, Longley, and Terry, *The Politics of Broadcast Regulation*, pp. 212–213.

21. Krasnow, Longley, and Terry, *The Politics of Broadcast Regulation*, p. 215.

22. Ibid., pp. 216–232.

23. William Richter, "Action for Children's Television: U.S. Citizens' Activist Group," in *Museum of Broadcast Communication Encyclopedia of Television*, ed. Horace Newcomb, Vol. 1 (Chicago: Fitzroy Dearborn, 1997), pp. 11–12; Nathaniel C. Nash, "White House Gets Bill Reducing Ads on Children's TV Programs," *New York Times*, October 2, 1990.

24. 359 F. 2d 994 (1966), p. 1009.

25. 425 F. 2d 543 (1969), p. 548.

26. Friendly, *The Good Guys*, pp. 43–50.

27. Ibid., pp. 50–72.

28. Robert D. Hershey Jr., "FCC Votes Down Fairness Doctrine in a 4-0 Decision," *New York Times*, August 5, 1987; Peter J. Boyer, "Fairness Doctrine," *New York Times*, August 6, 1987.

29. David Johnston, "Court Backs FCC's Repeal of the Fairness Doctrine," *New York Times*, February 11, 1989.

30. "Interview: Andrew Jay Schwartzman," Civil Rights Forum on Communications Policy website (www.civilrightsforum.org), September 1, 2000.

31. Andrew Schwartzman interview (telephone), December 16, 2002.

32. George Gent, "Church Protests Bias by Stations," *New York Times*, April 25, 1967.

33. Memorandum opinion and order and notice of proposed rule making, FCC, July 5, 1968, pp. 1–2, Docket 18244, author's files.

34. Stephen J. Pollak to FCC chair Rosel H. Hyde, May 21, 1968, Attachment A to memorandum opinion and order and notice of proposed rule making, FCC, July 5, 1968.

35. Memorandum opinion and order and notice of proposed rule making, FCC, July 5, 1968, pp. 11–12.

36. Eileen Shanahan, "TV, Radio Stations Warned on Bias," *New York Times*, July 6, 1968.

37. Henry Geller, E-mail to author, December 17, 2002.

38. "FCC Gets Tough on Equal Employment," *Broadcasting*, June 9, 1969, pp. 38–39.

39. Fred Feretti, "NAACP Fund and Church Score FCC 'Inertia' on Hiring," *New York Times*, February 26, 1970; "Double Trouble on Minorities," *Broadcasting*, March 2, 1970, p. 27.

40. Fred Feretti, "Foe of Bias in Broadcasting Is Hopeful," *New York Times*, July 1, 1970.

41. Lee Thornton, "Broadcast News," in *Split Images: African Americans in the Mass Media*, ed. Janette L. Dates and William Barlow (Washington, D.C.: Howard University Press, 1990), pp. 395–396; "Parker Assails Hiring Practices at TV Stations," *Broadcasting*, November 27, 1972, p. 26.

42. U.S. Commission on Civil Rights, *Window Dressing on the Set: Women and Minorities in Television* (Washington, D.C.: Government Printing Office, August 1977), quoted in Thornton, "Broadcast News," pp. 397–398.

43. Richard M. Levine, "We're On the Team, but We're Not Playing," *TV Guide*, July 18, 1981, p. 8, quoted in Thornton, "Broadcast News," p. 401.

44. "The Struggle Over Broadcast Access," *Broadcasting*, September 20, 1971, p. 35.

45. Thornton, "Split Images," p. 339.

46. David Honig interview (telephone), January 5, 2003.

47. Media Access Project website issues overview (www.mediaaccess.org).

48. Steven A. Holmes, "FCC Requirement on Minority Hiring Is Voided by Court," *New York Times*, July 30, 1998.

49. Neil A. Lewis, "FCC Revises Rule on Hiring of Women and Minorities," *New York Times*, January 21, 2000; John Schwarts, "FCC Unveils New Rules on Hiring," *Washington Post*, January 21, 2000.

50. Stephen Labaton, "Court Rules Agency Erred On Mandate for Minorities," *New York Times*, January 17, 2001.

51. Doug Halonen, "FCC OKs Rules on Equal Employment," *Electronic Media*, November 11, 2002, p. 4; Edmund Sanders, "FCC Is Expected to Readopt Rules on Equal Employment," *Los Angeles Times*, November 7, 2002.

EPILOGUE

1. Greg Braxton, "TV Study: Black Roles Are Mixed Bag," *Los Angeles Times*, June 5, 2002.

2. Dan Modisett interview (telephone), January 2, 2003.

3. Rose Ragsdale, "TV-3 Change Ends 15-year struggle," *Jackson Clarion-Ledger*, October 5, 1986; Wanda Cantrell, "WLBT Buyout Ended 22-year Siege," *Jackson Clarion-Ledger*, October 5, 1986; Frank Melton interview, October 4, 2000, Jackson, Miss.

4. Aaron Henry interview by Weyman Walker, February 23, 1996, Jackson, Miss.

5. Billy Watkins, "Frank Melton: The Angriest Man in Mississippi," *Jackson Clarion-Ledger*, January 19, 1992.

6. Patrice Sawyer, "WLBT Changing Hands," and Gary Pettus, "Hard- sought Minority Ownership Over," *Jackson Clarion-Ledger*, June 20, 2000.

7. "Number of Minority-Owned Stations Drops," *Quill*, March 2001, p. 33; "Commerce Secretary Mineta Releases Report Finding Gains in Minority Broadcast Ownership," U.S. Department of Commerce news release, January 16, 2001.

8. Dan Modisett interview, January 2, 2003.

ACKNOWLEDGMENTS

My thanks to all the people, in Mississippi and elsewhere, who agreed to be interviewed for this book. They are listed in the chapter notes, and they have my deepest gratitude for helping document this story.

Thanks, too, to Connie Curry for suggesting that I write this book; to Andrew J. Schwartzman of the Media Access Center for directing me to many good sources and warning me that I would have to wade through boxes upon boxes of files (he was right); to Mark Lloyd, whose Civil Rights Forum helped support my initial interview trip to Mississippi; and to Dr. James Capo, director of Fordham University's Donald McGannon Communication Research Center, who invited me to speak about this case and thus supported my research into it. Thanks to Tom Alexander, a former WLBT employee, who provided constant encouragement; to Patricia Derian, who gave me access to her papers at Mississippi State University and who told me that the WLBT interim operation files were located there as well; to the friends who fed me and lodged me as I was doing this research and to those who listened and encouraged; to Dean Mills, who read my entire manuscript and made invaluable editing suggestions; and to Susan Henry and Ann Seaman, skilled editors themselves.

These archivists were of invaluable assistance: David Pfeiffer at the National Archives in College Park, Maryland; Mattie Sink and Betty Self in the Special Collections Department of Mitchell Memorial Library, Mississippi State University in Starkville; Linda Seelke at the Lyndon Baines Johnson Library in Austin, Texas; and the staffs at L. Zenobia Coleman Library at Tougaloo College in Tougaloo, Mississippi, and at the state Department of Archives and History in Jackson, Mississippi. The New York Law School, especially Roberta Tasley, coordinator of the Communications Media Center, gave me complete access to the papers of Earle K. Moore. Everett Parker and Richard Sanders provided personal files that were of great assistance, and Martin Firestone and Frances Carter were most helpful, especially in arranging my interviews with Walter Hall.

Two dissertations and a research paper provided useful guideposts concerning questions to ask as I interviewed people involved in the WLBT case and its aftermath. These were Ed Meek's dissertation, "WLBT: Interim Operation, An Historical and Analytical Study" (University of Mississippi, 1973); Donald Ranley's dissertation, "The Challengers: Social Pressures on the Press, 1965–1975" (University of Missouri–Columbia, 1976); and a research paper by Robert B. Horwitz of the Department of Communication at the University of California, San Diego, "Broadcast Reform Revisited: The Rev. Everett C. Parker and the Standing Case," distributed by the Office of Communication of the United Church of Christ.

Last, but hardly least, I want to thank my agent, Heide Lange, and her assistant, Esther Sung, and the staff at the University Press of Mississippi, especially director Seetha Srinivasan and editor Anne Stascavage. Without them, this book would not have been published, and I am profoundly grateful for their efforts and those of copyeditor Robert Burchfield.

Changing Channels is dedicated to the memory of my father and mother, Morris and Mary S. Mills, and that of my friend and mentor, Eileen Shanahan, who covered part of this story and was as thrilled as I was with any research victories, large or small.

INDEX